The Dialogical Kindergarten

Molly Efrat
The Dialogical Kindergarten

Published by BooxAi
ISBN: 978-965-577-925-7

The Dialogical Kindergarten

Molly Efrat

Edited by
NAOMI GOLDSTEIN YALIN

Translated by
NAOMI GOLDSTEIN YALIN

MOLLY EFRAT

The Dialogical Kindergarten

Based on:

DOCTORAL THESIS:

Development of Children's Social-Communicative Patterns through a Multi-Dialogical Approach in the kindergarten

UNIVERSITATEA BABEŞ-BOLYAI CLUJ-NAPOCA

FACULTATEA DE PSIHOLOGIE ŞI ŞTIINŢE ALE EDUCAŢIEI

2016

DOCTORAL SUPERVISOR

Prof. Dr. MUŞATA-DACIA BOCOŞ

Contents

Acknowledgments

I would like to thank Professor Ungureanu and Professor Bocoş, my doctorate supervisors, for their professional and wise guidance.

Thank you to the doctoral committee.

And also my thanks to the staff of AD Atid Lekidum.

I would also like to express my gratitude to the research participants who provided the data for my study.

Last but by no means least, I am most grateful for the support of my beloved family throughout this journey, and especially to my husband Shay who joined me on this fascinating exploration.

Thesis structure

The thesis includes the following five chapters:

Chapter I presents The Theoretical Foundations for the research. This chapter analyzes, discusses and describes theories relating to the subject of the research.

Chapter II presents the methodology of the pedagogical research.

Chapter III presents the qualitative and quantitative findings of the research.

Chapter IV presents the discussion of the Findings of the research.

Chapter V presents the conclusions derived from the discussion of the findings and describes a practical and theoretical modular model that emerged from the research.

Abstract

The research examined the social-communication patterns of children learning in kindergarten according to the Multi-Dialogical Approach (MDA). It aimed to examine to what extent this approach contributes to the development of these social-communication patterns. The research goal was to fill a gap in knowledge relating to children's psychological development. The conceptual framework that underpinned the research included theories concerning social communication patterns, pre-school education, attentiveness, mediated learning, the Multi-Dialogical kindergarten and a model for activity planning in the Multi-Dialogical kindergarten.

This was a mixed method research. The qualitative part of the research was conducted in two parallel phases: conducting participatory observations on 25 kindergarten children learning according to the MDA; some of these observations were recorded in writing while others were video-filmed and transcribed. In addition, the researcher conducted semi-structured interviews with 15 kindergarten teachers, seven of whom work according to the MDA and eight who work according to the traditional educational approach. To supplement the qualitative study, a closed-ended quantitative questionnaire was constructed. This questionnaire was administered to 130 kindergarten teachers, 73 of whom were teachers working according to the MDA or undergoing training for the MDA and 57 teachers working according to the traditional approach. The data from this part were analyzed statistically.

The research findings indicate that the kindergarten children educated according to the MDA exhibited an obvious development of social communication patterns such as initiative, leadership, ability to give and accept feedback and the ability to converse and to be attentive to one another. A difference was found in social communication patterns between children educated in a kindergarten according to the MDA and children educated in kindergartens according to the traditional approach.

The significance of this study lies in the model it produced, which explains the development of the children's social communication patterns during early childhood through the MDA, showing how this approach can actually have an influence in the domain of children's developmental psychology. The modular-adaptive character of the developed model allows it to form a foundation for the development of children's social communication patterns in kindergarten since it allows the implementation of unique learning approaches. Moreover, the model can lead to alteration of the perceptions and character of work of different practitioners (kindergarten teachers, mentors and supervisors) responsible for the children and also of teacher education colleges. This change can be achieved by reducing the gap between declarations and actions that occurs in practice in kindergartens and colleges.

Keywords: social communication patterns in early childhood; multi-dialogical kindergarten, attentiveness, dialog, individual meetings, discourse, philosophical discourse, negotiation, collaboration, feedback and reflection, guidance, initiative, leadership, peer learning.

Introduction

The rationale that guided the research focuses on the gap that exists between the goals of education in general and the goals of education for early childhood as set out for the Israeli educational system, in particular. Those goals are presented by the Israeli Ministry of Education (2015a) along with the extent of their implementation in the field in the kindergartens. The present study focuses on the shaping of children's social communication patterns in early childhood, when they are educated according to the Multi-Dialogical Approach (hereinafter: MDA). These patterns, in fact, constitute important life skills that accompany the child from childhood through the different school stages and on into adulthood. According to the MDA, these life skills will form the foundation for the future citizen that the child will become in the society where he lives: a citizen with initiative, an independent thinker, reflecting on his actions, tolerant and flexible.

The Israeli Ministry of Education presents its educational philosophy in general and for early childhood in particular on its official Internet site. For example:

Deepening emotional, ethical and social education and promotion of personal and social involvement … fostering an optimal climate to reinforce resilience and personal growth and to promote containment of the other and acceptance of diversity (Ministry of Education, 2015a, p. 7).

Another example of the Ministry's declared goals of education is:

To reinforce powers of judgment and criticism, to foster intellectual curiosity, independent thinking and initiative ...to allow the children to develop according to their own path (Ministry of Education Internet site, 2015b).

These are important and meaningful goals for the development of significant social communication skills in early childhood. As an experienced kindergarten teacher, a Ministry of Education mentor and lecturer in a teacher education college, who also trains student-teachers for work with early childhood, I have come to realize that these goals are almost never implemented in practice in the field, meaning that they are almost never implemented in the kindergartens.

Background and context of the research

The research context is in early childhood, which is the first period that children spend in the Israeli education system, within the educational frame of the kindergartens for ages 3-6, that provide a developmental space responding to the needs of children in early childhood. The kindergartens that belong to and constitute an integral part of the public education system aim to establish a sense of confidence and trust for the child and his family, creating social interaction, so that the child can learn social rules, internalize behavioral norms, and develop emotional awareness and empathy, imparting values of morality and social justice and enabling the child to acquire world knowledge (Ministry of Education, 2010). The goals of the kindergarten, as they are stated by the Ministry of Education, are goals with significant weight for the social- communication development of kindergarten children. In practice, in the field of early childhood, in the kindergartens these goals are hardly expressed at all.

Various different educational approaches are implemented in the kindergartens for kindergarten children, including the Traditional Structured Approach, in which the teacher is the person that has the knowledge, which she transmits to the children (Kohn, 2002), and the Flow Approach that allows children to choose what they would like to deal with (Levine, 1989) and also the MDA (Firstater & Efrat, 2014). The implementation of the MDA in kindergartens relies on the general dialogical educational approach and expands its use to early childhood. According to this approach, the children participate in decision-making regarding the operation of all areas of the kindergarten through negotiation with the kindergarten teacher, who guides them. The distinction of this approach is that it relates to dialog at such an early age, in infancy and it provides the teacher with practical ways to do this in the kindergarten. Its innovation is expressed in the actual implementation, in practice, of the declared goals of education for infants in the kindergarten. Therefore, it is important to investigate the social- communication patterns of preschool children educated according to the MDA in order to determine whether Ministry of Education goals for kindergartens are actually achieved. For these reasons, the present study that conducts just such an investigation can provide vital information for various practitioners, including kindergarten teachers, mentors and supervisors working in the field. Additionally, the research findings and conclusions may be informative for the construction of courses for the professional development of those working with early childhood, and those who write learning programs for early childhood, and Ministry of Education policy-makers.

The gap in knowledge that this study aimed to fill is due to the fact that most studies that have been conducted in the dialogical learning field in various countries have focused on elementary school children. Others that related to kindergartens have mainly examined interactions between the kindergarten teacher and the child (Fumoto, 2011) and the influence of mediated learning on children (Tzuriel & Shamir, 2007). However, as far as can be ascertained, there has been no investigation of the implementation of different educational approaches in early childhood or of their implications for the children. The rationale for this seems to stem from the perception (that is not the subject for this research) that the educational stage of the kindergarten is a stage in the child's development of cognitive and emotional development for school. In any case, no studies were found relating to kindergartens working according to the MDA that focus on children's social communication processes in early childhood. Thus, this is the first research of its kind in Israel or worldwide to specifically relate to social and communication patterns within the context of a multi- dialogical kindergarten in early education.

Two research questions were investigated: (1) what unique social, behavioral and interpersonal communication patterns develop among kindergarten children in a multi-dialogical kindergarten? And (2) what social, communication and interpersonal differences can be found between children educated in multi-dialogical kindergartens and children educated in traditional kindergartens?

The research aims to examine the development of children's social-communication patterns, such as initiative, leadership, discourse, and the ability to give and receive feedback in a multi-dialogical kindergarten. More specifically, the research aimed:

- To ascertain the children's interpersonal communication patterns.
- To examine the implementation of the MDA in a kindergarten.
- To identify ways to implement the MDA in the kindergarten.
- To compare children's social-communication patterns in Multi-Dialogical kindergartens in contrast to children educated according to the traditional kindergarten approach.

The significance of the research

The significance of the research lies in its ability to inform a change in the perception and practical approach to early childhood education in the context of the Multi-Dialogical kindergarten. The research did indeed lead to the development of an original modular theoretical and practical model that explains the forces operating in a kindergarten that works according to the MDA. These forces serve as the foundation on which social communication patterns can be developed among early childhood children in the multi-dialogical kindergarten.

The structure of the thesis

Chapter 1: The Theoretical Foundations chapter describes, discusses and analyzes theories relating to the subject of the research. This chapter begins with main theories of the Dialogical Approach in education, continues with main fundamental theoretical perceptions in Dialogical Education and then discusses the main concepts of kindergarten children's social and communication skills. The chapter ends with a summary and description of the conceptual framework that underpinned the research.

Chapter II describes the pedagogical research. It details the methodological considerations taken into account in order to choose the most appropriate methodology to attain the research goals. The chapter begins by presenting a description of the funnel-shaped structure representing the research hypotheses and goals, and then describes the research procedure. The description of the procedure includes the type of research chosen for the study – mixed methods research, its validity and how it is expressed, a description of the research population that included kindergarten teachers and early childhood children, the location in which the study was conducted – the kindergarten, the timetable for the performance of the study, research methods employed to collect data – mixed methods including qualitative action research and quantitative study, the research tools – participatory observations (some video-filmed and transcribed and others recorded in writing) and semi-structured interviews in the qualitative part of the study and a closed-ended statistical questionnaire in the quantitative part of the study. It also describes the methods employed to analyze the collected data: content analysis for the qualitative data and statistical analysis for the quantitative data. The methodology chapter concludes with a description of the ethical considerations involved in the research and steps taken to address them.

Chapter III: The Findings presents the findings which emerged from the content analysis of the transcriptions of the video-films and structured participatory observations and the semi-structured interviews. It then describes the statistical analysis method used by the researcher and presents the statistical analyses of the quantitative findings.

Chapter IV: The Discussion of the Findings begins with the interpretation of the different types of findings discussing this interpretation in light of the theoretical foundations presented in the review of relevant literature in Chapter 1.

Chapter V: The Conclusions focuses on conclusions derived from the discussion of the findings, presenting a theoretical and practical modular model that was developed from the research findings and drawing general conclusions. In an additional discussion presented in this chapter, the thesis describes the contribution of the study to extant knowledge, the limitations of the research and recommendations for further research.

Chapter I below describes the theoretical foundations derived from the review of the relevant literature that underpinned the research.

Chapter 1

Theoretical Fundamentals: The Dialogical Approach and Kindergarten Children's Social-Communication Development

1.1 Preview

This work deals with the use of the Multi-Dialogical Approach (MDA) in the kindergarten. Its aim is to examine whether there is a connection between the implementation of the MDA in a kindergarten and the development of kindergarten children's social-communication skills. One of the purposes of preschool education is to allow the child to grow and to evolve into a person involved in society, who has the ability to judge and criticize and is a curious, independent thinker, demonstrating initiative. The basic assumption of Multi-Dialogical Education, which is the topic of the present thesis, is that a child, who learns about his world out of an inner interest, will evolve into that type of a person. The aim of this study is to examine the central aspects of this education, namely, the social-communication patterns and processes of children who learn in a Multi-Dialogical kindergarten.

The main contribution of the humanist psychologist Carl Rogers to the educational field was that:

...he located the educational process on two supporting beams: intellectual and emotional. In order to have effective learning, it is not enough to have the cognitive process of transferring information, solving a problem or phrasing a text; there has to be an experimental event, emotional and authentic, in order for the learning to be effective. Combining intellect and emotion for significant learning can be done only in a dialogical interphase which nurtures interpersonal relationships (Harari, 2008, p. 194).

This chapter will explain how this connection between learning and interpersonal relationships is reflected in practice in a Multi-Dialogical kindergarten.

The Multi-Dialogical kindergarten operates according to the principle that educational plans and children's activities are determined through negotiation with the children while cooperating with them. Therefore, the kindergarten teacher's role is not only to teach but rather to guide the children after checking with them what their interests are. Much emphasis is given to building a learning program in the kindergarten that is based on the children's knowledge and fields of interest, which the teacher identifies by paying attention to what they say and do. From this attentive phase, the teacher guides the children to achieve insight, to develop their autonomy and leadership skills, to lead educational and social processes, to develop their ability to hear other opinions, to receive feedback and to manage negotiation. It is important to mention that the MDA is a pioneering approach in kindergartens. The Italian Reggio Emilia kindergartens can serve as a model and basis for comparison. In these kindergartens emphasis is given to paying attention to children's ideas and helping them to develop their own theories to understand the world. In addition, in the Reggio Emilia kindergartens the children are involved in negotiating the educational program, which is built specifically towards each child's individual needs, relying on the educator's attentiveness and sensitivity to the child.

The theoretical and philosophical grounds for this educational approach stem from the theories of Socrates, Dewey, Buber, Freire, Rogers, Gardner, Vygotsky and Feuerstein, who share support for a dialog-based education, asking questions, listening, and conducting discourse between equals. The learner, the child, is not seen as an empty tool waiting to be filled but rather a true partner to the investigation and learning. Dialog and conversation are, therefore, basic components of all these theories. Dialog is enriched through discourse, in which the participants can exchange ideas, listen to other ways of thinking, investigate a problem in depth and understand its complexity, consolidate assumptions and open them to external criticism. In order to define the uniqueness of each of the above concepts, the difference between dialog and discourse is that during dialog, the communication can be made through talk or conversation, but the verbal aspect is not mandatory. Observation is an example of non-verbal dialog. In contrast, during discourse, communication is only verbal. This means that all discourse is dialog, but not all dialog is discourse. A specific type of discourse is philosophical discourse in which, for example, children raise questions regarding the world around them, and independently investigate their answers and theories, while acquiring discourse capabilities.

In Multi-Dialogical Education children are encouraged to develop social skills that lead to reflection in cooperation among themselves. This involves negotiation while independently trying to solve problems and conflicts, desiring to help a friend in need, and listening to others' ideas and responding to them while building a discourse culture. This MDA turns a spotlight on and encourages the development of children's social-communication skills in the Multi-Dialogical kindergarten. The Multi-Dialogical kindergarten encourages social interactions, shared initiatives, choices and self-guidance activities, as well as cooperation in partnerships. Other principles of this approach include the need to negotiate and solve conflicts without teacher involvement, as well as the ability to be considerate of others. It is helpful to examine how the MDA in the kindergarten conveys and contributes to the development of these skills. In order to understand the central role of discourse and dialog in the multi-dialogical kindergarten, it is necessary to look at the social and interpersonal communication patterns of the children in this type of kindergarten. The objective of the present research was to examine and investigate the social, behavioral and the interpersonal communications patterns that a multi-dialogical kindergarten encourages in children.

I.2 The dialogical approach in education

The MDA argues that the best learning takes place when it comes from the child's inner curiosity and is connected to his strengths (Firstater & Efrat, 2014; Hecht & Ram, 2008). The role of educators is to help each child learn according to his interests. The educators' decisions and the building of the curriculum originated from their attentiveness to the children and their cooperation with them in making these decisions (Lasri, 2004; New, 1998).

The Multi-Dialogical Educational Approach is presented below as well as the theories on which it is based. The review of literature on this approach focuses on the implementation of the MDA in kindergartens including its goals, its work methods, the leading staff, and the characteristic patterns of the kindergarten children's social-communication skills.

I.2.1 Negotiation between educators and children as the basis of the dialogical approach

Understanding ideas and not just repeating them requires a dialogical relationship in education (Wegerif, 2010); dialog enables us to analyze ideas, investigating, and not just accepting them as obvious (Alexander, 2006). At the heart of the dialogical approach is the concept that constant negotiation between the educators and the children on ideas and curriculum will facilitate the development of meaningful learning (Forman & Fyfe, 1998; Lasri, 2004). This means that educators and the children engage in active negotiation about the curriculum and the educational processes, contributing to one another (Jhong, 2008), in dialog based on open questions, reflections, feedback and rebuilding knowledge using each other's ideas (Callander, 2013).

Brain-storming is one of the means used to negotiate and organize knowledge in the dialogical approach. It can be defined as thinking about and exchanging opinions on a particular issue (Firstater & Efrat, 2014), in reciprocal interaction between participants (Ben-Yosef, 2009). In other words, brainstorming is "the knowledge and learning contents set out on the table between two knowledgeable subjects that meet around the table and used for the goal of shared learning" (Shor

& Freire, 1990, p. 107). This means that people develop their ideas and open up to new ideas through dialogical discussion (Feld-Elhanan, 2007), where brain-storming is one of the means for this process (Firstater & Efrat, 2014). This works well on condition that the instructor uses principles of justice and equality and does indeed facilitate the creation of such discussion (Sadan, 2008). Brainstorming plays an educational role (Firstater & Efrat, 2014), when dialog relies on the condition that knowledge of the other is given a place and allowed to be expressed (Feld-Elhanan, 2007).

The discourse in a dialogical learning session is flexible and dynamic. One of its purposes is to help children to construct tools for independent learning and to rouse interest (Ben-Yosef, 2009). Discourse like this begins with brainstorming on the studied subject so that the educators can understand what the children know and want to know on the subject (Firstater & Efrat, 2014). In this sort of discourse the children are given plentiful room to relate to the subject. The educators' role is to understand and ask the children what the intention of their words is in order to understand how and in which way they are thinking and to use this in planning the learning. The continuation of the learning dialog is then constructed in reliance on the children's knowledge and what they want to learn about the subject (Ben-Yosef, 2009). A dialogical learning discourse develops connections and social patterns (Ibid.) and highlights the children's empowerment (Firstater & Efrat, 2014).

According to the dialogical approach, educators and children learn together in dialog characterized by a sense of empowerment alongside an aspiration to produce both personal and general meaning regarding the subject they are discussing. The discussion is conducted in collaboration and in an egalitarian manner between them, so that each of them is fully involved and gaining a rich experience of the situation. Moreover, the subjects that they are discussing are open subjects, so that each subject may open into alternative subjects and they also discuss the implications that stem from their discussion. The significance of learning through dialog is that it encourages the children to ask questions, to think otherwise and to voice their reservations and discuss them without fear of making mistakes. It also encourages them to initiate subjects for discussion and activities. Thus, dialog between educators and students can create a space for thinking and empowerment (Ben-Yosef, 2009). It also creates cooperative thinking but requires clear rules for the dialogical process, which should be accepted by all participants (Fisher, 2007; Lipman, 2003). The dialogical interaction is therefore characterized by a feeling of safety, sympathy-based interpersonal relationships, and consideration and caring between the members of the group, who are able to acknowledge different points of view, but the child also learns to practice self-discipline and to assume his own responsibility for his learning (Aloni, 2008; Hecht & Ram, 2008).

Because of the uniqueness of each learner and the differences between learners, no one path suits everyone, but rather there are different routes which should be combined to create the educational act. Therefore, sharing opinions, peer study, mutual persuasion efforts and being open to the other are essential conditions for the success of this dialog (Aloni, 2008; Hecht & Ram, 2008). In addition, it can be observed that while the children learn the skills of dialog, an infrastructure is created for the learning of other communication skills such as management and leadership of discussions, attentiveness, problem-solving, reacting to other people's ideas, and being ready to change their personal point of view after hearing others' points of view alongside independent thinking (Fisher, 2007).

Independent thinking constitutes an important additional characteristic of the dialogical approach to education and it develops out of negotiations between the educator and the children (Firstater & Efrat, 2014). It is based on the provision of a supportive space where dialog can take place out of respect for the learners (Murphy, 2010). It represents freedom and it is expressed as a resource available to the individual throughout their life experiences and assists them in coping with new situations. In order to attain independent thinking, an individual needs to train to be able to examine themselves from the broadest possible viewpoints and ways of interpretation. An additional ability that should be developed through the dialogical process is the ability to make decisions and to try to realize them out of loyalty to their own path and personal thinking (Aloni, 2013).

One of the roles of education is to enable learners to develop the ability to learn independently and to initiate (White, 2007). In practice, using dialog in learning enables the learner to practice decision-making and to employ independent and caring thinking (Murphy, 2010). In other words, children who experience a sense of commitment and responsibility in their learning will develop independent thinking (Greene, 1995). More specifically, it seems that their personal consideration of contents that are being dealt with leads the children to use and adopt individual concepts such as: what I consider to be interesting, what excites me, with whom I feel it is appropriate to cooperate, the activities in which I would like to participate, what is my opinion on a particular event or subject, what I learn from the event. In other words, when the child gives personal meaning to subjects and contents, he/she assimilates a pattern of constructing a personal worldview (Ben-Yosef, 2009).

This links up with the present research when it is understood that independent thinking is expressed in a person's ability to think in an individual, reflective and critical manner, out of the ability to take responsibility for one's choices, decisions and their implications (Aloni, 2013). When an individual develops independent thinking, this will contribute to their social abilities and improve their ability to integrate within society that is often characterized by uncertainty (Barnett, 2007). Moreover, a person who enjoys independent thinking will consider his thoughts and opinions and try to realize his choices even in the face of strong social pressures (Aloni, 2013), so that he will be able to become an active citizen in the society in which he lives (Murphy, 2010). Thus, when investigating whether the MDA has an effect on social-communication patterns of kindergarten children, one of the skills that should be noted is the children's ability to develop independent thinking.

I.2.2 The educator's role in the dialogical approach

It is important to understand that the dialogical approach is not an educational program but a philosophical belief which implies a change in the conceptualization of the educator's role (Callander, 2013). This study adds another level of understanding, arguing that the use of dialog enables children and educators to learn from each other as a result of their interactions (Alexander, 2006; Wells, 2000), and allows the educators to become part of the learning process since they act to understand the children's motives and lead and guide them accordingly (Jhong, 2008; Rinaldi, 1999). According to this approach, the educators should direct the procedure of the activities and the learning process on the foundation of the children's reactions to contents that emerge and not according to a pre-determined and closed program that principally serves to teach the children what is correct and what is not correct (Ben-Yosef, 2009). At this stage, they discover the children's beliefs, theories and knowledge of the study topics and analyze them, to understand the way that the children think and their meanings (Forman & Fyfe, 1998). In other words, in order to conduct a dialog, the educators must understand the real meanings underlying the children's words (Wells, 1986) to document the children's work and use this documentation as a tool to guide them and as a basis for the curriculum. By doing so, they become investigative educators, who study along with the children, and who ask the children about their future work planning in order to build their work programs (Jhong, 2008; Rinaldi, 1996; Wong, 2009). In contrast, meticulous planning of learning by the educators could stultify the children's development. Structured adherence to predetermined plans leads to the educator's lack of attention to the children's unanticipated reactions, and they fail to consider these reactions, so that no real dialog is enabled (Ben-Yosef, 2009). In contrast, educators working according to the dialogical approach find it very important to plan their meetings with the children in a flexible and dynamic manner. This enables the learning path to progress, yet allows deviations from the subject to be discussed in line with the children's reactions and improvisation, if necessary, to add additional learning paths (Ben-Yosef, 2009). It seems, therefore, that the dialogical approach to education necessitates that the educator should be able to manage and organize time in a flexible manner (Ben-Yosef, 2009; Firstater & Efrat, 2014).

Philosophers agree that, in order to learn, learners should take an active part in their learning process (Ciot, 2009; Palinscar, 1998) and learn to explain their thoughts and ideas on different topics (Alexander, 2006; Skidmore, 2006). Therefore, in dialogical education the learning program is considered as a program that grows out of the children and is constructed by the educators (Forman & Fyfe, 1998) based on what interests the children. Such a program enables the learner to take an active role and also provides options for choice and development of decision-making skills (Seung, Susan & Min, 2005). This is also the reason that according to this approach, the children and educators cope with assignments together as a collective. The children can freely formulate and propose their ideas with the educators' support. The dialog between educators and children is characterized by mutual relations, so that those who participate in the learning listen to each other's ideas, while sharing and observing alternative viewpoints and going deeper into ideas that are developed on the subjects discussed (Alexander, 2006).

The educators' consideration of the children is a very significant element in the MDA. Educators do not assess the children's learning in terms of "correct or incorrect", rather they take the approach that the goal is to understand and learn about the children's reactions to the organization, and starting from this point to allow the children to encounter different viewpoints. As part of this consideration, they are aware that the children's seemingly "incorrect" reactions concerning a particular subject are usually based on creative thinking (Ben-Yosef, 2009). Their role can be seen as identifying the children's initiatives, supporting them and developing them together with the children through mediation (Lasri, 2004). Therefore, part of their role appears to be to stimulate the children's curiosity and desire to learn, to assist them in coping with difficulties that they encounter in the learning process and thus help them to develop. In order to help them to perform this kind of educational work, educators need to be aware of the diversity among the children that is expressed in each child's individual learning style, thinking and areas of interest (Ben-Yosef, 2009).

I.2.3 Observation and attentiveness

Dialog contributes to an individual's emotional and social-communication development. This is because, through dialog, the individual can share his experiences, emotions and actions with others and by doing so, create a basis on which he can develop self-awareness, self-control and thinking tools (Tomasello et al., 2004). Children practice and develop their social skills as a result of activities in which they participate (Berk & Winsler, 1995). By doing so, they use their experiences to create meaning (Vygotsky, 1978), and learn to take responsibility, cooperate, initiate and lead (Claxton & Carr, 2010).

The concept of dialog is not complete without attentiveness. Attentiveness is active communication that includes listening, interpretation, and construction of meaning. It is important to point out that it is not limited to the spoken word and is not passive but rather active. Dialog in education involves attentiveness as part of a dynamic process shared by the children and adults, discussing meanings, and including verbal and non-verbal expressions (Clark & Moss, 2005). In line with this conceptualization, it may be said that, as children possess a hundred languages to express themselves (Malaguzzi, 1998), educators must find a hundred ways to listen (Edwards, Gandini & Foreman, 1998).

Observation and attentiveness are at the basis of the dialogical approach in education and are meant to support and assure mutual communication and investigation by both children and educators (Fiore & Suares, 2010). Despite the notion that attentiveness is mainly connected to what you hear, it is important to understand that attentiveness is also expressed in observation. Attentiveness and observation lead children to take part in social interactions, communication, and cooperation with peers, on the one hand, and allow differences, strengths, and leadership skills to develop, on the other (Seung, Susan & Min, 2005). Thus, we may say that children develop an investigative culture with the help of the educator's guidance through dialog, attentiveness, asking questions, and through the recording of the children's activity. Thus, the educational process evolves from attentiveness, observation and recording, a process which emphasizes the development of social and cognitive skills and talents of the learners (Fiore &

Suares, 2010). The main nexus of the educational process is the meeting between the children and educators, where knowledge is used to serve this purpose (Aloni, 2008). It is therefore important to put the emphasis on how knowledge is acquired rather than on what it actually is. This links up to the current study, which clarifies how this process is carried out by partners in the education process, educators and children, who meet for a mutual activity and mutual processing of the investigated topic or project. Together they propose and discuss theories concerning the involved subject (Edwards, Gandini & Forman, 1998); and negotiate different perspectives and concepts of the investigated realm (Forman & Fyfe, 1998). As a result, children learn out of their own interest and activity in the environment while the educators mediate and help them conceptualize phenomena and situations (Caspi, 1979). With regard to the educational environment, it has been found that children are constantly learning regardless of the educational location, and not only in classrooms (Holt, 2004; Rogers & Freiberg, 1994).

I.2.4 Discourse and dialog

Dialog is a type of interpersonal conversation, speech or communication, characterized by good intentions and reciprocal trust, by openness towards the other and respect for their personality, that over time expands to become self-awareness, awareness of the other, to the subjects of discussion and the relationship between the participants (Ben-Yosef, 2009, p. 150).

Dialog is characterized by the fact that it allows the participants to express their opinions, and any subject can be examined from various viewpoints. Moreover, dialog enables its participants to relate seriously to each other and to develop the ability to understand the thinking, goals and reasoning of others, and so it leads to the development of sensitivity to diversity between different people or different cultures (Lam, 1996). In practice, it can take place in various fields of knowledge and different cultures. In any case it seems that practicing dialogical discourse leads allows the child to develop independent thinking (Firstater & Efrat, 2014). The uniqueness of this type of discourse is expressed in the fact that, on the one hand, there is no intention that the child should reach the "correct" answer, nor does the educator try to persuade the child what is correct or not. On the other hand, it exposes the child to various viewpoints, training him to express his personal opinions and experiences, paying attention to the child and providing the child with feedback. Moreover, with the educator's guidance the child is assisted in producing meaning from his experiences and opinions so that they become part of the child's own world and world view and tools for life (Ben-Yosef, 2009).

Investigating the term "discourse" in education, Bakhtin (1984) distinguishes between two discourse types: one is dialogical and the other monological. It is important to point out the differences between the two terms in order to understand how discourse is connected to dialog. It seems that monological discourse blocks real dialog (Skidmore, 2000). In this discourse, the educator's purpose is to pass knowledge on to the children, and by staying true to these aims, educators gain a large extent of control over the discourse. In fact, it is a discourse that focuses on the educator's power and suffocates dialog, reciprocal relations between the participants of the discourse, and their ideas (Lyle, 2008). In contrast, philosophers note that dialogical discourse fosters the investigation of a subject (O'Connor & Michaels, 2007); and enables adults to pay attention to children's ideas and events (Fisher, 2007). Here the educator's role is not to be the knowledge provider but rather to be the discourse instructor. It can be argued that, in some cases, children have more knowledge than educators on the investigated subject and they learn together. This study adds another level to understanding the concept of reciprocity in education, where the reciprocal relations during discourse expose participants to challenges and changes (O'Connor & Michaels, 2007). There is an understanding among philosophers that the purpose of dialogical discourse is to promote communication by creating a place where many equal voices can participate in discussions. It implies a genuine will to understand the opinions of each of the discourse participants and to build meaning together through cooperation and attentiveness towards one another (Lyle, 2008). This means all participants have a sense of shared experience (Gutierrez & Larson, 1995).

To summarize: Dialogical discourse and dialog are the main characteristics of the dialogical approach in education (Cohen, 2008). What are the commonalities and differences between the two concepts? Both dialog and discourse are based on investigation and developing a subject (O'Connor & Michaels, 2007); both of them constitute a kind of true human partnership whose objective is not to accomplish something but rather to establish reciprocal relationships. The difference between them is that while in dialog the partnership is expressed in both verbal and non-verbal ways, in a dialogical discourse, the partnership is only expressed verbally (Buber, 1980). In practice, the children should be taught the rules of discourse: timing – when to enter into the discourse and say their words, speaking without interrupting the speech of others, respectful consideration of the words of their discourse partners, even if they contradict their own opinions, giving feedback with reasoning and without aggression and without any attempt to enforce their opinions on others (Blum-Kulka, 2008; Cohen, 2008). This forms the foundation for the dialogical approach, allowing the child to practice skills for dialog through dialogical discourse.

I.2.5 Philosophical discourse

With regard to the age appropriate for initiating philosophical discourse, it has been found that even kindergarten children have the ability to conduct a philosophical discourse (Cohen, 2008). There are many similarities between the components of philosophy and education (Lipman & Sharp, 1985). They both focus on investigation, study, examination, reaching conclusions, dialog and are both based on critical thinking and questioning. In sum, there is no way to separate education and philosophy and it can even be argued that philosophy is education. Thus, developing philosophical discourse with children helps them to develop an intellectual and social approach to life (Cohen, 2008).

Philosophical discourse helps to promote children's ability to ask questions and explore the world. There is agreement among philosophers that dialog develops communications skills, curiosity and cooperation among children (Fisher, 2007). This connects to the current study in the way it perceives the importance of discourse as an important component of the educational dialog and in that there is an understanding that in a philosophical discourse, children should have room to ask their own questions, raise topics for discussion, explore their ideas, develop opinions and theories, and listen and voice different points of view on the same learning subject (Fisher, 2007, Lipman, 2003). Despite the different opinions concerning the age at which it is possible to take part in a philosophical discourse, it was found that kindergarten children are indeed able to participate in philosophical discourse, to ask and deal with philosophical questions (Fisher, 2007).

In order to create a philosophical discourse, practical matters must be considered, such as seating arrangements and discourse rules. The seating arrangement during a philosophical discourse is a circle, enabling everyone to see each other. In addition, for the discourse to be fruitful and based on attentiveness, several rules must be enforced: children must listen to each other inside the philosophical discourse circle; only one child talks at a time; children should think before speaking and say what they mean; they are allowed to disagree with another's idea and ask him about his opinion; they must respect one another. Every meeting of philosophical discourse begins with repeating the discourse rules and ends with feedback on how the participants felt during the discourse. Following the rules enables children to explain their opinions, while the educator's role is to mediate the discourse circle (Firstater & Efrat, 2014; Fisher, 2007; Lipman, 2003).

The aim of philosophical discourse with children is not to teach children philosophy but rather to encourage them to create their own philosophy, which will be exploratory, dynamic, investigational, and creative (Cohen, 2008). During a philosophical discourse, an experience is shared and meaning is investigated. As philosophical discourse is based on attentiveness, listening, understanding, empathy, and joint activity (Fisher, 2007), it can be argued that this discourse develops the children's self-awareness and their awareness of other circle participants. In addition, in this way, children develop social and communication skills like reading social situations, persuasive abilities, abilities to lead negotiation, accepting others' opinions and the ability to cooperate (Fisher, 2007; Lipman, 2003).

The dialogical education approach enables children to exercise listening skills, make mistakes and learn from them; give feedback and evaluate one another, and cooperate with one another (Alexander, 2006; Boyd & Markarian, 2011; Jones, 2007). The current study reinforces the understanding that when this approach is implemented, children clearly define their words, learn to ask questions, express themselves in a clearer way, and consolidate points of view that most suit them; all of which help them to develop initiative and leadership (Lyle, 2008).

The educator's mediation plays a significant role in a community that is conducted through dialog with the children. Dialog mediation can bring the children to a higher level of cognitive development at an earlier age. In mediating the dialog educators enable the children to share ideas and options and consequently to challenge one another's thinking (Lyle, 2008). Knowledge and understanding are learned and developed when both educators and children conduct mutual examinations, seeking proof, analyzing ideas and investigating values.

It is understood that during the learning process, the children's contribution to the learning is equal to the educator's, whereas the educators should understand the children's thinking, letting them develop their thoughts and speak about them (Alexander, 2006). They should also enable the children to ask questions and bring their own points of view. At this stage of the dialog, the educators should be able to recognize and respond to the children's ideas by listening to them and be able to develop them into learning subjects. It is important to emphasize that children will be more involved in the development and learning of these subjects, together with the educators, because the subjects have originated from their fields of interests (Alexander, 2006). Meaningful activity guided by the educator's mediation supports the development of the children's social skills, such as commitment, responsibility, self-confidence and independence (Lyle, 2008).

The key to a successful dialog is listening, self-recognition and mutual understanding, but not necessarily mutual agreement (Lyle, 2008). Philosophers who deal with dialog and education agree that the basic characters of dialogic approach in education are: negotiation between participants in the educational process, attentiveness to children's theories which is used to create the foundation for learning, understanding that the meeting of children and educators is the main learning process and that knowledge is only a learning tool. This approach has deep roots in history (Aloni, 2008; Forman & Fyfe, 1998; Lasri, 2004) as is described in the next section.

I.3 Main fundamental theories in dialogical education

The ideas behind the dialogical approach in education, especially the term "dialog," have been well known throughout human history and in philosophical theories. In the fifth century BC, the Greek philosopher Socrates defined the dialog as conversation, conducted with the purpose of developing independent thinking (Cohen, 2008). The philosopher Buber defined dialog as a situation that allows a person to acknowledge himself through contact with another, aiming to create a partnership on the way to reaching the truth (Buber, 1980). Dewey, a twentieth century educational philosopher, an educator himself, and one of the designers of progressive education, referred to the dialog as negotiation between an individual and society (Cohen, 1983). Rogers, a twentieth century psychologist, writing in the 1950s, saw the dialog as a meeting between equally-valued people (Rogers & Freiberg, 1994). Freire, a twentieth century educator, declared that dialog is an egalitarian discourse between educators and learners, based on mutual respect and originates from the learner's life (Gur, 2007). According to the Multiple Intelligences theory developed by the psychologist Gardner, dialog recognizes strong intelligence within a child and helps to nurture it (Gardner, 1996).

Vygotsky, a developmental psychologist, and Feuerstein, a professor of educational psychology, have contributed to conceptualization of the term "mediation". Vygotsky developed the "zone of proximal development" and Feuerstein expanded this theory into his "mediated learning" theory (Feuerstein, Klein & Tenenbaum, 1991).

This part of the chapter details these theories and philosophies and indicates their affinity to education and dialog.

I.3.1 The dialog and Socratic discourse

Dialog and Socratic discourse are conducted through asking questions and the answers to these questions provide material for investigation and the drawing of conclusions. This study adds another level of understanding to extant theory on such dialog, explaining how this dialog can be used among kindergarten children. This type of dialog is possible only when the educators enable the children's self-comprehension without instilling their personal opinions and allow the children to learn from their own mistakes (Tauber, 2008). In Socratic discourse, the conversation leader learns from the participants. The questions, based on prior knowledge, are key to this discourse and reveal much more about the person asking the question and his world than do the answers. Putting the emphasis on the questions proves that knowledge is not determined but rather is constantly evolving and subject to investigation. The questions are not divided into minor or major questions and there is no one right answer. The essence of the question, the investigation and examination, awaken goodness in a person, give perspective to his life, establish his autonomy and nurture his intellect (Cohen, 2008). This interpretation leads us to understand that by asking questions, people can become aware of themselves, their nature, and their inner potential. By doing so, they actually develop their social and intellectual skills. This training develops tools for better decision-making, examining every subject from many different angles and enabling the investigation of each subject with a question. This discussion of many different aspects eventually improves the individual's ability to use decision-making skills (Phillips, 2004).

Deep observation of Socratic discourse indicates that this is a structured discourse, although not a rigid one, and it is not based on random questions. It has a direction and focuses on a certain subject. In this discourse, assumptions are made, theories are built, and answers are investigated, which can also be denied if they do not contribute to the discussion or add to the investigated subject. Therefore, it is important for the discourse leader to know how to maintain the discourse structure and evolvement without letting it turn into the small talk of an exchange of opinions (Cohen, 2008).

The Socratic dialog is serious and strict and focuses on seeking the truth, although its atmosphere might seem light, relaxed, humoristic and ironic (Phillips, 2004). The strict nature of the discourse is reflected in a critical dialog in which both leaders and participants are aware of mistakes and wrong thoughts. As soon as mistakes are recognized, they are acknowledged, not by ruling them out but rather by bringing opposite examples and dealing with them (Cohen, 2008). The participants should take responsibility for the dialog and the discourse. They should question their own questions, correct their own mistakes, investigate their discourse and examine the way they think (Reed & Johnson, 1999).

It is important to understand that Socratic discourse does not teach consensual truths or lecture the listeners. Rather, it is a dialog that aims to promote independent thinking (Tauber, 2008). During this discourse, participants' comprehension and ideas are revealed, and others point out where they are wrong. Participants become aware of their contradictions and may reach the conclusion that they do not have a clear knowledge of the discussed subject (Cohen, 2008). The purpose of this discourse is to shed participants' confidence in their knowledge, expose the underlying hidden truth, and clear the way for thinking (Tauber, 2008). Socrates said that the success of a pedagogic dialogic process depends on several factors connected to the educators and children and to address these aspects both educators' and children's views should be taken into account. The educators should believe in the children's ability to explore, learn, discover and reach conclusions. They should help the children to discover their own ability to study and learn, assuming that the children have the intellectual and mental ability to do so. On the other hand, in order to have a pedagogic dialog, the children should be encouraged to have a passion for learning and the educational process and have curiosity and interest in the investigated subject (Phillips, 2004).

Another important aspect of the Socratic dialog is silence. Silence during dialog can be very powerful as it allows for the birth of the answer, challenges thinking and opens it up. In order to go deeply into this thinking, it should be acknowledged that both educators and children have a place in the dialog, and educators should learn never to reach new insights instead of the children. Their job is to enable the children to learn by themselves, for themselves, and from themselves, and not to tell the children what is right and what is wrong about the subject being studied. Therefore, they should guide the children and wait for the answers to come from them. A question may be raised as to how the educator is to react to children's wrong answers. The answer is that, if the children give wrong answers, the educator should continue to guide them by asking additional guiding questions. They should continue to do so until the children come to their own conclusions about their wrong answers (Cohen, 2008). In order for children to learn by themselves, for themselves and from themselves, they need to abandon wrong conclusions, understand that they do not know everything, and from this point, start a quest to acquire the right knowledge. No learning process or dialog is completed before children go through these stages. It is therefore suggested that whatever children learn by themselves will become part of their personality (Tauber, 2008).

I.3.2 The Buberian dialog

Martin Buber, the noted philosopher, saw "dialog" as a situation that allows a person to get to know himself through the encounter with others, aiming to create a partnership that will reveal the truth (Buber, 1980), where each participant aspires to realize their own uniqueness (Cohen, 2001). Buber distinguished two modes of being: a dialog state which he named a state of "I-You", and a mode which is the opposite of a dialog, reflected by the term: "I-It". In the "I-you" mode, there is a true dialog in an encounter between two peers, which does not necessarily have to be through direct conversation. Each of the peers acknowledges the other and addresses him with respect in order to have a true reciprocal relationship. Through the dialog, true responsibility develops (Cohen, 1976; Friedman, 2002) and relationships are experienced through attentiveness to oneself, to peers and to the world (Avnon, 2008). In an encounter of this kind each person brings with him a presence, which in many ways is incomplete. This may be expressed in intellectual, spiritual, historical, physical, emotional terms (Ben-Yosef, 2009). On the other hand, in the "I-It" mode, there is no dialog but rather a conversation between people with no real attentiveness (Aloni, 2008; Buber, 1980; Friedman, 2002). Monologue is disguised as a dialog, and people seem to be talking to each other while really just talking to themselves. It is important to emphasize that a person cannot be forced into a dialog, which should develop out of a free will.

Dialog is not restricted to educator-children relationships (Bartholo, Tunes & Tacca, 2010) but is a genuine process which exists with or without words and is based on reciprocity. Specifically, a true dialog exists when a true reciprocal relationship is developed between one person and another, and this relationship is reflected in a mutual experience in which at least one of the participants takes an active role. The reciprocal relationship, i.e. the dialog, allows each participant to experience events through another person's point of view. Another aspect of the dialog is trust. To summarize, reciprocal relations in dialog help to develop trust between educators and children and allow both educators and children to be open to new ideas and to learn from each other (Baniwal, 2014; Buber, 2002).

Educators play an essential role in Buberian dialog. Although the educator does not see it as his role to change the children or replace their own truths; it is his job to nurture and develop each child according to his unique inner-character (Harari, 2008).

In relation to the current study, it can be stated that an educational perspective that argues that it is not the educator's role to provide, design, pass over, or deliver, but rather to create true interaction while trying to be in constant dialog with the children within an "I-You" mode. The definition of the educational act is that the educators hold great responsibility for the children's souls and inner-worlds, and should influence them without inducing force but through a gentle balance between closeness and distance (Avnon, 2008). This leads to the understanding that the affinity between the educators and the children is not through influence over the not-fully developed mind by a fully developed one, but a soul to soul affinity, where the emphasis is on real partnership between the two (Buber, 1980).

The minor difference, which is sometimes unnoticeable, between guidance and interference, is critical when creating a dialog. This understanding is relevant for the current study, which examined the effects of dialog as part of the MDA in kindergarten; there is an emphasis on the fact that educators should maintain this gentle balance. On the one hand, educators should not interfere with children's choices and with their autonomous learning, but on the other hand, they should guide the children by pointing out directions that will further develop their learning (Baniwal, 2014). In other words, a direct order is negated in the Buberian dialog. Therefore, the educators' main role is turning children's hearts towards reality, not by direct order but rather by paving the way towards it. In addition, educators should not force an accepted value-system on the children or give them ready-to-use solutions (Cohen, 1976); but rather show them the way to find their own solutions, and while doing so, contribute to the children's spontaneous and appropriate development. Therefore, the educators' main role is to help the children help themselves. This does not mean they should be completely neutral and stand on the side, but they should guide the children towards a directed path. The educators' role is to allow the children guided freedom so that the children can explore and walk carefully through trial and self-expression, accompanied by the educator, who should help and guide the children (Aloni, 2008).

One of Buber's basic educational concepts is the educational meeting, which lies at the core of the educational process (Avnon, 2008). This human encounter is based on the significant dialog which leads to a sense of confidence, empathy, relativity and support (Ministry of Education, 2010). To be more specific, the relationship formed in the encounter between a child and an educator acts as a guiding force, which helps to develop and support the child's abilities. Through this meeting, the child's reality becomes more real and the components of their reality change from abstract to immediate and concrete (Buber, 1980).

Buber indicates that in order to have a meaningful dialog with another, the individual should be in a true dialog with himself first (Harari, 2008). A dialog cannot be forced on a person, but the dialog is open to everyone. The dialog originating from within a person will grow into an "I-You" dialog with the other if it is based on a reciprocal relationship and mutuality. When a person learns to be true and responsible for himself, for others and for reality, he will be able to make decisions and fulfill any goal (Cohen, 1976).

I.3.3 Educational theory of John Dewey

John Dewey, an educator and educational philosopher of the twentieth century, who was one of the designers of progressive education, created the concept of negotiation between an individual and society. He indicated that society's demands for law keeping depend on a person's freedom to evaluate, examine, doubt, judge, act, choose, investigate and fulfill (Cohen, 1983). Education should therefore offer the learner the freedom to explore and experience (Dewey, 1938). Learning through problem-solving and practical coping with different issues helps children to take on a more active role as members of the society and develop social skills like initiative, problem-solving, the ability to take a stand, and listening (Aliakbari & Faraji, 2011; Gover, 2008).

Dewey addressed social and communication skills as a significant part of his philosophy. He theorized that the purpose of education is to help children to develop social and communication skills such as sensitivity, honesty, generosity, empathy, self-restraint, and good judgment (Dewey, 1997). This aim can be reached by providing real life experiences for children, even at a preschool age, experiences which necessitate character building and good judgment, and from which the children can learn. Two methods should be used for learning: first, self-example (modeling) by the educator's behavior and second, by experiencing daily social dilemmas under guidance from the educator (Aloni, 2008). Life is seen as an experience-based adaptation process and children can be made more aware of these processes by the educators' guidance and trained to develop social-communication skills which will help them to adapt (Dewey, 1961). Adherence to habits, routine acts and impulsivity do not prepare a person to cope with changing situations and are in conflict with the Dewey's theories regarding negotiation about curriculum development (Cohen, 1983).

Childhood is not seen as a preparation for adulthood but rather has a purpose in itself (Hecht & Ram, 2008). Childhood has a value of its own and is a present time process. Education is the essential act of productive living and not a means to prepare for life (Dewey, 1956). This relates to the current study by clarifying the nature of the kindergarten as a representation of present time, similar to the home, similar to the environment and similar to the playground, that is, a realistic educational presence for the children (Cohen, 1983).

The responsibility for the educational process rests on the educators. The children do not have, nor should they have, total freedom (Dewey, 1988). Therefore, the educators' role is to train children's intelligence in various areas: intellectual, social, and communication with the environment. This does mean the limitation of freedom; training the children helps them to increase their freedom (Dewey, 1997). Despite the concept of partnership between educators and children in defining the educational content, it is important to understand that educators are the ones responsible for negotiation about the curriculum and to ensure that it represents the present life of the children. It is their responsibility to create the reciprocal acts and the mutual connections within their mutual group with the children (Hecht & Ram, 2008).

Dewey's approach to education emphasizes the importance of nurturing individual personalities. This is achieved by allowing the children's activity to be free; this permits them to develop internal discipline, and the children's learning will be derived from their experiences. There is an underlying assumption that education should be about seizing present opportunities and not about preparation for future life. Therefore, not all children will reach the same intellectual, communicational, and social intelligence within a certain time frame (Cohen, 1983). Education gives the children the ability to think; its purpose is not to teach the child how to think. According to this theory, by nurturing and developing children's thinking, they will be given the tools to develop their social, communicational and intellectual lives in the present and in the future (Cohen, 2008).

It is true that education should originate from children's needs and interests, but these are not aims in themselves, but rather means for children's development. The natural impulses of children should be maintained and directed towards growing (Dewey, 1988). The term "grow" refers to bringing the children's strengths into play and raising them to a higher level of social, communicational, and intellectual skills, including judgment, perception and behavioral habits. This is under the understanding that it is only when educators recognize children's impulses and interests that they will be able to guide them through curriculum negotiation (Dewey, 1997). In relation to the present study, this perspective emphasizes the need to support the diversity that exists among children by building and embracing pedagogic tools that will nurture these differences (Wolensky, 2014).

This approach to education, which is based on the children's experiences, is not easy to implement because the educators' guidance is not enforced but rather comes from negotiation. When considering the organization of the environment, the educators' place in it should be considered as well. They should create the best environments to support the performance of experiments that will lead to growth; take account of environmental elements and take advantage of them (Cohen, 1983).

It is important to note the difference between external and internal conditions, as this type of education can only evolve by assuming that internal conditions precede external conditions. External conditions include the teacher, books, equipment and other tools that, in fact, represent the adult's experience. In contrast, internal conditions are the feelings and immediate tendencies of the child (Dewey, 1997). It can be concluded that, at a certain point, the existence of these internal conditions will determine the educational process. Understanding that growth, which is a goal in itself, encompasses a person's life, allows us to determine that the purpose of education in the kindergarten is to create conditions which will assure continuous lifelong education by promoting strengths that ensure growth (Dewey, 1997).

I.3.4 The Rogerian Dialog

Karl Rogers, a psychologist writing in the 1950s, considered dialog as meeting between two equal human beings whose connection is based on care, trust and honesty. They try to understand each other's agreements and disagreements (Rogers & Freiberg, 1994). A central part of his theory is "active listening", meaning a mental activity that involves the listener's strong concentration, and in which the listener does not only hear but also senses the message; succeeds in hearing both what is actually being said, and what is said between the lines, and then acknowledges, while listening, the verbal and non-verbal messages delivered by the speaker (Zamir, 2006).

In order to understand Roger's interpretation of "dialog", it is important to recognize that a person has an internal need to meet with others and to conduct dialog. Meaningful dialog and discourse can only be realized if the person meets his inner-self first, parts within him that are not always familiar to him. In other words, as soon as he is aware of himself, he will be able to succeed in creating a meaningful dialog with the other (Harari, 2008). The reason is that his awareness, which comprises an important part of his personality, must be brought to the meeting with the other. In education, this means that a dialogical discourse between an educator and a child, which occurs in a respectful, non-judgmental environment, brings reciprocity and equality (Zamir, 2006). In order to go deeper into this subject, it is important to understand that in any discourse of this kind, there are meaningful moments that serve as turning points. These moments, which are characterized by attentive communication, begin the growth process. During these moments, equilibrium is formed between the educator and the learner, and change is manifested in both of them as a result of their interaction. This study adds another level to the understanding that for this growth to happen, positive elements should exist during the discourse, such as empathy, acceptance and equality (Harari, 2008).

According to Rogers, a dialog enables self-realization, growth and development. Children, by their nature, can grow and seek challenges while striving for freedom. Meaningful learning, using dialog, provides the means for the children to gain self-recognition, to grow and to develop; and this will be achieved if the educators respect the children, value them and enable their learning (Harari, 2008; Rogers & Freiberg, 1994). Meaningful learning occurs when both emotional and intellectual aspects are addressed and expressed in learning. Meaningful learning originates from experiential learning which is based on emotion and intellect. The emotional aspect is manifested by emotional involvement, arousal, intention, excitement and re-defining the experiences and the emotions. The intellectual aspect is manifested by exploring existing perceptions and acquiring new ones. Combining the two during the experiential learning helps the learner to re-organize the self and leads to meaningful learning (Harari, 2008).

Children possess natural potential for learning that must be realized, retained and not suppressed. In order to safeguard this potential, children should be given the opportunity to determine their own educational goals, goals which they aim to progress to, and they should be involved in determining their assignments and the evaluation of these assignments (Zamir, 2006). This means that the educational curriculum should be determined in line with the children's areas of interest, where the educators are involved and assist them in building and implementing it. Children, by nature, have internal drive, motivation, and curiosity for learning. They consider their environment as a challenge which holds great opportunities for exploration and learning, and they know how to think independently and reach new understandings (Harari, 2008).

A central part of Rogers's theory is the "freedom to learn". The educators' role is to allow children the freedom to learn. The experiential aspect of the learning is gained through children's actions, while learning, which leaves everything in educators' hands, is passive and freedom-less. In contrast, in dialogical learning, the educators aim to create conditions that will assist children's learning, but not teach them directly. Children should be trusted and believed, granting them the freedom to learn (Rogers & Freiberg, 1994). In order for this freedom to be realized, the learning curriculum should be relevant to the children, while the educators allow them to choose what they learn independently and help them to learn out of the experience. If they are granted this kind of learning, they will have greater knowledge of the subjects being taught and will be more persistent in their learning (Rogers & Freiberg, 1994).

Dialog between educators and children is realized by direct personal and humane encounters between one human being and another, based on honesty, credibility and authenticity. In this context, the interaction and dialog between the educators and the children plays a significant role in learning. This interaction demands that the educators, who are assisting the children in their learning, enter the learning process without pretense, being attentive to and aware of the children's emotions (Anderson & Cissna, 1997). In addition, they should be capable of expressing their own emotions to the children when needed, and share their feelings (Ibid.).

Dialog and learning are connected to each other. As meaningful as one can be, the other can be even more meaningful. As noted above, the way to make dialog more meaningful is through appreciation, acceptance and respect by the educators for the children, which are the crucial conditions for the existence of this dialog (Zamir, 2006). Educators should be able to comprehend the children's emotions with all their experiential elements during learning including: frustration, boredom, excitement, anger, indifference, spiritual elevation; without being judgmental or critical. This sends a message to the children that they are not perfect but possess potential and ability, and this, in fact, signifies the basic trust between them. Another condition for the existence of a meaningful dialog is the educators' empathetic understanding towards the children. This understanding will be realized when educators are able to understand the children's inner world, and the children's own perceptions of the learning process (Harari, 2008).

Rogers's theory on dialog is based on the emotional involvement of the educators that is expressed by their enthusiasm and their sensitivity to the children during the learning process, and which is a condition for experiential learning. In this way, the educators lead the children to their emotional standpoint which is very important for real learning (Rogers & Freiberg, 1994). In addition, the educators' role is to create a climate of acceptance by offering their points of view in a non-judgmental manner, expressing their trust in the children, and giving legitimacy to the children's expressions of their points of view and emotions (Anderson & Cissna, 1997). All of the above strategies create dialog that can help the children improve their overall functioning and improve their ability to develop themselves in their own way. These strategies contribute to the development of the children's communicational and social life-skills, by allowing them to become more open people, more at peace with themselves, more autonomous, and with a greater capability to feel empathy with others (Harari, 2008).

I.3.5 Paulo Freire's pedagogical dialog. Critical pedagogy

Paulo Freire, an educator of the twentieth century, also dealt with dialog from an educational viewpoint. According to his approach: "Dialog is a state in which people meet in order to think together about their reality, about its creation and design …dialog helps us to think together about the things that we know and those that we do not know, and to act, out of a critical opinion, to change the reality" (Shor & Freire, 1990, p. 160).

Freire claimed that dialog is an equal discourse between learners and educators, based on mutual respect and originates from the learners' life (Gur, 2007). The dialog is at the heart of the educational process and its purpose is to bring a change in reality, where acquisition of knowledge allows a person to reach a higher state of awareness and self-esteem, gives him a sense of control over his life and the ability to struggle for change in the face of society (Darom, 1989; Gover, 2008).

In order to understand Freire's theory, a clear difference must be drawn between the two terms discussed by him: the "banking" concept of education and "conscientization". According to the banking concept, the learner is considered an empty vessel that should be filled by the educators and be deposited with facts, values, knowledge and beliefs; this means that the learners passively absorb knowledge. The educational process is imagined as depositing knowledge in a bank and it is assumed that the learners possess no opinions, no creativity and no understanding. Therefore, if the educator is the subject of the learning process, the learners are only the objects, and the process results in them taking a passive object role in society. The second term, conscientization, refers to education that brings up problems and originates from a dialog. This term is the complete opposite of the banking concept of education. Conscientization is a dialogic process that builds a bridge between the educators' role and the learners, who are usually considered to be opposites. In fact, they are not opposites, as both of them simultaneously teach and learn. Therefore, the concept of teaching educators and learning children does not exist. Moreover, in this educational dialog, a form of partnership is formed, involving mutual examination, reciprocal influence and dialog between equals (Aliakbari & Faraji, 2011; Darom, 1989; Freire, 2000; Gover, 2008).

The educators are not the center of knowledge; rather they deliver knowledge in the process of dialog with the children (Aliakbari & Faraji, 2011). To do so, they should give up total control of the learning process in order to create such a dialog (Freire & Freire, 2004; Foley, 2007). This type of dialog is employed by educators, who present children with problems in accordance with their areas of interest and their lives (Gover, 2008). These educators strengthen the children and treat them, from the early stages of learning, as significant learners. In practice, it means that the educators need to explore the children's world in order to recognize it, acknowledge it, and respect it. In addition, they are required to learn the children's languages, and their special phrases, and by doing so, empower them by hearing their unique voices and seriously consider these voices from the beginning of the dialog (Gover, 2008). Moreover, the educators should possess the ability to initiate a critical process with the children, acknowledging their point of view, and this will eventually engender a true dialog leading to a contribution to society (Sadeghi, 2008).

Learning has dual goals: one – understanding reality, and second – a struggle to change the reality (Darom, 1989). According to this conceptualization, children and educators need each other to re-learn, and to explore their knowledge and opinions, in order to create new knowledge that will lead to change. In any event, it can be argued that as long as children are part of the creation of knowledge, they will grow to understand reality (Gover, 2008). This study will add another aspect to the understanding that in order for children to understand reality, their learning should be based on authentic materials (Ohara, Safe & Crookes, 2000) which have originated from their experiences. At this point, educators and children, using their dialog, should analyze these materials, discuss and critically think about them. They should bring their experience into the educational dialog as well as their mutual learning (Kincheloe, 2005).

It seems that children's interest in the explored subjects is critical. If the learning contents are relevant and meaningful for the children, and originate from their areas of interest (Okazaki, 2005), the children will learn to connect their knowledge to existing problems of society, and this can lead them to change it. All of the above strategies help the children to develop their social skills such as leadership, initiative, and taking a stand (Ares, 2006; Dheram, 2007).

I.3.6 Dialog and mediation – Lev Vygotsky and Reuven Feuerstein

Lev Vygotsky, a developmental psychologist and Reuven Feuerstein, a professor of educational psychology, have greatly contributed to an understanding of the term "mediation" in education. Vygotsky developed a mediation theory involving learning in the "zone of proximal development". Feuerstein broadened and further developed this theory. Feuerstein's theory of "mediated learning" originated from the concept of "learning in the zone of proximal development", coined by Vygotsky, and the understanding that social interaction influences thinking development (Feuerstein, Klein & Tennenbaum, 1991).

I.3.6.1 Lev Vygotsky's Mediation and Dialog

The concepts of "learning" and "development" are central to Lev Vygotsky's mediation theory. Learning and development have reciprocal relations. Learning enables development, meaning that it comes first. Children possess consciousness functions that have not been fully developed but are in developmental stages. Through their interaction with their human environment, which is in fact the learning process, these pre-developmental functions are turned into thinking abilities that define the level of the child's development (Klein, 1986). This study will shed light on the educational implication of this theory, which is the understanding that whatever children can perform at present, with assistance, they will be able to perform by themselves in the future. Therefore, the best learning is learning that comes before the development and that leads it forward (Feuerstein, Klein & Tennenbaum, 1991).

Vygotsky's conception of learning relates to the fact that it is performed during children's daily activities within their world. As a result, children gain knowledge about the world and about themselves at the same time. In addition, the learning should be acquired by the children in an active and independent way, so that they can build knowledge and not just receive it from the educators. In other words, when children are passive recipients of information, while teachers are active, serving as tools to deliver knowledge, no learning will take place (Stetsenko, 2009). This concept emphasizes that the educational process is the source of learning, and not the cognitive result that follows (Vygotsky, 1999). The term development has an important place in Vygotsky's theory. The developmental process starts with the interaction between educators and children, which is internalized over time, and which becomes an inner cognitive tool that a child can use when facing other tasks. The interaction between the children and educators is, in fact, the basis of the development of a child's cognitive tools (Vygotsky, 1978, 1999). The explanation of the nature of development and its central role in the learning process is characterized by the term "zone of proximal development" which represents the distance between the current developmental stage and the potential next stage (Vygotsky, 2002; Bodrova & Leong, 2007). Looking deeply into this concept it can be argued that children are at a certain developmental level where a wide range of educational interventions is open to the educators. These interventions will advance development to a higher level. In other words, the "zone of proximal development" defines the distance between the children's level of development at present and the level they will reach following the educators' mediation. This is, in fact, the zone where learning is taking place (Tzuriel & Shamir, 2007). Developmental processes and learning processes are not identical: the learning process is followed by the developmental one. The learning process occurs in the "zone of proximal development" and upon being internalized, it becomes a developmental process (Klein, 1986; Bodrova & Leong, 2007).

There is a strong connection between an educational process and a social process; one cannot exist without the other. More specifically, it can be argued that the educational aim is not to acquire knowledge but to generate a process that motivates and contributes to the social aspect of individual development (Stetsenko, 2009). Moreover, the purpose of learning is to establish a person's identity through the social skills he acquires during his learning process (Kozulin, 2004; Stetsenko, 2009; Vianna & Stetsenko, 2006). This personal development arises from the interaction and cooperation with society (Vianna & Stetsenko, 2006).

Social adaption leads to learning. This means that the development of social and communicational skills is very significant for a child's learning (Tzuriel & Shamir, 2007). According to this conceptualization, there are constant social and cultural influences on children's learning; every learning process is influenced by its social context. This understanding is very important, as children are active and energetic learners who build their knowledge mainly on social interactions (Rahim & Rahman, 2013). True learning, accomplished by exploring and discovering, will give children active knowledge and the opportunity to practice the acquisition of social and communicational skills, which will be needed for the next educational level (Stetsenko, 2009; Vianna & Stetsenko, 2006). It can be argued that cognitive development takes place following the reciprocal relations between the spontaneous development of children and their social interaction with their peers and the adults around them (Tzuriel & Shamir, 2007).

Dialog that originates from mediation develops high mental abilities in children's social and communicational areas (Vygotsky, 1978). In order for children's learning to be effective, they need organized mediation, integrated and implemented in accordance with their level of knowledge; this is, in fact, the role of the educators. In order to achieve effective mediation, the educator should cooperate with children in mutual activities that possess cognitive aspects, and which are adapted to the children's level of development (Wertsch & Rogoff,

1984). In addition, educators should analyze the children's knowledge at each level and use this analysis to assist the children in continuing their developmental steps according to their own pace and ability (Tzuriel & Shamir, 2007); by doing so, they will advance and develop the children in practice (Wertsch & Rogoff, 1984).

The great art of educators is to realize when to be the mediator, to recognize when mediation is not well suited to the child's developmental level and to allow the child to understand and further grow by dealing with the learning problem he is facing (Tzuriel & Shamir, 2007).

The rationale of Vygotsky's theory is that any individual, including a child, is a social creature and therefore establishes relationships with those around him: his family, his friends, and his educators. With a little assistance and mediation, he can learn from social contexts much more than he would without this mediation. This leads to Vygotsky's conclusion that, by receiving the right mediation through language, the child's social world will become the main toolbox for his actions and learning. This mediation should be accompanied by attentiveness and dialog, which will help the educators understand how the children see the world (Lyle, 2008; Tzuriel & Shamir, 2007).

I.3.6.2 Reuven Feuerstein's Mediation and Dialog

Feuerstein envisaged two channels of development and learning: one channel is learning through direct experience with objects which originate from the direct meeting of the person with environmental stimulations. The second channel is learning through mediation. This learning originates from a mediated meeting between a person and his environment, which leads to change in understanding that can be implemented in future new situations and stimulations, which is, in fact, development (Klein, 1986; Isman & Tzuriel, 2008).

The main concept established by Feuerstein is "mediated learning". Mediated learning is defined as the valuable interaction between a person and his environment. The uniqueness and importance of mediated learning is that it does not serve merely as stimulation for the children, while letting them know about the focus of this stimulation, but rather it enables the learning of tendencies, approaches and general techniques upon exposure to stimulations, which will be used by the children in future exposure to stimulations (Feuerstein, Klein & Tennenbaum, 1991). With regard to the current study, it can be argued that mediated learning allows children to learn to "see" more and learn more when encountering future stimulations (Isman & Tzuriel, 2008).

Feuerstein's conceptualization suggests that mediated learning is the factor responsible for the development of flexible thinking. Flexibility ensures the signification of a stimulus. To deepen this idea, it may be suggested that mediated learning creates flexible adaptation, which we call intelligence. Intelligence, in its broader meaning, is a person's ability to adapt, to fit, and to change his reaction to a new situation or stimulus that requires such a change. This ability to adapt, fit and change one's reaction is, in fact, the measure of his intelligence (Feuerstein, Klein & Tennenbaum, 1991; Klein, 1986).

One of the main areas to be considered is the quality of mediation. When creating a dialog, the quality of mediated learning is based on three criteria that should come into action: First, intentionality and reciprocity. Second, transcendence, and third, mediation of meaning. "Intentionality and reciprocity" refer, on the one hand, to the guided interaction between educators and children that can be considered mediated learning only if educators intend to be mediators and succeed in transferring this intention to children. On the other hand, the mediation act will be successful only if the children accept the educator's invitation, once it is brought to their attention, which creates the reciprocity. This criterion indicates that this kind of learning occurs by children's choice, and its internalization will result in a significant change of thinking (Isman & Tzuriel, 2008). Another main criterion, transcendence, links the mediation to the stimulus and to what lies beyond this specific stimulus. This means that every educator's mediation to the children serves as a model for the children that will be used to learn something beyond their immediate needs. In other words, this learning creates distance in both time and space from the instant needs of the child: it "implants" the goal of stepping away from the immediate and visibly seen. The result is, therefore, that transcendence enables the transfer of learning to new stimuli and situations. The third and last criterion is mediation of meaning. The goal of mediation of meaning is that children will learn to search for meaning based upon the mediation delivered to them. It is important to stress that meaning can originate from different fields: emotional, values, social, cognitive, and cultural. This meaning can be realized in many ways, such as choosing the learning materials, accentuation, and time dedicated to a specific subject, tone of the voice. The unique contribution of the mediation of meaning to children is that it passes on the mediator's values and culture to them and also deepens their need to search for meaning in things, experiences and information on the other hand (Feuerstein, Klein & Tennenbaum, 1991; Klein, 1986).

To summarize the theory of mediated learning, children who experience a meaningful mediation in an active way, succeed in internalizing this mediation and transferring it to make their own meanings that originate from new information they encounter. In order to assist them, educators should organize the educational environment to enable the children to succeed, so that the children can develop the feeling that they can operate independently and can succeed in doing so (Feuerstein, Klein & Tennenbaum, 1991; Klein, 1986). These educational and philosophical theories of Feuerstein and Vygotsky form the basis for the multi-dialogic education approach.

I.3.7 Howard Gardner's multiple intelligences theory

The psychologist Howard Gardner developed the Multiple Intelligences Theory. According to this theory, "dialog" relates to the recognition of the child's strong intelligence and support for this intelligence by strengthening it. This dialog is realized through the educator's evaluation of the child's tendencies and self-abilities, and by finding specific ways to teach him suitable subjects accordingly (Gardner, 1996).

Gardner's conceptualization of Multiple Intelligences originates from the study of awareness, which has been elucidated in cognitive science and study of the brain, and the nervous system. It relates to the different ways in which people develop life skills, indicating that each person has his strong areas of intelligence which are manifested in a number of areas. In practice, it must be understood that the individual, even children, can be strong in one area while being less strong in another (Retting, 2005).

The intelligences Gardner refers to are not abstract and can be easily recognized (Gardner, 1996). There is agreement among researchers that individuals all have different unique intelligence profiles with which they are born and by which they are eventually characterized (Gardner, 1996; Retting, 2005; Willingham, 2004). While every individual possesses all intelligences at a certain level, each person has his stronger and weaker ones. Most tasks that a person performs will require more than one type of intelligence. The different intelligences are not used independently but rather complement one another, meaning there is no way to totally differentiate one from another (Willingham, 2004). It was also found that each of the intelligençes can be divided into sub-intelligences. In any event, it can be stated that the Multiple Intelligences Theory's main contribution is to recognize the diversity of the intellect.

More specifically, there are eight intelligences (Willingham, 2004) that are used concurrently as each individual develops skills or solves problems. They are also used to produce entire social areas such as professions, hobbies, etc. *Linguistic intelligence* is a high ability to master the language area, verbal or written. *Logical-mathematical intelligence* is associated with scientific and mathematical thinking, and consists of the ability to think logically. *Visual-Spatial intelligence* provides the ability to create mental images. *Musical intelligence* encompasses the high ability to create music and rhythm and is based on certain areas of the brain that function in the comprehension and creation of music. *Bodily-kinesthetic intelligence* is the ability to use the body or parts of it to coordinate or solve problems. *Naturalistic intelligence* is strongly connected to nature; it is the ability to understand natural phenomena, forces of nature, knowing how to be aware of the natural environment and to act accordingly. There are two personal intelligences which are not totally characterized but which have great importance: the *interpersonal intelligence* and the *intrapersonal intelligence*. The intrapersonal intelligence includes the ability to understand one's acts and motivations, and how to cooperate with them. The interpersonal intelligence has a higher correlation to the intrapersonal one and refers to inner abilities. It is one's ability to create an accurate and realistic image of oneself, and being able to effectively use this image to operate in the world he lives in (Gardner, 1996; Willingham, 2004; Retting, 2005).

Considering Multiple Intelligences Theory in relation to education, it can be concluded that since each child's mind operates differently, the education system should take that into consideration. The purpose of education should be to define each boy's or girl's specific strong intelligences. This definition will pave the way to true learning, based on interest and investigation, and as is noted in the current study, should be based on the child's strong abilities. Therefore, there is no need to flood the children with information and challenges, which necessitate use of all intelligences, as this will result in superficial learning and not deepen it (Willingham, 2004). It is important to emphasize that although all eight intelligences are considered basic, in Western society, the linguistic and the logical-mathematical intelligences have become the ones which are considered most important. Therefore, evaluations in many educational institutions are based on a high valuation of linguistic and mathematical skills. This can be referred to as a one-dimensional concept in evaluating people's intelligence. This type of evaluation is observed in the hard core of educational programs in educational institutions, which include an outline of facts that everybody should know and memorize but which include very little choice (Gardner, 1996).

Gardner's approach focuses on the individual child (Retting, 2005); and on the dialog conducted with him, considering his strengths and areas of interest. Relying on Multiple Intelligences Theory, this approach recognizes the child's main intelligence and reinforces it (Willingham, 2004). The prominence of this approach lies in its objective, defined as developing the intelligences and assisting the individual child to reach professional and hobby goals, which best suit each child's unique range of intelligences. Another purpose of this approach is the ability to understand and best establish the cognitive profile of each child. Here, the dialog between the educator and child takes place in accord with the child's strengths and areas of interest (Gardner, 2011).

To consider the application of Multiple Intelligences Theory to dialog with children, it should be recognized that this type of dialog is based on two assumptions: the first is that not everyone learns in the same way, not everyone holds the same areas of interest and has the same abilities. Therefore, the child's strong areas must be considered (Willingham, 2004), and these should direct the learning process. The second is that at present, no one can learn all that there is to know, and as this ideal is not possible, a choice is inevitable. According to this theory, the dialog will be realized by assessing the child's tendencies and self-abilities, and by letting him make choices on his own (Retting, 2005; Gardner, 1996).

The current study relates to two main influences of Multiple Intelligences Theory on education. The first is the concept of "personal suitability" and the second involves "multiplicity". "Personal suitability" means that the educator should know as much as possible about each child, nurture and prepare him, using suitable means that will allow the child to express himself and his understandings in the best possible way. The term "multiplicity" refers to the educator's need to consider what are the important elements of the child's knowledge, and to present them to him using as many ways as possible to take advantage of the largest possible range of intelligences. This will help each child manifest his unique and special intelligences (Harpaz, 2014).

By strengthening the child's strong abilities and using them to start the learning process, the child develops social patterns. A child that is in such a dialog with his educators will feel more adequate, more committed, and will possess a greater tendency to be a part of and contribute to society. By deepening his studies and taking advantage of the interest he finds in studies which use his stronger intelligences, the child will gain the opportunity to practice these abilities (Gardner, 2011).

I.4 Discussion of the main concepts in early childhood education

The kindergarten in Israel is an educational-learning framework, aiming to promote children's development as active, initiating, decisive, independent and social individuals (Levine, 1989; Ministry of Education, 2010). Multi-Dialogical Education is based on the principles of dialogical education and expands the term dialog. To define the Multi-Dialogical Approach (MDA) to education it is first necessary to define Dialogical Education. Dialogical Education is the development of a culture of research among the children while the educator listens to the children, asks them questions, mediates and documents their activity (Fiore & Suares, 2010). This enables the children to conceptualize phenomena and situations which arise from activity in their environment (Caspi, 1979). Multi-Dialogical Education is characterized by the fact that the children are partners in decision-making about how the kindergarten operates, not only in the area of studies but in all aspects of the kindergarten. This decision-making, based on negotiation between the kindergarten teacher and the children (Efrat & Ungureanu, 2015), includes discourse about behavioral norms, focuses of activity and how these should be advanced, holidays, and how they should be celebrated, and the kindergarten way of life. Thus, the MDA adds another dimension to dialogical education which is expressed as attentiveness and in how the dialog operates in the kindergarten (Firstater & Efrat, 2014).

The teacher's attentiveness to the way the children think, and the theories and ideas coming from them form the basis of the dialog which develops and which is applied in the kindergarten (Jhong, 2008; Firstater & Efrat, 2014). According to the MDA, attentiveness is expressed in every aspect of the kindergarten and not only in spoken words. The partners are the entire kindergarten community which includes the children, the kindergarten teacher, the kindergarten staff, the parents, and the larger community in which the kindergarten exists. The staff's attentiveness to the children's activity in the various areas of kindergarten life leads to a multi-disciplinary dialog. This enables the child to be a partner in the practice, in planning and applying the curriculum which has been constructed together as a result of the negotiation process. The kindergarten community of which the child is a member, is responsible for the implementation of the curriculum. In practice, this approach is performed by involving the children in planning kindergarten activities, by letting them instruct their peers in small groups and in the general meeting, by encouraging them to give feedback to other children on instructed activities, and by the kindergarten teacher's personal meeting with them to plan activities that will be presented by them. In other words, the basic concepts on which the MDA is based are as follows: attentiveness, children's guidance, negotiation in all aspects of kindergarten life with the participation of the children, feedback which the children learn to give and to accept, reflection that the children apply to their guidance, peer learning and discourse skills taught to the children. The MDA is founded on negotiation between all the partners in the educational process: the children, the kindergarten teacher, the staff and the parents (Firstater & Efrat, 2014). The parents also play an important role in the multi-dialogical process as participants in the research based on their children's interests and in its implementation. Parents may also stimulate and identify their children's areas of interest and bring this to the attention of the kindergarten staff. The research process then continues in the kindergarten (Firstater & Efrat, 2014).

Since the MDA is an innovative approach, previous philosophical theories implemented in the Reggio-Emilia kindergarten in Italy, which inaugurated dialogical education in all of its kindergartens, can serve as a basis of comparison. The Reggio-Emilia approach in Italy is based on attentive pedagogy, and relationship pedagogy (Rinaldi, 2006); where emphasis is put on observing and focusing on children's enriched activity as a means of attentiveness (Edwards, Gandini & Forman, 1998). There is an understanding that children possess different languages to express themselves, and that they should be treated as equals and as experts in their areas of interest. It is connected to the current study in its focus on the children's experiences as the basis for learning that occurs as a result of the exploration process and gained knowledge. The entire kindergarten community is part of the educational dialog and the learning process: the children, the educational staff and the parents (Clark & Moss, 2005). According to the Reggio-Emilia approach, the educator is an investigator who is committed to a steady, continuous process of building knowledge along with the children, and researching as a way of thinking. The research is done by the educator on a daily basis, together with the children, based on subjects relating to children's interests, while the investigation is carried out through negotiation between all participants in the research (children and educator) and by documentation (Rinaldi, 2006). Table I.1 below draws a comparison between the characteristics of the different dialogical approaches to education.

Table I.1: Comparison between the Different Dialogical Approaches to Education

<table>
<tr><th>Approach / Characteristic</th><th>Dialogical Education Approach</th><th>Reggio Emilia Educational Approach</th><th>Multi-dialogical Education Approach</th></tr>
<tr><td>Age</td><td>School age</td><td>Nursery school children</td><td>Ages 3-6</td></tr>
<tr><td>Areas of Interest</td><td colspan="3">The children's areas of interest constitute the basis for the curriculum (Firstater & Efrat, 2014; Rinaldi, 2005)</td></tr>
<tr><td>The teacher's attentiveness as the basis for identification of the children's areas of interest</td><td colspan="3">The teacher identifies the children's areas of interest by paying attention to and observing the children (Firstater & Efrat, 2014; Jhong, 2008; Rinaldi, 1999).</td></tr>
<tr><td>Perception of the teacher's role</td><td colspan="3">The teacher sees himself as the children's facilitator and partner and not as a source of knowledge (Firstater & Efrat, 2014; Jhong, 2008; Rinaldi, 1999).</td></tr>
<tr><td>Negotiation</td><td colspan="2">Participation of the children in learning through negotiation with them about the curriculum (Forman & Fyfe, 1998).</td><td>Participation of the children in the learning and decision-making regarding what happens in the kindergarten, through negotiation with them (Firstater & Efrat, 2014; Forman & Fyfe, 1998).</td></tr>
<tr><td>Investigative learning</td><td colspan="3">Learning is investigative, and is derived from the areas of interest that the children suggested (Firstater & Efrat, 2014; Jhong, 2008; Rinaldi, 1999)</td></tr>
<tr><td>The teacher learns with the children</td><td colspan="3">The teacher is an active participant together with the children. The teacher learns with the children (Firstater & Efrat, 2014; Jhong, 2008; Rinaldi, 1999)</td></tr>
<tr><td>Documentation by the teacher</td><td>Literature on this theory does not relate to documentation</td><td colspan="2">The teacher documents the children's areas of interest and their ideas in order to continue to plan the subject and go deeper into it (Firstater & Efrat, 2014; Jhong, 2008; Rinaldi, 1999; Wong, 2009)</td></tr>
<tr><td>Documentation by the children</td><td>Literature does not relate to documentation by the children</td><td>Literature does not relate to documentation by the children.</td><td>Together with the child, the kindergarten teacher documents the plan for activities that emerged from their area of interest. The teacher writes and the child draws, so that he understands what is written and learns independently (Firstater & Efrat, 2014).</td></tr>
<tr><td>Examining children's knowledge as a foundation for learning</td><td>Literature does not relate to this.</td><td>Literature does not relate to this.</td><td>When he begins the subject, the kindergarten teacher asks the children three questions: what do they know about the subject? What would they like to know about the subject? And what would they like to do on this subject? The children's answers constitute the basis on which the kindergarten staff will plan the subject (Firstater & Efrat, 2014).</td></tr>
</table>

The children's leadership	Literature does not relate to children guiding their peers.	Literature does not relate to children guiding their peers.	The children learn to guide their peers during kindergarten meetings, to guide work in small groups and to lead activities at the "creativity tables" according to their suggested ideas and after planning sessions with the kindergarten teacher (Firstater & Efrat, 2014)
Teacher-child planning sessions	Literature does not relate to meetings between teacher and child to plan activities.	Literature does not relate to meetings between teacher and child to plan activities.	Before each activity that the children want to guide they meet with the teacher to plan the activity and its implementation (Firstater & Efrat, 2014)
Feedback	Literature does not relate to children giving feedback to peers.	Literature does not relate to children giving feedback to peers.	The children learn to give and accept feedback concerning the activity that they guide (Firstater & Efrat, 2014)
Rules of discussion	Literature does not relate to learning discourse rules as life skills.	Literature does not relate to learning discourse rules as life skills.	The children sit in a discourse circle and learn how to conduct discussions without being managed and given permission to speak by a teacher and to express their opinion respectfully, even if it differs from other children's opinions (Firstater & Efrat, 2014)
Philosophical discourse	Literature does not relate to philosophical discourse for dialogical education.	Literature does not relate to philosophical discourse.	The children learn that they may raise philosophical questions and conduct a philosophical discussion about these questions. (Firstater & Efrat, 2014)
The kindergarten community	Literature does not relate to the concept of an educational community.	Literature does not relate to the concept of an educational community.	The kindergarten community including the children, the teacher, the kindergarten staff and the children's families, all participate in the educational process by implementing the children's initiatives (Firstater & Efrat, 2014)

I.4.1 Definition of Multi-Dialogical Education

The foundation for multi-dialogical education in kindergarten is identical to the foundation of the dialogical and Reggio-Emilia approaches and primarily focuses on the teacher's attentiveness towards the children (Efrat & Ungureanu, 2015; Fiore & Suares, 2010). Although these three approaches have similar characteristics, there are also significant differences. What is common to all three is that the children's own areas of interest constitute the basis for the curriculum. The children's areas of interest are identified by the teacher's attentiveness and observation and the teacher sees himself as the children's facilitator and partner rather than as the source of knowledge. Learning is investigative and stems from the areas of interest suggested by the children, while the teacher is an active participant in the children's learning process (Clark & Moss, 2005; Firstater & Efrat, 2014; Rinaldi, 2005).

Both the dialogical and the Reggio-Emilia educational approaches require the participation of the children in the learning process through negotiation about the curriculum (Forman & Fyfe, 1998; Lasri, 2004); while in the MDA the kindergarten children participate not only in determining and deciding about the areas of learning but also in how the kindergarten operates (Firstater & Efrat, 2014).Common to the Reggio-Emilia approach and the MDA is the documentation by the kindergarten teacher of the children's topic of interest and the program for its implementation in order to continue to plan further in depth study (Clark & Moss, 2005; Firstater & Efrat, 2014; Rinaldi, 2005).

There are many significant areas completely unique to the MDA. The basis of this approach is the involvement of the kindergarten community including the children, the teacher, the kindergarten staff and the children's families, who all share in the educational process by implementing the children's initiatives (Firstater & Efrat, 2014).

The activities include four main stages:

1. When introducing the subject, the kindergarten teacher asks the children three questions: What do they know about the subject? What would they like to know about the subject? And what do they want to do about this subject? The children's answers constitute the basis on which the kindergarten staff plans the subject.
2. Before each activity that the child volunteers to guide, he meets with the teacher and discusses the activity and how he will conduct it.
3. Together with the child, the teacher documents the plan for

the activity. The teacher writes and the child draws so that he can understand what is written and will be able to conduct the activity independently.

4. The child guides the activity himself, but with the assistance of the kindergarten teacher, and receives feedback concerning the activity from the children in the discourse circle.

I.4.2 What do the children learn from the MDA?

1. They learn to guide the circle time of the entire kindergarten, to guide group work and to guide creative activities emanating from the ideas that they suggest after planning these activities with the teacher.
2. They learn to conduct discussions without being managed by adults or given permission to speak. They learn to express their opinions respectfully even if it differs from the opinions of others.
3. They learn to raise philosophical questions and discuss these questions among themselves.
4. They learn to give and accept feedback on the activity that they have guided.

In conclusion, it can be said that the main innovation of the MDA is that it includes all domains of kindergarten life, since it is simultaneously oriented to teacher-to-child dialog and child-to-child dialog and the dialog is conducted with a patient and tolerant approach towards others (Firstater & Efrat, 2014).

I.4.3 Attentiveness as the basis of the approach

Two of the main goals of the multi-dialogical kindergarten are to develop life skills and social-communicational abilities. Salient among them are abilities and skills such as caring and consideration for others while safeguarding children's personal rights, cooperation and attentiveness to new ideas, critical observation of things and ability to cope with conflicts, ambiguous situations and frustration, as well as the ability to control and postpone instant gratification (Aloni, 2008; Efrat & Ungureanu, 2015; Malaguzzi, 1998). The main hypothesis in multi-dialogical education is that a child who learns about his world through inner interest will grow to be this kind of person, since he has acquired the ability to reach learning conclusions by himself (Firstater & Efrat, 2014; Lasri, 2004; Tauber, 2008).

In practice, the MDA emphasizes attentiveness to children's ideas, and the kindergarten discourse is based on them (Firstater & Efrat, 2014; Jhong, 2008). Attentiveness is not just "listening on the way to acquiring knowledge", but rather a reflective process aimed at thinking about new meanings, making connections, and discovering new concepts (Clark & Moss, 2005). This study adds another level to the understanding that this pedagogy has many facets and all are attentiveness-based. The study points up that there is an inner-attentiveness or inner-reflection; there is attentiveness to the many languages spoken by children, and there is the open attentiveness which is created by documentation and interpretation by the educators, to the deepening of mutual learning between them and the children. In other words, documentation enables open attentiveness on the way to building meaning. In practice, documentation can be executed in many ways, such as writing, photographing, recording or any other means, and this is done by both the kindergarten teacher and the children, so that their mutual learning becomes available and accessible for all of them (Rinaldi, 2005). In any event, educators deal with three main questions in regard to their attentiveness: first, how are we, as educators, able to assist children in finding meaning in their experiences? Second, how are we, as educators, able to assist children in finding meaning in what they encounter? Third, how are we, as educators, able to assist children in finding meaning in what they are doing? (Rinaldi, 2005).

Young children convey their thoughts and feelings and express themselves in many unexpected different ways (Bae, 2009); they can express themselves through actions, drawing or through other ways, not considered by the kindergarten teacher, as long as the teacher does not restrict their thinking, but rather pays attention to them and conducts dialog about their ideas (Jhong, 2008). Therefore, the kindergarten teacher should develop the ability to listen to the children, to observe them and to interpret their body language. In order to assist them in expressing themselves, she should respect their life experience and try to understand their way of thinking and intentions. In addition, while listening to the children, she should pay attention to their acts and the verbal communication between themselves. Through the teacher's attentiveness children learn to express themselves (Bae, 2009).

I.4.4 The kindergarten teacher: The place and role of the teacher working with the MDA

How the teacher perceives her role in the kindergarten is critical. If kindergarten daily activities are dictated only by the teacher, this will become an obstacle to children's influence on their daily lives in the kindergarten (Emilson, 2007). In this type of situation, the teacher is the decision maker and plans kindergarten activities and the areas of study are determined according to her point of view. This creates distance between the children's point of view and that of the teacher. This distance means that the children have a low level of influence on the way in which they learn and what they learn (Arner & Tellgren, 1998; Aspan, 2005; Ekholm & Lindvall, 1991; Selberg, 1999; Sheridan, 2001). This leads to theoretical and practical consequences. Theoretically, it can be argued that if the teacher wishes to allow the children's influence on a daily basis, she should surrender some of her complete control over them, over the activities and over the learned subjects within the kindergarten, and while doing so, become practically more available for observation and attentiveness. This will allow her to listen to the children, to look at them and their actions with a deeper perception, to come closer to their world and to their points of view, and from this point to guide them through their areas of interest. By doing so, she enables them to be responsible learners in their studies (Bengtsson, 2005; Emilson, 2007; Fiore & Rosenquest, 2010; Johansson, 2004; Sheridan, 2001). In other words, it can be said that the kindergarten teacher needs to define her educational goals and be aware of the gaps between what should be done and what is actually being done from an educational perspective (Claudie, 2012).

The educational work in the multi-dialogical kindergarten focuses on observation and identification of the children's areas of interest and their initiatives (Firstater & Efrat, 2014; Jhong, 2008). When addressing learning in a kindergarten that functions according to the MDA, it is important to note that learning based on children's areas of interest will be significant learning (Renninger, 1992), where the level of children's influence and participation depends on the teacher's standpoint and approach (Arner & Tellgren, 1998; Emilson & Folkesson, 2006; Sheridan, 2001). According to the dialogical approach, the teacher's ability to recognize the children's areas of interest and use them for their learning plays a significant role (Fumoto et al., 2004; Hobson, 2002). Using dialog, the kindergarten teacher can get to know, reveal and meet the children's reactions and contents (Firstater & Efrat, 2014). This allows the teacher to plan the work and the learning contents that are suitable for the children (Ben-Yosef, 2009). This means that the unique contribution of the kindergarten teacher during her dialog with the children is based on her ability to connect to the children's experiences and use them as the basis for further learning (Fumoto, 2011); The current study relates to the use of these techniques to increase the children's involvement in the kindergarten subjects, which can be accomplished by guidance and support. Therefore, the teacher should maintain flexibility through her attentiveness to the children and the children's involvement helps her to plan the kindergarten curriculum (Fumoto, 2011).

The educational environment and the educational contents are formed together with the children and originate from their world, and not only from the kindergarten teacher (Rogoff et al., 2001); and this process has reciprocal influences for all participants, the children and the teacher (McLean, 1991). In order to allow children to develop their areas of interest, an educational environment should be created which will allow them to develop self-exploration and a sense of trust in their abilities (Lasri, 2004). This will generate their communicational and social skills, which can be implemented by their assumption of responsibility, initiative and leadership, choice, perseverance, focusing and delaying gratification (Levine, 1989). There is a direct relationship between the sense of trust implanted in children and their daily contribution. A kindergarten teacher who trusts children's abilities will be able to elicit children's contributions to their daily interactions and allow the children to be responsible for them, both with other children and with adults, while she gives them space to participate in their activities and their areas of interest (Rinaldi, 2006). The partnership between the kindergarten teacher and the children during activities and during learning is a relationship of equal partners, where the teacher should be alert and open to the children's initiatives and their areas of interest (Rhedding-Jones, Bae & Winger, 2008). It, therefore, seems that the greatest obstacle for children at young age to be involved, to express their opinions and to contribute their point of view is the educators' standpoint, which can either allow or deny it (Council of Europe, 2011).

Recent studies regarding kindergarten children's attitudes and opinions (Harcourt, 2011; Sargeant, 2008) indicate that children possess the ability to express their opinions and to explain important personal experiences (Harcourt, 2011). In this context, the current study adds another level of understanding indicating that the children's point of view is based on their personal experiences and the connections that they make as a result of their life experiences. This insight implies that the kindergarten teacher cannot change children's points of view but should rather try to reach out and understand it (Johansson, 2003). However, understanding a child's point of view depends on the teacher's approach (Emilson & Folkesson, 2006); this approach should award value to children's culture and to the way they perceive the world, and in practice, the teacher's approach will determine the learning framework and the extent to which children participate in their learning (Pramling-Samuelsson & Sheridan, 2003). It seems that for children's learning to be conducted in a significant manner, it should be based on the teacher's attentiveness and be conducted through a communicational relationship between the kindergarten teacher and the children (Fumoto, 2011), where children can be active partners in their learning process. This partnership is based both on the children's point of view and the teacher's ability to understand that point of view (Pramling-Samuelsson & Sheridan, 2003).

The above-mentioned studies also indicate that kindergarten children can mediate personal experiences to their surroundings as well as personal feelings and thoughts, provided that the educators try and recognize it, observe and interpret it. To assist the children, the educators should mediate their activities through recognition, observation, attentiveness and interpretation of these activities. In this way they, in fact, allow the children true participation in their personal learning (Pramling-Samuelsson & Sheridan, 2003) enabling them to acquire social skills such as cooperation and decision-making (Emilson & Folkesson, 2006). Mediation is a key concept in the implementation of the MDA in kindergartens (Firstater & Efrat, 2014), where it is understood that educators' mediation contributes to the quality of education (Bowman & Donovan, 2001; Klein & Yavlon, 2007; Pianta, LaParo & Hamre, 2008). It is argued that the kindergarten teacher is the main mediator to the children (Fisher, 2007); her enthusiasm for learning together with that of the children encourages her meaningful mediation and enables true discourse with them (Fumoto, 2011). It is important to emphasize that if the kindergarten teacher knows how to mediate, learning is at its best, so that mediation is one of the most substantial elements in the development of skills and social interaction between children (Cornu & Peters, 2005; French, 2007; Stance & Kao, 2010).

It can thus be concluded that the role of the kindergarten teacher working according to the MDA includes: planning and allocating time in the daily schedule for attentiveness, observation and identification of the areas of interest suggested by the children, finding each child's area of strength and reinforcing it (Gardner, 1996); planning activities that the children initiate together with them, and conducting personal meetings with them. The teacher must also impart leadership, feedback and discussion skills to the children, mediate their ideas and initiatives and document them. In this way, the teacher learns together with the children and avoids the desire to teach by supplying all the learning material. In addition, the teacher should know how to correctly organize and manage time in the kindergarten in order to reach each and every child (Firstater & Efrat, 2014).

I.4.5 Negotiation between all participants, including the children, in learning and decision-making in the kindergarten

One of the prominent aspects of the use of the MDA in kindergarten is the children's participation in decision-making concerning their activities in the kindergarten. The possibility of being partners in decision-making allows children to create an open and significant world by expressing their opinions in the group. The inevitable question is whether this is even possible at such a young age, and indeed some studies have supported and proven that kindergarten children are capable of reporting, analyzing and reaching decisions on situations and problems that arise in the kindergarten. Additionally, they can lead, execute projects, debate and guide others. In the context of the current study it is noted that children's participation in decision-making in the kindergarten is not symbolic but rather real. In practice, it is manifested by determining rules of conduct in the different areas of the kindergarten and by preparing and guiding activities for the entire kindergarten. The children participate in choosing, planning, and leading projects in the kindergarten, according to their areas of interest, guiding meetings and group activities by the children for the entire kindergarten and managing discourse and debates about subjects that are of interest to them (Danner & Jonyniene, 2012; Firstater & Efrat, 2014; Rinaldi, 2006). With regard to the MDA it can be argued that true inclusion of the children, their peers and the kindergarten teacher creates a sense of excitement in learning and developing communicational relations between all those participating in the learning. In fact, children-teacher relationships are human encounters that involve meaningful communication, and experience and shared understanding (Efrat & Ungureanu, 2015; Fumoto, 2011). Learning takes place in these encounters through the dialog between the participants when the children and teacher conduct reflection on the processes they have experienced and examine themselves in order to improve in the future (Firstater & Efrat, 2014, Ben-Yosef, 2009). This learning is a long, dynamic and reflective process. Many people can participate in it and it involves cognition together with emotion, expressed in curiosity and daring (Ben-Yosef, 2009). In practice, this type of education involves a pattern of interaction, which is characterized by the asking of relevant questions raised by the dialog participants, the children and the kindergarten teacher, by answers that are not defined in advance, and which are given during the dialog and can change the discussed subject (Nystrand, Gamoran, Kachur & Prendergast, 1997). The present study adds another level of understanding, since it indicates that the above process is possible as a result of a basic understanding that children at the kindergarten age possess knowledge and experience that allows them to develop their own ideas and opinions that can be delivered during the dialog (Lansdown, 2001). This approach may change the perspective of children-teacher relationships in education when this system is characterized by negotiation between all those participating in the learning process (Lyle, 2008).

Working in the multi-dialogical kindergarten involves less teaching and formal knowledge provided by the teacher and more attentiveness to the children and their ideas (Firstater & Efrat, 2014; Rinaldi, 1999). Therefore, there is no detailed teaching plan and no fixed and structured daily routine; only the environment is planned and what occurs within it is random (Inan, 2009; Lasri, 2004; Levine, 1989). More specifically, the teacher's work plan changes in accordance with the activities developed by the children, understanding that the children have to explore and learn, and it also allows originality and differences between the children (Inan, 2009; Rinaldi, 1999).

I.4.6 Children's participation in planning and guidance of kindergarten activities

The process of planning the activities and the learning is a significant part of the kindergarten teacher's work (Ojala, 2010). In order to include the kindergarten children in that process, the teacher should understand how children think and what their points of view are (Pramling-Samuelsson & Sherdan, 2003). Importantly, combining the children's points of view in the planning, execution and evaluation of activities and learning within the kindergarten should be done with them and not over them (Leinonen & Venninan, 2012); recognizing the children's point of view and focusing on their world and their way of thinking, enables the dialog and the inclusion of children in planning and in their learning (Emilson & Johansson, 2009; Pramling-Samuelsson & Sheridan, 2003). Children's participation in planning kindergarten activities creates interaction between all participants in the educational act: the children, the teacher and the educational environment (Pramling-Samuelson & Sheridan, 2003). Forming a trusted pattern between children and teacher is the basis of the approach in which children plan kindergarten activities. In order for this to happen, children should communicate with the teacher in an optimal way that originates from basic trust and from the clear knowledge that she trusts their abilities (Thomas, 2002).

In the MDA, children learn to take part in planning their activities and their learning (Firstater & Efrat, 2014). In practice, children's participation is observed in daily involvement in the kindergarten routine, as well as larger things, such as leading research processes and kindergarten projects (Clark & Moss, 2005; Leinonen & Venninan, 2012). It is important to emphasize that children's exposure to and their involvement in the research of new ideas and new points of view gives meaning to their ideas, and dialog enables them to become involved in a meaningful research and learning process. There is no need for them to memorize the information but instead, the information helps to advance their understanding (Fisher, 2007). In the context of the current study, it was noted that the ability of children to be active individuals in their groups requires practice and experience (Leinonen & Venninan, 2012); this becomes possible when their voices are recognized and respected (Hill, Davis, Prout & Tisdall, 2004; Sinclair, 2004).

Group guidance is one of the practical applications of the MDA. Kindergarten children learn and are able to assimilate the ability for group guidance. This guidance empowers them (Firstater & Efrat, 2014). It strengthens their self-confidence and their social standing and they learn how to guide without controlling or being aggressive. In order to assist them in learning how to guide, the educator guides them on this subject and allows each child who wishes to do so to guide an activity under their mentorship. Moreover, the educator constitutes a model both for the guidance role and for the role of the learner when the child guides the group (Ben-Yosef, 2009).

The development of social-communication skills in kindergarten children depends on the teacher's respect for the children and belief in their abilities to lead, plan and be a part of their learning. This has great influence on children in the present and influences the type of adults they will become in the future (Smith, 2002). Thus, that children's participation in the process in planning activities in the multi-dialogical kindergarten is based on the teacher's significant role, which is manifested by observation, as part of her attentiveness to the children and her support for their social skills (Berthelsen, 2009). Children's participation in planning their activities and their learning in the kindergarten is a personal experience in which they develop social abilities such as listening and involvement, expressing personal opinions, acquiring methods to learn, to share their experience with their peers, to practice daily decision-making, to conduct negotiation, to learn to wait for their turn and to share with friends (Clark & Moss, 2005; Leinonen & Venninan, 2012; Venninen, Leinonen & Ojala, 2010). It is important to understand that all children can participate in their learning; it depends solely on the teacher's approach and the extent to which she allows their participation (Nyland, 2009). If the teacher's actions do not provide opportunities for participating in planning their own activities and their own learning, children will not choose to do this by themselves (Emilson & Johansson, 2009).

I.4.7 Children's feedback as an integral part of activity guidance in the kindergarten

For children to become responsible partners in their learning in the kindergarten according to the multi-dialogic approach, they must acquire the ability to initiate, plan, and guide activities for the entire kindergarten community. Feedback is an integral part of this activity and, in fact, is a part of the discourse circle. In practical terms this means that the children learn to give non-judgmental feedback to their peers at the end of each activity, with the goal of learning and further building from it, and the kindergarten teacher also models such feedback to them (Firstater & Efrat, 2014). Feedback given to the child who guided the activity for his friends relates to focused points that the child guide made or to feelings that he aroused for the participants. In order to help the children to do this, they learn how to give focused and specific feedback and to avoid generalizations. It is noted that not all those present need to give feedback, although it is desirable that each of them should give feedback to their friend who guides the meeting. Moreover, it is important to coach the children to give positive feedback. The rationale for this being that one learns out of successes and the understanding that genuine and positive feedback without criticism can effectively guide the child's learning and constitute a very powerful tool to empower the child, since it focuses on the strengths of each child and not their weaknesses. Nevertheless, if there is criticism regarding the guiding child, then the educator will find a way to transmit it without focusing specifically on the child rather by relating in general to certain principles (Ben-Yosef, 2009).

The kindergarten teacher also constitutes part of the feedback circle and she also gives feedback to the child (Firstater & Efrat, 2014). It is noted that the feedback that she gives to the child does not aim to make any covert assessment of the child's performance (Lasri, 2004). Therefore, the feedback should be optimistic (Firstater & Efrat, 2014), while on the other hand, it should also be dynamic. In addition, although it should focus on successes, it should also not ignore difficulties. In other words, when successes are emphasized, even if they are not complete, no labeling occurs, rather there is a positive development (Ben-Yosef, 2009) for the person receiving the feedback (Firstater & Efrat, 2014). This means that the teacher needs to learn how to provide feedback that helps the child to grow (Firstater & Efrat, 2014).

Feedback should comply with several principles: (1) the feedback should focus on the process and progress that the child underwent and also on the life skills that the child demonstrated (Ibid). (2) The child should be addressed in a containing and personal tone from one person to another and not from a position of all-knowing authority. (3) The process that the child undergoes should not be compared with that of other children, but only compared with regard to the child's own development and abilities along the time axis (Ben-Yosef, 2009). (4) The feedback should not "label" the child, rather it should be optimistic and transmit a sense of participation (Firstater & Efrat, 2014).

It is important for feedback to be given in the form of dialog (Ibid), meaning that it should express an equality between all the participants and should create mutual relations between them (Ben-Yosef, 2009). In order to facilitate this, it should be transmitted in an egalitarian, warm, open, calm, respectful and supportive manner (Firstater & Efrat, 2014). However, it should also stimulate and challenge the receiver (Ben-Yosef, 2009). More specifically, various types of manipulation such as moral preaching, emotional blackmail, silencing or coercion should be completely avoided (Ben-Yosef, 2009; Firstater & Efrat, 2014).

It is important to consider that feedback plays a significant part in peer study and is given in order to improve children's efforts and their future learning (Topping, 2005). In addition, such feedback enables the partners (children and teacher) to propose how things should be done differently in their opinion (Mercer & Littleton, 2007), in addition to learning to see the other and to complement a friend (Firstater & Efrat, 2014). The current study adds another level to the understanding that positive feedback has significant consequences which are reflected in the development of children's communicational and social skills; because it points up that when expressed in the right way, feedback can advance the social abilities both of the child providing the feedback and the child who is receiving it, and can also improve their self-esteem (Topping, 2005). Children learn and understand realities around them through dialog (Sadeghi, 2008). This understanding is important to the education process they undergo in the multi-dialogical kindergarten and can be acquired through the feedback that the children learn to give (Firstater & Efrat, 2014).

I.4.8 Peer study as a dialog

Research findings have indicated that effective peer study is possible in young, kindergarten-aged children (Fuchs, Fuchs, Mathes & Simmons, 1997; Mathes, Howard, Allen & Fuchs, 1998). Peer study is one of the main aspects of the MDA (Firstater & Efrat, 2014). Peer study is defined as the acquisition of knowledge and skills with assistance and support from equal-status participants, with the goal of sharing and helping each other to learn (Topping, 2005). During peer study, which is also mutual learning, the value of self-responsibility is reflected in each of the participants, working together towards a purpose defined by the peer group (Buchs, Butera & Mugny, 2004).

Trust and reciprocity are two central concepts in this type of learning. This study adds another level to the understanding that peer study is based on reciprocal-relations between participants, since it relates to the active participation of both children and educators in the learning process, and group success originates from their efforts. In addition, the emotional side should be considered, relying on trust between participants that leads to group consolidation, with no authoritative and managerial acts by any of them (Topping, 2005).

Peer learning allows each child to express themselves in their own personal manner and yet to pay attention to the consideration and opinions of their friends, which may differ from their own. This practice allows the children to develop skills so that they learn to see a subject simultaneously from several angles and provides a unique contribution to the children's perceptions and the development of their ways of thinking. In practice, the children learn to pay attention to each other's words with much patience, not to reject an opinion that differs from their own and to express their opinion during their learning without wrangling or loud arguments (Ben-Yosef, 2009). Moreover, peer study leads to the development of participants' life skills. Peer study encourages social communication between its participants, intensifies students' learning and strengthens their emotional side. In practice, it contributes to the development of social-communication skills such as attentiveness, independence, mutual assistance, consideration, cooperation, acceptance of new opinions and their exploration, the ability to grant and accept feedback, and the ability to initiate and lead the peer group. Moreover, it enhances self-confidence and self-acceptance, as well as the motivation and loyalty to the group, the ability to value and cherish the learning partners, and the sense of belonging to a unified meaningful group. Thus, peer study can contribute to its participants' emotional development. In addition, group members' ability to enjoy and go deeply into the investigated or debated subject during peer study their skill in reaching a more abstract level of thinking, also indicate educational development (Cohen, Kulik & Kulik, 1982; Johnson & Johnson, 1986; Rohrbeck et al., 2003; Sharpley & Sharpley, 1981; Slavin, 1995; Topping, 2005).

I.4.9 Conversation between equals: Acquiring discourse skills

Discourse enables an individual to have a presence in the world. It incorporates words, beliefs, theories, values, acts, opinions, gestures and eye contact (Gee, 1989). Discourse helps to develop communication patterns of attentiveness, listening and tolerance for the words of others out of a desire to understand their viewpoints. It also helps to develop the ability to restrain judgmental reactions even when things are said which contradict the opinion of the listener (Ben-Yosef, 2009). In kindergartens in Western society, discourse appears in general meetings of the kindergarten community. During these meetings, a teacher sometimes asks that a child express his opinion or share an experience while other children listen. Nevertheless, it can be said that children do not really listen to each other. The reason is that they are often mindful of the need to receive the teacher's approval and obtain permission to speak about what is on their mind (Sela, 2002). In addition, it is difficult for them to convey their thoughts in a practical and clear way, and even more difficult to sit still and listen to their friends (Aram & Shlak, 2007). In order to conduct discourse the children need to acquire the rules and the skills of participation in discourse, and they need to learn the social norms required for participation (Ben-Yosef, 2009).

Discourse skills can be acquired and developed among children (Firstater & Efrat, 2014); through the educator's true attentiveness (Sela, 2002). Studies have shown that kindergarten children can be taught how to conduct a conversation (Mercer & Dawes, 2010; Mercer & Littlton, 2007); but this requires the teacher's awareness, and both children's and teacher's need to practice and exercise being discourse participants (Wells, 1986; Wells & Ball, 2008). One of the main concepts of the MDA in the kindergarten is the learning and usage of discourse skills (Firstater & Efrat, 2014) due to the understanding that discourse gives children many chances to express and talk about their ideas and theories, meet different points of view and explore their thoughts with other children (Callander, 2013). With reference to the current study, while the children learn and acquire discourse skills in the multi-dialogical kindergarten (Firstater & Efrat, 2014), emphasis is given to actual meaningful expression and not just on how things are being said and what they mean (Gee, 1989). As part of this process body language, tone of voice and gestures give meaning to the discourse (Jewitt, 2008; Kress, 2007).

Acquiring discourse abilities is very important since discourse is crucial for children's social and communicational development (Alexander, 2006). The children practice and develop these skills and learn how to use words to communicate with their environment (Wells, 1986; Wells & Ball, 2008). In order for these skills to actually develop, the discourse subjects should rely on the children's areas of interest, on philosophical questions they raise (Firstater & Efrat, 2014); and on real situations and relevant goals, they find interesting (Boyd & Galda, 2011; Wells, 2000, 2006). The discourse skills acquired in the multi-dialogical kindergarten (Firstater & Efrat, 2014); include learning how to listen to each other (Jones, 2007); and with reference to the current study, how to speak in a respectful way towards each other. More specifically, while speaking, they learn how to use exploratory words such as: "in my opinion"; and "I think that" (Callander, 2013); they learn not to dismiss their friends' ideas but rather to express their opposite opinion in an accepting way, using phrases such as: "I think differently" or "my opinion is different than yours because" (Firstater & Efrat, 2014).

In discourse, according to the MDA, there is no need to raise hands to obtain the teacher's permission to speak. When children raise hands and await permission to speak, they do not really learn how to listen to each other because they constantly seek ways to get the teacher's attention in order to be granted permission to speak. In addition, because they are busy thinking and planning what to say when they receive permission to speak, they do not learn to take responsibility for the timing of when to enter the discourse, which should originate from attentiveness. On the other hand, when children conduct conversation without raising hands and are aware of the fact that only one child can speak at a time, they are more attentive to one another, as they wish to be a part of the discourse (Firstater & Efrat, 2014).

This rationale has a direct consequence for the teacher's role in the discourse. She is a part of the discourse circle, the guide, but not the manager. Children learn not to look at her or to address her, as she is not the center of discourse. In practice, her role is to initiate and conclude the conversation (Firstater & Efrat, 2014) and to guide children on how to speak in a respectful way that includes exploratory phrases (Callander, 2013). She also assists them in acquiring skills relating to appropriate timing for entering the discourse, as well as teaching them how to speak in turn and doing all of the above without raising hands or receiving her permission to speak. Another role the teacher plays in guiding the discourse is to accommodate children that have not been integrated into the discourse, asking if they wish to add something to the conversation while they are given the choice to reply or not. By doing so, she acknowledges the differences between children in the group (Firstater & Efrat, 2014).

Kindergarten children are curious, have originality and have the courage to ask questions regarding essential things that adults do not always consider and give obvious answers to. They wish to know why and how different things happen, while the answers are also questioned. These are, in fact, philosophical questions, so typical of kindergarten children (Cohen, 2008). One of the concepts of a multi-dialogical kindergarten is philosophical discourse (Firstater & Efrat, 2014). The current study adds another level of understanding, noting that in order to guide philosophical discourse among kindergarten children, the teacher needs to develop her attentiveness and allot time for dialog. It is important to emphasize that knowledge is not constant, therefore the child learns to ask questions about the world around him, asking why it is the way it is and how it can be proven. This suggests that thinking steps are being conducted by the participants, the children and the teacher during the discussion. Another aspect to be considered is that when guiding children's philosophy, what is "different" is valued and new ways of thinking are welcomed (Firstater & Efrat, 2014; Lipman, 2003).

Children can develop high levels of trust among themselves by speaking and listening to each other in a sensitive manner, based on values of respect and attentiveness while others speak. This creates a space in which all participants' voices are heard and the group listens to these voices (Lipman, 2003). One of the main concepts of the MDA in the kindergarten is the discourse in general and the philosophical discourse in particular (Firstater & Efrat, 2014). The contribution of this approach is expressed in developing children's cognitive and social-communication skills. These skills are reflected by children learning how to conduct negotiation, raising new points of view together with their discourse colleagues, developing their ideas based on attentiveness to their colleagues' ideas, and asking questions that inflict thinking and investigation (Callander, 2013). In addition, while practicing discourse, children develop the ability to use empathy and care towards other participants, as well as critical thinking (Fisher, 2007).

To summarize this chapter, learning in a multi-dialogical kindergarten is based on children's experiences (Firstater & Efrat, 2014), and the curriculum is built personally for each child. In the first step, the child is observed, his activities are documented, and discussion is conducted with him. In the second step, a staff meeting is conducted, where analysis of the observation, documentation and discussion is made, and personal educational work is determined for each child (Given et al., 2010; Jhong, 2008, Lasri, 2004). The goal is to assist, guide, and create a dialog and not to teach or lead the child in predetermined paths (New, 1998; Caspi, 1979). The MDA offers and develops communicational and social skills both between the child and the educator and between the child and his friends. This is discussed further in the next section.

1.5 Discussion of the main concepts in the development of kindergarten children's social-communication skills

Studies indicate that the human brain is shaped in interaction with the social-cultural world (Bruner, 1996). These interactive processes have theoretical and practical consequences: the development of social-communication skills in early childhood forms the basis for successful development of these skills in adulthood (Lopez et al., 2000). More specifically, it seems that giving children the opportunity to try egalitarian and meaningful interpersonal communication helps them to develop social patterns and skills (Ben-Yosef, 2009). In the context of this study, this leads to the understanding that the development of interpersonal relationships between children and social-communication skills contributes to the quality of education, including early childhood education (Bowman & Donovan, 2001; Klein & Yavlon, 2007; Pianta, LaParo & Hamre, 2008).

The acquisition of social-communication skills by kindergarten children involves deepening, broadening, and enriching content and improving children's level of interest in learning subjects and in activities in the kindergarten (Bodrova & Leong, 2005; Firstater & Efrat, 2014). These skills enable children to acquire independence. Early childhood children wish to and are able to develop and attain independence. In particular, they aspire to the sense of self-control that comes with independence. To establish this stage in their lives, it is important to understand that developing initiative and independence among children is directly connected to their participation and involvement in decision-making about themselves and their everyday lives (Hill et al., 2004). Moreover, this independence develops a sense of personal empowerment, self-confidence and security, and is built through interactions with the teacher, who includes the children in decision-making and negotiation, and gives children the opportunity to choose, explore and deal with problem-solving (Firstater & Efrat, 2014; Erhardt-Weiss, 2008).

The ability to communicate with others requires mastery of language, understanding of discourse rules and participation in conversation. More specifically, children should be able to express their opinions, to ask questions, to wait their turn in the discourse circle and to learn how to listen (Wolf, 1998). Studies have indicated that children at kindergarten age start to develop these communication skills and tend to speak in a less egocentric way, reflecting not only their personal point of view (Sroufe et al., 2004). Therefore, they are able to initiate conversation, take responsibility for it, say what they mean and respond to what their friends in discussion are saying (Blum-Kulka, 2008). Moreover, they develop abilities such as speaking in accord with the listener's needs, explaining and passing on their ideas in a structured way using age-appropriate words and verifying that the listeners have understood their meaning (Sroufe et al., 2004). It can be argued that an attentiveness-based discourse which emphasizes reciprocity among children and their abilities to ask questions, to observe, and to initiate, greatly contributes to their social skills (Rahim & Rahman, 2013; Rhedding-Jones, Bae & Winger, 2008).

With regard to children in early childhood, they possess strong abilities at kindergarten age and even before that, to develop social skills, accept differences they have with others, accept mistakes and learn from them (Malaguzzi, 1998). Studies show that their social skills are developed through social interactions among themselves and between them and the adults (Carpendale & Lewis, 2004; Han & Kemple, 2006). Understanding social maps and developing social-communication skills stems from cooperation between children and their mutual assistance (Wright et al., 2003). In addition, regarding the current study, it can be understood that social interactions are essential to the development of cognitive, social and moral knowledge. Thus, children who experience social interaction based on their personal experiences and who take part in social activities build their knowledge of the world. Their practical understanding of social interaction and the establishment of their experiences and beliefs is gradually built from the connection created with others. This very important understanding that the nature of social interaction that children experience influences their understanding of the social-world supports the rationale that the knowledge they acquire in this way provides them with tools for cooperating, initiating and conducting negotiation (Carpendale & Lewis, 2004).

Reciprocity is an important element in social interaction among kindergarten children. It can be argued that social interaction is based on reciprocity and this helps to build the children's sense of comprehending the world. Thus, children build new concepts of reality from their connections with other people. Through this interaction they discover that other people have other points of view and beliefs about the world that are different from their own. Their beliefs are then weakened, and they can change their expectations and understanding of the world, followed by a change in their concept of reality (Carpendale & Lewis, 2004). More specifically, by letting children speak, they come to realize that they are human beings with aspirations and they learn to engage in mutual respect (Jhong, 2008). The act of speaking develops communication skills (Blum-Kulka, 2008).

Knowledge is built through peer study when the children become teachers for one another through negotiation that is conducted among themselves and the feedback they give each other. Moreover, peer learning respects comprehensions which are dissimilar; the children's power to conduct negotiations with others will eventually lead to a better understanding of the learned topic and acquisition of communication and social skills (Forman & Fyfe, 1998).

At kindergarten age, social fitness is in the process of being developed, enabling children to integrate among their age group (Becker, 2009). In practice, early childhood social abilities are acquired as a result of developing the ability to adjust behavior and to be considerate towards others, while the children adopt a positive identity towards themselves and practice decision-making (Han & Kemple, 2006). Moreover, the dynamics among children at that age influence their leadership abilities (Seung, Susan & Min, 2005). More generally, it can be said that their social abilities are reflected in a few areas such as communication, social integration, dealing with emotions, the ability to cooperate and conduct negotiation (Sroufe et al., 2004); and developing leadership skills (Seung, Susan & Min, 2005). It is important to mention additional social skills such as effective expression of aggression, which is reflected in the child's ability to stand up for his rights, and planning and coordination, which are reflected in the child's ability to consider different modes of action, understanding their advantages and disadvantages, in order to choose the best way to act, and act accordingly (Sroufe et al., 2004).

Key concepts, which pave the way to acquiring communication and social skills are attentiveness and participation, two connected skills. The current study adds another level of understanding to these concepts indicating that in order to establish these skills, it is important to understand the connection between them: Attentiveness is a crucial step in participation, and during participation, children are involved in different situations in an active way, but this cannot take place without developing their attentiveness (Miller, 1997). Studies indicate that kindergarten children can mediate personal experiences to their surroundings, as well as their feelings and emotions, provided that the educators try to recognize this ability, to observe, listen to and interpret it. If they succeed in doing so, the children will experience true participation in their learning (Pramling-Samuelsson & Sheridan, 2003), while strengthening their self-esteem and acquiring social skills such as cooperation and decision-making (Emilson & Folkesson, 2006).

Children of a young age are influenced by other children in their age group and influence them in return (Seung, Susan & Min, 2005). In some studies it was found that kindergarten children are capable of understanding that everyone possesses feelings, wishes and different thoughts, and that this ability to understand the difference originates from interaction between peer groups (Astington & Jenkins, 1995; Slomkowski & Dunn, 1996). This suggests that kindergarten children's social-communication skills develop among peer groups (Aram & Shlak, 2007). The unique contribution of the peer group is that within it, children can practice relationships of equality and social-communication skills such as problem-solving, cooperation, leadership and discourse (Sroufe, Cooper & DeHart, 2004). This practice requires them to address their friends' points of view, which may be different than their own, while they should learn to speak their mind in a respectful and understandable way (Campbell, 2002). In other words, they acquire social values such as caring, responsibility, seeing the other, choosing, planning, and problem-solving based upon the social interaction they experience (Han & Kemple, 2006). The obvious conclusion is that interactions and reciprocal relationships with others build their social world, their social understanding skills, and knowledge with regard to the society in which they live (Becker, 2009). It is also important to state that in their relationships with their age group and by sharing a game or a personal area of interest, as well as receiving feedback from the group members, the children gain a sense of satisfaction and develop social and leadership skills (Seung, Susan & Min, 2005).

With regard to the kindergarten children's social-communication skills, it is noted that dialog and discourse are crucial for the learning and development of social values (Egan, 1992). This insight includes the understanding that involving kindergarten children in the kindergarten's decision-making encourages the development of acquired social-communication skills (Danner & Jonyniene, 2012); because through them they learn how to share, respect the other, listen and accept different points of view (Egan, 1992).

In early childhood, social ability is defined as the ability to develop, initiate and maintain relationships with adults and with same aged peers (Odom, McConnell & Brown, 2008). As noted, practicing different types of social experiences allows children to acquire substantial knowledge and social-communication abilities (Stanton-Chapman, Denning & Jamison, 2012). They learn to understand friends' and adults' wishes and develop social skills such as attentiveness, sharing with the group, cooperation between children and their peers and between children and adults, initiative, leadership, discourse, and the ability to give and receive feedback (Firstater & Efrat, 2014; Han & Kemple, 2006; Missall & Hojnoski, 2008).

Empowerment also contributes to the development of kindergarten children's social communication skills (Firstater & Efrat, 2014). "Empowerment" can be defined as activity intended to help the other to grow in different directions and dimensions. Empowerment allows the people who are empowered to understand that their voice is significant, valuable and relevant, that it is worthwhile listening to their voice attentively. This understanding produces personal and social implications expressed in a sense of self-efficacy, in the growth of ability to function better under self-direction, with self-control and in becoming more autonomous while developing empathy and sensitivity to others, involvement and social tolerance (Aloni, 2013).

Nevertheless, it is important to note that this empowerment is not a one-time event, rather it is a process leading to higher self-esteem and consequently to the desire to act and to have an influence (Mullender & Ward, 1991). The importance of empowerment is expressed in its influence on skills, relationships and social processes. Empowerment allows those who are empowered to feel that they can have an influence, can contribute to the shaping of reality and realize their inherent potential and eventually leave their mark. Moreover, it makes them want to act for and join intervention processes, partnerships and commitments in order to attain goals that are important to them. It improves their sense of control and leads them to collaborate (Sadan, 2008), and act to improve social consolidation, cohesion and mutual responsibility (Ben-Yosef, 2009). The understanding that the child's empowerment contributes to the development of the child's social and communication skills was relevant for the present study, which related to the ability of the MDA to empower kindergarten children (Firstater & Efrat, 2014).

To summarize, the principles of multi-dialogical education in the kindergarten (Firstater & Efrat, 2014) include attentiveness to children's ideas, discourse, and learning based on the children's areas of interest (Jhong, 2008; Rinaldi, 1996), with the aim of allowing them to practice interpersonal communication and other social patterns (Ben-Yosef, 2009). This connects to the current study in that it clarifies the role of the kindergarten teacher, which is to build the curriculum according to these principles, assist, guide, create a dialog and not teach or lead the children in pre-determined roads (Caspi, 1979; Rinaldi, 1999). Consequently, this approach encourages communication and investigation within peer groups through cooperation and relationships that allow children to develop social skills such as caring for and helping others, cooperation and acceptance of new ideas, critical observation of reality, ability to deal with conflicts, ambiguous situations and frustrations, as well as the ability to control and postpone, as required, immediate satisfaction of needs (Aloni, 2008; Malaguzzi, 1998). This study examines the aspect of social-communication skills and how they are reflected in the multi-dialogical kindergarten and poses the question: What are the interpersonal social-communicational and behavioral patterns that the multi-dialogical kindergarten conveys to kindergarten children?

I.6 An innovative model of multi-dialogical kindergarten activity planning

The child's innovation and planning of activity are seen as especially important in this type of kindergarten. The multi-dialogical kindergarten has developed a clear method for the planning of activity with a child who initiates an idea. The structured planning works according to a model that implements the principles of dialogical education, developed by the kindergarten teacher-researcher, who was also the researcher leading the present study. The model is based on the philosophical theories of Socrates, Dewey, Buber, Freier, Rogers, Gardner, Vaygotsky and Feuerstein. What is common to these theories is their support for education based on dialog, asking questions, being attentive and conducting discourse between equals. The child-learner is not an empty vessel that needs to be filled; rather, he is a real partner in investigative learning (Aloni, 2008; Avnon, 2008; Gardner, 1996; Gover, 2008; Harari, 2008; Tauber, 2008). The model relates to the planning of activities between the child and the kindergarten teacher. A child who has an idea for an activity or discussion comes to the teacher and asks for an activity planning meeting. The teacher and child set a date that is suitable for them both and write it on the calendar, and the meeting takes place at the appointed date. At the meeting, they discuss what the child would like to do in the activity, how he intends to do it and how it would be possible to guide the activity in practice. The teacher uses a very open style of instruction in the meeting: She asks the child what he wants to talk about, requesting that he describe the activity as he sees it. She discusses with him how he would like to prepare the activity and asks what assistance he needs to prepare it and who might be able to help him. After they make these decisions, they turn to the organizational aspects and together, they examine what the child needs to guide the activity: the necessary materials and resources. Together they consider where they can obtain them and who will be responsible for bringing them. At the next stage they record their decisions on a page that serves as a memo: the teacher writes in words and the child draws so that he can understand what is written (See Appendix 7). After everything is ready for the activity, the child guides the activity in the kindergarten on the predetermined date. He receives feedback from the children who participated and reflects upon the activity with the teacher.

Figure I.1: Model of child-teacher activity planning (personal model)©

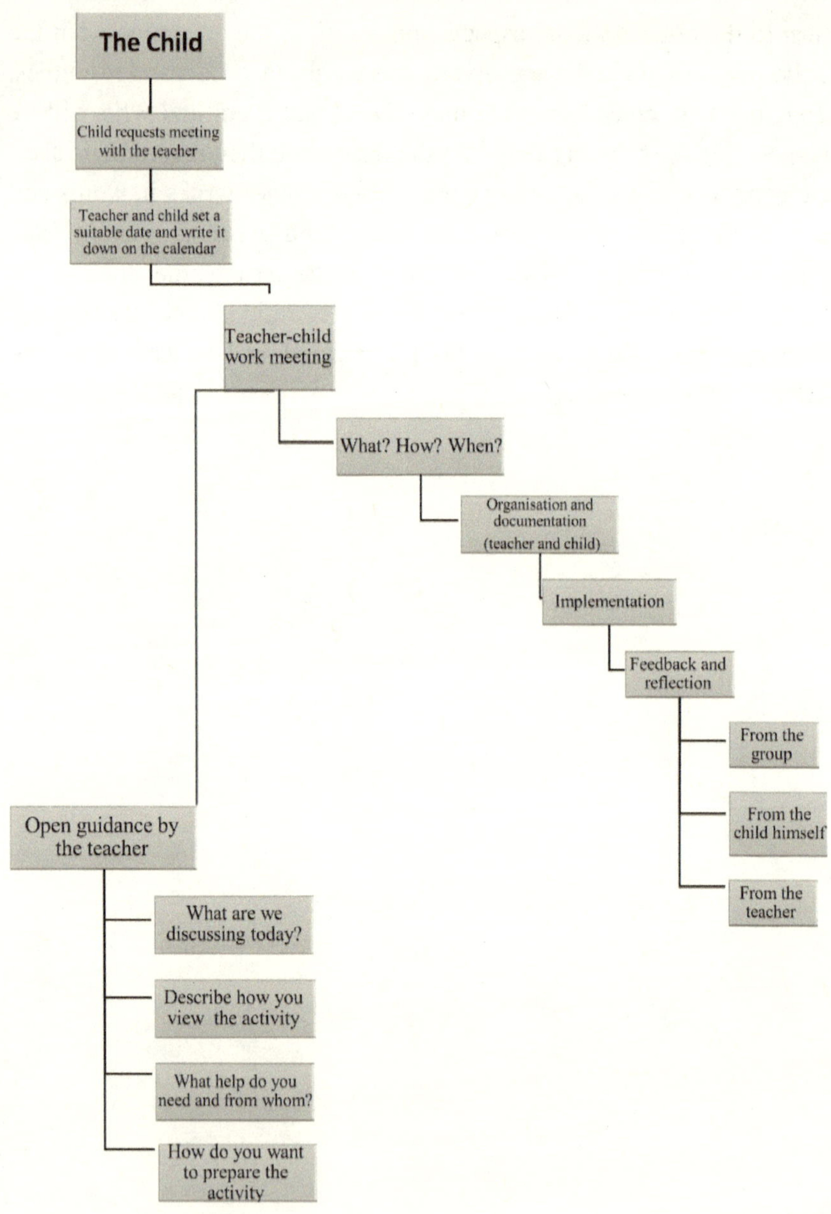

I.6.1 The conceptual framework

This research focuses on the development of social-communication patterns among children in a kindergarten operating according to the MDA.

The research aim was to examine the development of children's social-communication patterns, such as initiative, leadership, discourse, and the ability to give and receive feedback in a multi-dialogical kindergarten. The specific research aims were:

- To ascertain the children's interpersonal communication patterns
- To examine the implementation of MDA in a kindergarten
- To identify and examine ways in which the MDA can be implemented in the kindergarten.
- To compare children's social-communication patterns in multi-dialogical kindergartens in contrast to the patterns of children educated according to the traditional kindergarten approach.

The research questions were: (1) what unique social, behavioral and interpersonal communication patterns occur among kindergarten children in a multi-dialogical kindergarten? And (2) what social, communication and interpersonal differences will be found between children educated in multi-dialogical kindergartens and children educated in traditional kindergartens?

The research draws on the premise that a connection exists between the MDA in kindergartens and the development of social-communicative patterns in the kindergarten children. **Differences will be found in social and communicative patterns between children educated in multi-dialogical kindergartens and children educated in traditional kindergartens. Differences will be found mainly in the extent of participation by the children in their learning processes, peer education: the extent to which the children guide their colleagues on a learning subject, the feedback, the manner of discourse and the extent to which philosophical discourse is conducted.**

This research will contribute to the educational understanding of age-appropriate development of preschool children's social-communicative patterns following the MDA. It will contribute to the understanding of how preschool children learn to conduct discourse, negotiations, and conversation and how they develop the ability to give and receive feedback, the ability to initiate and to lead, and the skills to consider others. The research findings may also be informative for any preschool in another country and/or culture.

In order to achieve the research aims, and based on the literature review above, the conceptual framework included the following elements:

1. Social communication patterns.
2. The multi-dialogical kindergarten.
3. A multi-dialogical kindergarten activity-planning model.
4. Early childhood education.
5. Attentiveness.
6. Mediated learning.

Figure I.2 below illustrates the conceptual framework that underpinned this study.

Figure I.2: The conceptual framework of this research ©

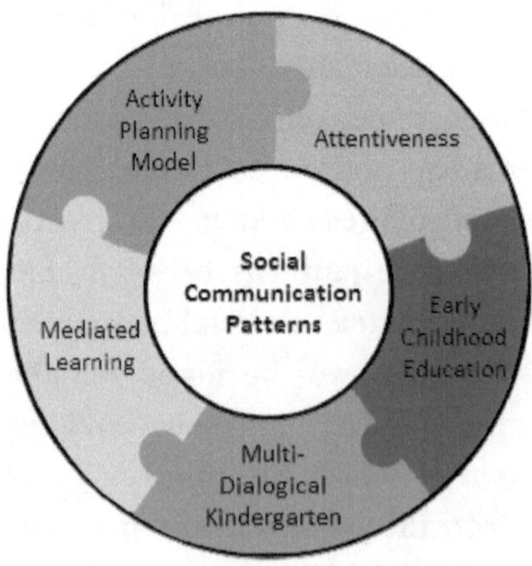

I.6.2 The elements of the conceptual framework in detail

Social communication patterns can be found at the center of the figure as it represents the focus of the research. Education is based on the learner's freedom to explore and experience (Dewey, 1938). Learning through problem-solving and practical implementation of issues lead children to take on a more active role as people within society and develop social communication skills like initiative, problem-solving, the ability to take a stand, and listening (Aliakbari & Faraji, 2011; Gover, 2008).

Multi-dialogical kindergarten aspects have been chosen for the conceptual framework because this type of kindergarten represents the setting in which the research takes place. The educational work in the multi-dialogical kindergarten is focused on observation and identification of the children's areas of interest and their initiatives (Firstater & Efrat, 2014; Jhong, 2008). When addressing learning inside a kindergarten that functions according to the MDA it is important to state that learning based on children's areas of interest will be significant learning (Renninger, 1992), where the level of children's influence and participation depends on the teacher's standpoint and approach (Arner & Tellgren, 1998; Emilson & Folkesson, 2006; Sheridan, 2001).

Multi-dialogical kindergarten activity planning has been chosen for the conceptual framework as it is the model which is unique to this type of kindergarten. The innovation and planning of activity by the child is seen as an important component of this type of kindergarten. The multi-dialogical kindergarten has developed a clear method for the planning of activity with a child who initiates an idea. The model is based on the philosophical theories of Socrates, Dewey, Buber, Freire, Rogers, Gardner, Vaygotsky and Feuerstein. What is common to these theories is their support of education based on dialog, asking questions, being attentive and conducting discourse between equals (Aloni, 2008; Avnon, 2008; Gardner, 1996; Gover, 2008; Harari, 2008; Tauber, 2008).

Early childhood education is included as it provides the umbrella for understanding the research. Children at a young age are influenced by other children in their age group and influence them as well (Seung, Susan & Min, 2005). In other studies it was found that kindergarten children are capable of understanding that everyone has feelings, wishes and different thoughts and that this ability to understand the difference originates from interaction between peer groups (Astington & Jenkins, 1995; Slomkowski & Dunn, 1996).

Attentiveness is also included as a component in this conceptual framework as it is the basis of the MDA. When working according to the MDA, emphasis is given to the teacher's attentiveness to children's ideas and the discourse is based on them (Firstater & Efrat, 2014; Jhong, 2008). Attentiveness cannot be comprehended as "listening on the way to acquiring knowledge", but rather as a reflective process aimed at thinking about new meanings, making connections, and discovering new concepts (Clark & Moss, 2005).

Mediated learning is important as a fundamental constituent of the multi-dialogical kindergarten approach. According to the theory of mediated learning, children who experience meaningful mediation in an active way succeed in making connections to meanings that originate from new information they encounter. In order to assist them, educators should organize the educational environment to enable the children to succeed, leading to the children's feeling that they can operate independently and can succeed in doing so)Feuerstein, Klein & Tennenbaum, 1991; Isman & Tzuriel, 2008).

In summary, the research sought to develop a theoretical model which can explain the unique approach in kindergartens operating according to multi-dialogical education and may serve as a practical modular method to be used by all kindergarten teachers.

Chapter 2

Description of the Pedagogical Research entitled: Development of Children's Social-Communicative Patterns through a Multi-Dialogical Approach in the Kindergarten

II.1 Preview

This chapter describes the methodology chosen for the current research, understanding that research is a systematic and meticulous attempt to produce reliable and trustworthy knowledge (Lavie-Ajayi, 2013, p 10). Mixed-methods data-collection tools were chosen to collect quantitative and qualitative data that could be used to respond to the research question. Part of the qualitative data was collected through action research, including transcribed videotapes and protocols from structured participatory observations performed in a multi-dialogical kindergarten. These observations were used to clarify the different types of kindergarten children's interpersonal communication. In addition, the research employed semi-structured interviews and closed questionnaires. Semi-structured interviews were administered to a small number of kindergarten teachers in order to collect qualitative data that would help to examine the effect of the application of the Multi-Dialogical Approach (MDA) in kindergartens. Closed questionnaires were administered to a large number of kindergarten teachers in order to collect quantitative data that would help to identify and explore ways to implement the MDA in kindergartens. The qualitative research data were analyzed by qualitative content analysis based on the formation of categories, while the quantitative data underwent statistical analysis using t-test variance tests in a purposeful sample.

Mixed-methods research relies on the collection and analysis of both quantitative and qualitative data, and the two types of data are collected simultaneously or sequentially, and integrated in a research process (Creswell et al., 2003). Mixed-methods are mostly used in educational research because this complex research field requires a thorough examination of both quantitative and qualitative aspects of the studied issues (Assaf, 2011; Bocos, 2007). It provides a unique added value as it is conducted in context and within relationships and experiences in an attempt to understand them (Bocos, 2007; Gidron, 2011). The contribution of mixed-methods research is that qualitative findings may add validity to the quantitative findings while the quantitative findings can examine and help to strengthen the reliability of the qualitative findings (Fetters, Curry, & Creswell, 2013). The disadvantage of mixed-methods research is the fact that the use of more than one method may lead to problems of focus.

The multi-dialogical kindergarten also constitutes a group in which social, academic, communicative and group processes occur. The researcher is a teacher in a multi-dialogical kindergarten and regards herself as a member of the group of children who are the subjects of this research. Her research objective was to examine the development of children's social-communication patterns, such as initiative, leadership, discourse, and the ability to give and receive feedback in a multi-dialogical kindergarten. Thus, it appears that the mixed-methods approach was the most appropriate method to answer the research question and provide valid and reliable data for the research. The research examined the assumption that there is a connection between the use of the MDA in kindergartens and the development of kindergarten children's social-communication patterns.

II.2 Research aims

The main research aim was to examine the development of children's social-communication patterns, such as initiative, leadership, discourse, and the ability to give and receive feedback in a multi-dialogical kindergarten. In order to achieve this aim, the subsidiary aims were:

- To ascertain the children's interpersonal communication patterns
- To examine implementation of MDA in a kindergarten
- To identify and examine ways of implementation of the MDA in the kindergarten.
- To compare children's social-communication patterns in multi-dialogical kindergartens in comparison with children educated with the traditional kindergarten approach

II. 3 Research hypothesis

Differences will be found in social-communication patterns among children educated in multi-dialogical kindergartens and children educated in traditional kindergartens. Differences will be found mainly in the extent of participation by the children in their learning processes, peer education: the extent to which the children guide their colleagues on a learning subject, the feedback, the manner of discourse and the extent to which philosophical discourse is conducted.

II.3.1 Research variables

Independent variable: Implementation of a multi-dialogical kindergarten approach for children aged 3-6.

Dependent variables: Social-communication pattern level:

- Participation: the extent of participation by the children in their learning processes (***the implications for participants***).
- Peer education: the extent to which the children guide their

friends on a learning subject (***the implications for children's leadership abilities***).

- Feedback: the extent of planned feedback provided by the teacher to the child regarding activities initiated by the child; the extent to which children are asked by the teacher to give feedback to the child that guides the activity (***the quality of the feedback***).
- The manner of discourse: the extent to which children participate naturally in the educational process (***the quality of open dialog***).
- Philosophical discourse: the topics developed from the children's theories which are discussed in the kindergarten ***(implications for children's ability to develop philosophical concepts***).

II.4 Research design

This research is a mixed-methods study. It uses a qualitative approach that sees reality as a multifaceted phenomenon whose different interconnected levels should be investigated together because of the connection between them (Lavie-Ajayi, 2013). The qualitative study is complemented by a quantitative study, which contrastingly examines the implementation of theory in order to provide data relating to the existing reality (Raphaeli, 2011). As noted above, this mixed-methods research investigated the development of children's social-communication skills in a kindergarten working according to the MDA.

II.4.1 Research type

As noted above, the first part of this mixed-methods research was an action research. This qualitative study aimed to enable a profound examination of the implementation of the MDA in the kindergarten and increased the validity of the research. It aimed to add an additional layer to understanding the use of the MDA in the kindergarten and how the implementation of this approach influences the development of the children's social-communication skills. The second part of the research was a quantitative study in which the researcher examined the implementation of this method and its consistent nature in order to represent it and provide data relating to the existing reality (Raphaeli, 2011; Westerman & Yanchar, 2011).

II.4.2 Research population

The research population consisted of three groups: the first group included 25 children aged 3-6; the second group included 15 kindergarten teachers and the third group included 130 kindergarten teachers. Participants were selected according to the purposive sample method to represent the phenomenon under study. This is a method commonly used in case studies such as this one (Stake, 1995; Shkedi, 2003; Mason, 1996).

The first population group for the qualitative study consisted of children, learning in a kindergarten that operated according to the MDA, in a kibbutz in the North of Israel. A kibbutz is a type of communal settlement that exists uniquely in Israel. Kibbutzim are scattered throughout Israel and located in rural areas. This form of settlement began more than 100 years ago in Israel and its lifestyle was based on three fundamental values: full reciprocal responsibility between the members, complete equality and participation of all members in all areas of communal life including assets. In recent years this picture has altered: on the one hand, equality is no longer complete and kibbutz members are awarded differential earnings. On the other hand, the property is still shared and the level of reciprocal responsibility varies from kibbutz to kibbutz (Palgi, 2008; Shapira, 2010).

The participatory structured observations (some of which were documented in writing while others were video-filmed and transcribed) were conducted during the school years 2013-2015 and focused on one kindergarten class which had 25 students (12 girls and 13 boys) aged 3-6 years (8 aged 3, 8 aged 4, and 9 aged 5). The children learn in the kindergarten over a three-year period, entering at age 3 and moving to schools at age 6. There are sibling couples in the kindergarten who are not twins, and one set of female twins. Most of the children come from the kibbutz's families and have a medium socio-economic status. The researcher, who acted in this part of the research as an insider conducting action research, serves as a teacher in the kindergarten and works according to the MDA. This status was one of the strong considerations for her choice of the children as the population for this part of the research.

The second and third population groups were composed of kindergarten teachers.

The second group used for qualitative research was composed of 15 kindergarten teachers. Seven of them work and receive training in the multi-dialogic approach, while the other eight work according to the traditional approach. All of the participants in this group work in kindergartens in kibbutzim and community settlements in the North of Israel. Community settlements in Israel share social activities but do not share economic or occupational roles as in the kibbutzim. Yet like each kibbutz, each community settlement has a common vision determining its character (religious or secular) and decisions concerning the community are decided by a general assembly of all community members and not by publicly elected representatives.

It is noted that all the studied kindergarten teachers have academic education. Most had a first academic degree and one had a second degree. They also all had teaching certificates and they were employed by the Israel Ministry of Education in the state education system.

The number of children in the kindergarten classes, in which the teachers worked, ranged from 14 to 32. The ages of the children in their kindergartens ranged from 3-6. The teachers are assisted in the kindergarten by assistants and young women serving in compulsory civil service, who are assigned to civilian duties. The role of the assistants is both educational and operational. They act in cooperation with the teacher as a team. However, the teacher is the one who manages and is responsible for the operation of the kindergarten, and the assistant is her right-hand man in all pedagogic functions, helping to prepare the kindergarten for various events (for example, festivals and birthdays) and performing cleaning duties etc. (Guberman, 2009: Ministry of Education, 2001). The young women who serve in civil service are of an age for compulsory enlistment into the army (18 years) but are exempted from military service due to religious beliefs or medical disabilities and instead serve in civilian functions, in places where the state needs extra manpower such as educational institutions or hospitals. During the period of their service, the state supports them financially as it supports soldiers. Their role in the kindergartens is identical to that of the assistant-teachers, but they are younger than them.

The similarity between the kindergartens where the studied teachers worked in terms of composition of the kindergartens, employer, the number of assistants, and the age of the children, constituted one of the considerations for the selection of these kindergartens as a source of teachers for the research population. An additional consideration for selection was the teachers' training or lack of training in the use of MDA in kindergartens.

The third group of the research population, which was employed for the quantitative research, consisted of 130 kindergarten teachers employed by the Ministry of Education as kindergarten teachers in state kindergartens. This population included 73 kindergarten teachers who use and receive training in the MDA. Most of these kindergarten teachers are enrolled in an in-service professional framework which provides knowledge and skills regarding the MDA. This means that this educational approach appears to be gaining power and popularity. The remaining 57 teachers in this group use the traditional approach. The main criterion for the selection of this population was the educational approach used by the kindergarten teachers.

The sample of the research population, with its three component groups is an intentional sample. "Intentional sampling methods are non-probability procedures that select a group of individuals for a sample with the purpose of meeting specific prescribed criteria" (De Souza et al., 2012, p.189). The researcher using intentional sampling should be aware of its advantages and disadvantages. The advantage of such sampling is that it provides validity for the research since it selects a sample from those who actually experience the studied phenomenon. The main way to examine the development of social communication skills of children learning in a multi-dialogical kindergarten, which is the purpose of this study, is through the experience of an individual participating in this process (Shkedi, 2003), and even though there are many participants, in fact, each of them constitutes a unique case and represents the phenomenon under study (Stake, 1995). The disadvantage of the purposive sample is its low reliability, since the sample reflects the approach that the studied phenomena are investigated through the subjective experience of people who experience it. In the present study, to accurately explain the reasons for selection of the sample, it is noted that it focused on the choice of participants, children and kindergarten teachers, who would succeed in representing the population from which they were selected in the most significant way, so that they could clarify the studied phenomenon (Mason, 1996).

II.4.2.1 Research population profile

As noted above, the research population was divided into three groups. Details of the first group appear in Table II.1 below that presents the profile of the research population for the qualitative action research, kindergarten children who were filmed on video-film that was then transcribed and were the subject of structured participatory observations.

The second group is described in Table II.2 below, which presents the profile of the research population for the qualitative part of the research, 15 kindergarten teachers, who filled out semi-structured interviews. This is followed by a description of the profile of the third group in Table II.3, the population who participated in the quantitative part of the research and filled out an anonymous closed-ended questionnaire. 130 kindergarten teachers participated in this latter part of the research.

Table II.1: Background details of the first group of the research population

Characteristic / Age group	Boys	Girls	Children resident in kibbutz where kinder-garten is situated	Children coming from surrounding localities	Siblings who are not twins in same kinder-garten	Twin siblings in same kinder-garten	Medium socio-economic strata
Age 3	4	4	7	1			8
Age 4	4	4	8			1	8
Age 5	5	4	9				9
All ages					2		
Total	13	12	24	1	2	1	25

Table II.2: Background details of the second group of the research population

Teacher's fictitious name	Academic education	Has teaching certificate	Years of teaching experience	Employer	Studied MDA	Type of locality in which they work	Number of children in kinder-garten	Ages of children in years	No. of staff in kinder-garten
Anat	1st degree	Yes	2	Education Ministry	No	Kibbutz	26	3-4	**Teacher + 3 ass.**
Bilha	1st degree	Yes	14	Education Ministry	No	Kibbutz	20	3-4	Teacher + 2 ass.
Carmel	1st degree	Yes	3	Education Ministry	No	Kibbutz	14	3-4	Teacher + 1 ass.
Dina	2nd degree	Yes	11	Education Ministry	No	Kibbutz	20	3-4	Teacher + 2 ass.
Edna	1st degree	Yes	3	Education Ministry	No	Community Settlement	29	3-6	Teacher + 1 ass. + 1 civil service
Frieda	1st degree	Yes	2	Education Ministry	No	Kibbutz	29	4-6	Teacher + 2 ass.
Gali	1st degree	Yes	4	Education Ministry	No	Kibbutz	20	3-4	Teacher + 2 ass.
Hana	1st degree	Yes	15	Education Ministry	No	Kibbutz	15	3-4	Teacher + 2 ass.
Irit	1st degree	Yes	8	Education Ministry	Yes	Kibbutz	25	3-6	Teacher + 2 ass.
Judith	1st degree	Yes	10	Education Ministry	Yes	Kibbutz	35	3-6	Teacher + 3 ass.
Karen	1st degree	Yes	5	Education Ministry	Yes	Kibbutz	32	3-6	Teacher + 3 ass.
Liron	1st degree	Yes	3	Education Ministry	Yes	Kibbutz	24	3-6	Teacher + 2 ass.
Michal	1st degree	Yes	23	Education Ministry	Yes	Kibbutz	25	3-6	Teacher + 2 ass.
Noam	1st degree	Yes	13	Education Ministry	Yes	Community Settlement	28	4-6	Teacher + 2 ass.
Ora	1st degree	Yes	5	Education Ministry	Yes	Kibbutz	14	3-4	Teacher + 1 ass.

Table II.3: Background details of the third group of the research population

	MDA teachers	Traditional teachers
No. of teachers studied	74	58
Employer	Ministry of Education	
Education		
Senior teachers with no academic degree	1	2
Bachelor's degree	60	55
Master's degree	13	1
Years of experience as kindergarten teachers		
1-10 years	20	16
10-20 years	15	18
20-30 years	38	23
30-40 years	1	1
Type of settlement where kindergarten is situated		
Kibbutzim	52	17
Community settlements	19	26
Urban settlements	3	15
Number of children in the kindergarten		
10-20 children	10 kindergartens	12 kindergartens
20-30 children	48 kindergartens	32 kindergartens
30-40 children	16 kindergartens	14 kindergartens
The children's ages	3-6 years old	
No. of staff members in kindergarten		
2 members of staff	19 kindergartens	23 kindergartens
3 members of staff	40 kindergartens	25 kindergartens
4 members of staff	15 kindergartens	10 kindergartens
Total number of teachers	130 teachers	

II.4.3 Location - the research field

The research was performed in 73 kindergartens located in the North of Israel, in kibbutzim and community settlements. More specifically, the research field for the first two stages of the research was a kibbutz kindergarten in the north of Israel. The kindergarten is located in a rural area and the surroundings abound with natural scenery: woods, fields, orchards, and vegetable gardens. The kindergarten operates throughout the year, nine hours a day. The children spend three consecutive years in the kindergarten: from ages three to six. During the daily program, the children play inside the kindergarten and in the adjacent playground. They take part in dramatic play-acting, work in creative workshops, go out for nature walks and eat in the kindergarten. The kindergarten staff includes a kindergarten teacher and two assistants. The kindergarten is recognized by the Israeli Ministry of Education.

The unique multi-dialogical method used in the kindergarten means that the children participate in the planning of the kindergarten's content and curriculum. They invent ideas for activities and discussions, talking about them with the kindergarten teacher, guiding the activities for the kindergarten children and receiving feedback from the group and reflecting on their activities with the teacher. The activities may include all of the children or only a small group. The special approach is expressed in any of the kindergarten activity areas: a meeting, creative activity, a walk, a game, and work in a small group, drama or any other area that the children can suggest.

II.4.4 Timetable

Table II.4: Timetable of the research

Target	Action	Timetable for performance
Progress report 1	Writing Presenting the report	End of February 2015 March 2015
Constructing the research tools	Conducting a pilot study, drawing conclusions and final version of semi-structured interviews and questionnaires.	September-October 2014 (Semi-structured interviews) February-March 2015 (closed ended questionnaires)
Performing the research	Implementing semi-structured interviews Conducting observations and video-filming and photography Implementing closed-ended questionnaires	November-December 2014 March 2014-March 2015 April-June 2015
Data analysis and presentation of findings	Quantitative and Qualitative	August-December 2015
Writing up and editing thesis		Until May-June 2016

II.5 Research Methods

II.5.1 Paradigm

The research paradigm is a mixed-methods approach and includes three stages.

- At the first stage, videotaping (that was transcribed) and participatory structured observations (that were documented) related to the activities of 25 children in the multi-dialogical kindergarten.
- At the second stage, semi-structured interviews were administered to 15 kindergarten teachers. These interviews

were drafted by the researcher and related to the kindergarten teacher's work and her educational approach in an attempt to examine the implementation of the MDA in a kindergarten.

- At the third stage, a closed-ended questionnaire was administered to 130 kindergarten teachers. This questionnaire was composed by the researcher using categories that emerged from the content analysis of the qualitative part of the research. Its goal was to identify and examine ways to implement the MDA in the kindergarten and to compare between the traditional method and the multi-dialogical method as they were reflected in the opinions of participating kindergarten teachers.
- At the first and second stages, qualitative content analysis was used to identify main themes in the documentation of the observations, video-films and semi-structured interviews (Bryman, 2004; Creswell, 2013). At this stage, it was important for the researcher to conduct a deep clarification of the interpersonal communication patterns of the children in the multi-dialogical kindergarten and also to examine how this approach was applied in the kindergarten.
- The above-described paradigm was found to be suitable to respond to the research questions.

Table II.5 details the sample populations, aims, tools and data-analysis methods used at the different stages of the mixed methods research design.

Table II.5: Mixed-methods research design

Method		Aim	Tools	Origin of the tool	Data analysis	Sample population
Action Research	**Stage 1a** **Qualitative study**	To ascertain the children's interpersonal communication patterns	Filmed and transcribed participatory structured observations.	Original tool	Content analysis	25 children learning in the kindergarten
	Stage 1b **Qualitative study**	To examine implementation of MDA in a kindergarten	Semi-structured interviews	Original tool	Content analysis	15 kindergarten teachers: 7 of the teachers had undergone training for the MDA. 8 of the teachers had not undergone training for the MDA.
		Extracting categories				
Stage 2 **Quantitative study**		To identify and examine ways of implementation of the MDA in the kindergarten. To compare children's social-communication patterns in multi dialogical kindergartens in comparison with children educated using the traditional kindergarten approach	Close-ended questionnaire	Original tool	Statistical analysis	130 kindergarten teachers: 73 of them undergone training for the MDA. 57 of them use the traditional approach.

The researcher chose to use a mixed-methods approach for the present research to gain deep understanding of the research field that, in this case, was a kindergarten, and to investigate how the MDA influenced its work; the rationale for this decision being that it was important to attain a high level of reliability, validity and generalizability and this approach enabled the researcher to respond to the research question: What are the unique social, behavioral and interpersonal communicative patterns occurring among the kindergarten children in a multi-dialogical kindergarten? Table II.6 below summarizes the research methodology:

Table II.6: Research Methodology

Paradigm	**Mixed-methods**
Approach	Constructivist
Research Design	Two Stages: Stage 1: Qualitative Action Research Stage 2: Quantitative
Population	Stage 1a: 25 kindergarten children Stage 1b: 15 kindergarten teachers Stage 2: 130 kindergarten teachers
Research Tools	Stage 1a: Filmed and transcribed participatory structured observations; Stage 1b: Semi-structured interviews. Stage 2: Closed questionnaires devised from the categories that emerged from the content analysis of the qualitative part of the research.
Hypothesis	Differences will be found in social-communication patterns between children educated in multi-dialogical kindergartens and children educated in traditional kindergartens. Differences will be found mainly in the extent of participation by the children in their learning processes, peer education: the extent to which the children guide their colleagues on a learning subject, the feedback, the manner of discourse and the extent to which philosophical discourse is conducted.
Data Analysis	Stage 1: Qualitative content analysis Stage 2: Quantitative statistical analysis
Ethical Considerations	Discretion, anonymity, informed consent form, blurring faces in films.

II.5.2 Mixed-methods research

When referring to mixed-methods research, it is important to understand where it developed, what it is based on and how it makes use of the combination of qualitative and quantitative research methods (Bocos, 2007). Qualitative research represents a constructivist-interpretive approach that places the emphasis of research on understanding and reconstructing the meaning of reality by those who interpret it. In contrast, quantitative research represents a positivist approach where the emphasis is on scientific investigation, which seeks to explain the regularity of reality and discover the truth. In other words, the positivist approach regards the learner as someone to be infused with knowledge by those who possess knowledge, meaning that the learner is considered to be an empty container, into which knowledge is transferred from an outside source. Conversely, the constructivist-interpretive approach regards the learner as someone who takes an active part in learning and creating knowledge and thus, in effect, constructs meaning.

It is important to note that the interpretive approach grew out of opposition to the positivist approach. According to this newer approach, research in social sciences should be regarded differently from natural sciences research, for each kind of science has different characteristics that require a different approach to the research field. There is much criticism directed towards each approach by advocates of the other approach (Assaf, 2011; Howe, 1988). Quantitative researchers criticize the low generalizability of qualitative research findings, as well as the researcher's biased involvement in data collection and interpretation of results, which they do not consider objective. In contrast, qualitative researchers do not attribute much value to the "truth of the reality" which quantitative researchers try to uncover, and they dismiss the concept of objectivity as it is perceived in quantitative research (Assaf, 2011). In summary, it is important to note that each research approach emphasizes a different worldview, and they consequently disagree on the methods that should be used to conduct research. Qualitative researchers perceive knowledge as a personal product emerging from the interaction with language, norms and history of the culture in which the individual operates. Thus, qualitative research is perceived as unique and subjective. On the other hand, quantitative researchers perceive knowledge as representing reality, and therefore, this research is perceived as comprehensive, objective and generalizable (Assaf, 2011).

In the last two decades an additional research approach has developed: mixed-methods research, but it is important to note that the two methods that are combined in this new approach developed as two separate traditions and researchers would choose one of these approaches as their research method, according to their beliefs and approach (Assaf, 2011). Mixed-methods research involves collecting and analyzing both quantitative and qualitative data, collected simultaneously or in sequence, and during the research process the data from both sources is integrated (Creswell et al., 2003).

This orientation has developed in the social sciences in general (Tashakkori & Teddlie, 2003), and in educational research in particular as policy makers, teachers, researchers, and professors who train educators have become interested in educational research that is based on mixed-methods (Assaf, 2011). The unique contribution of this research approach includes two main understandings: (1) questions about meaningful ways to promote values and social skills are based on the understanding that patterns that can be explored, uncovered and explained, allowing for prediction of the impact of these patterns in broader contexts. (2) The understanding that the education system consists of people: children, parents and educators, belonging to national, community or school cultures. Therefore, both social and academic processes take place within these cultures, influenced by interaction and different traditions, and significantly influencing the way people behave and act.

Mixed-methods research is usually applied in complex research fields and this is the reason why it has become popular for educational research (Bocos, 2007), which requires a thorough examination of both quantitative and qualitative aspects (Assaf, 2011). In recent years mixed-methods research has been widely used in the global research arena of social sciences (Assaf, 2011; Tashakkori & Teddlie, 2003).

To help understand the advantages and disadvantages of mixed-methods research for research validity, it should be remembered that the use of more than one method provides validity for research. In qualitative research, the use of different sources for data collection and the use of a variety of research tools means that the data gathered from these different sources and research tools can be cross-checked (triangulated) one with the other to reinforce the validity of the data.

However, the validity of data from psychological measurement tools used in quantitative research is examined through correlations between different tools designed to test the same features, alongside additional features (Assaf, 2011). The great contribution of mixed-methods research is the fact that qualitative findings validate quantitative findings, whereas quantitative findings can examine, help and strengthen the reliability of the qualitative findings (Fetters, Curry, & Creswell, 2013). Regarding the question of validation through the use of multiple methods, advantages can become disadvantages. If a large number of methods are used within the boundaries of one approach, this could be an advantage. However, if the multiplicity of methods exceeds the boundaries of that approach that is regarded as a disadvantage, with the main criticism being the lack of a clear research philosophy.

When examining the advantages and disadvantages of mixed-methods in terms of quality and depth of research, critics have noted that mixed-methods research is rather shallow. The claim is that because the perception of knowledge and reality is so different in the two approaches, it is impossible to bridge between them without harming the quality of the research and the researcher's integrity. Researchers who wish to refute the claim of 'shallowness' in this type of research consider using action research (Assaf, 2011).

In conclusion, it seems that the main advantage of mixed-methods research is in the integration of methods, since this leads to the collection of behavioral, numerical, visual and verbal sources, and consequently builds a thick description of the phenomenon (Assaf, 2011), which could not be achieved by using only one research approach (Tashakkori & Teddlie, 2003). This thick description is the result of the integration of quantitative and quantitative data (Creswell & Plano-Clark, 2011). An additional major advantage is that the elements of one research method can make up for the disadvantages of another and thus shed light on various topics related to field research (Assaf, 2011). Hence, the unique contribution of mixed-methods research is that it presents a more valid image, a complex and more generalizable picture, than studies that rely on a single research approach.

In the current research, I chose to use the mixed-methods approach in order to understand the research field, which in this case is kindergarten, more deeply and to examine how the use of the MDA affects the kindergarten and its products. I consider this research to be educational action research, which aims to address the educational contexts, and the effect they have on learners' development when they are managed with the use of the MDA. The mixed-methods approach was chosen in order to reach a profound understanding of these contexts and to provide a broader picture of the research field, which in this case was a kindergarten, through empirical data collection, analysis and interpretation.

II.5.3 Qualitative research – As part of mixed-methods research

Qualitative research attempts to understand how participants perceive reality and what meaning they attribute to it. It aims to identify and explore the various layers and meanings of reality, including the perceptions, actions and processes that participants experience (Lavie-Ajayi, 2013). "Qualitative research is a situated activity that locates the observer in a particular location in the world and involves an interpretive, naturalistic approach to the world. This means that qualitative researchers study things in their natural settings, attempting to make sense of or interpret phenomena in terms of the meanings people bring to them" (Denzin & Lincoln, 2000, p. 3). A broader definition is given by Strauss & Corbin (1990) "by qualitative research we mean any type of research that establishes findings not through statistical processes or other quantitative means" (p. 17).

From these definitions it seems that qualitative research is conducted in people's natural surroundings and in their language. The researcher tries to become involved in and to relate closely to the studied phenomena, including expressing empathy towards the studied population, while as a human being himself, the researcher also acts as the research tool and tries to maintain his distance, criticizing himself and conducting reflection throughout the entire research procedure (Shkedi, 2011).

Human and social phenomena are dynamic and variable, and they are not pre-determined, so that only a human researcher can cope with such a vague and unclear situation while absorbing the complexity and perpetual variability that characterizes human experiences (Lincoln & Guba, 2000). In qualitative research, the researcher's interpretations have a strong weight. This is expressed in the structure of the research, its organization, the choice of research arguments and the presentation and writing up of the findings. A qualitative researcher observes data in depth, compares them and discusses the possibilities that arise from them, either accepting or rejecting them. Moreover, the qualitative researcher's interpretation is supported by evidence, indicating trust-worthiness, since he goes deep into the data, and searches for and relies on other sources for inspiration. The researcher's interpretation is also supported by their own worldly knowledge, experiences, wisdom and deep familiarity with literature on the studied topic (Alpert, 2011).

The qualitative researcher (like the positivist researcher) needs to follow certain ethical criteria and principles that will influence the conduct of the research in a substantive way. However, the consideration of ethics has not always been seen as an obvious necessity in qualitative research studies (Dushenik & Sabar Ben-Yehoshua, 2002).

Qualitative data collected in this research added another layer to the understanding of the use of the MDA in the kindergarten and how it influences the kindergarten children's development of social-communication skills.

II.5.3.1 Action research

Action research is a type of self-reflection research, performed by participants who themselves act in order to improve their work in a rational way, to understand the personal and social situations in which their work exists and to be able to explain them in a public manner (Salmeier, 2011, p.42).

In action research collaboration is most important since this collaboration leads to reflection on the research and the construction of pedagogic theory out of the research itself. This theory serves the researcher enabling him to apply it in the future, and so it is a powerful tool for the construction of future pedagogic knowledge (Whitehead, 2009).

The present study was action research in the sense that the researcher investigated the contribution of the MDA which she had developed, for social communication patterns among kindergarten children. Also, as part of her work as kindergarten supervisor, the researcher conducted professional development courses in MDA for kindergarten teachers affiliated with the Ministry of Education in Israel. The researcher, in this case, was acting as an agent of change from bottom-up and top-down.

II.5.4 Quantitative research – As part of mixed-methods research

Quantitative research is about explaining phenomena by collecting quantitative data, which are analyzed by mathematically based methods… Many researchers take a pragmatic approach to research, and use quantitative methods when they are looking for breadth, want to test a hypothesis, or want to study something quantitative (Muijs, 2010, pp. 9-10).

Quantitative research is based on the positivist approach that examines regularities, assuming that the world is built on regularity (Raphaeli, 2011; Westerman & Yanchar, 2011). It examines the causative relation between things and aims to test theory, and is used to collect and present data relating to the existing reality in order to examine regularity. Quantitative research examines and takes an interest in a phenomenon on the condition that it is able to represent a general law. It does not deal with one-time, specific and concrete phenomena, since they do not represent the general rule. Thus it is usually possible to draw conclusions and generalize from its findings for other contexts than the context in which the particular study was conducted (Raphaeli, 2011).

The advantages and disadvantages of a quantitative study should be considered before commencing such a study. The advantages of quantitative research are its objectivity and strong reliability, its generalizability and the connections derived from it, its ability to reveal new trends and to replicate the research data in future studies. The disadvantages of this method are its low validity, and the fact that it must be based on prior knowledge, and also the fact that a study of this sort does not develop theory but rather it tests existing theory (Muijs, 2010).

Quantitative research relies on numerical data collection in order to test hypotheses. The way to test hypotheses is through questionnaires, observations and surveys, and the data that the researcher collects are quantitative, under the assumption that new trends can be revealed through numerical data. Quantitative study begins with a particular theory that expresses regularity, which the researcher tries to investigate and to distinguish. The investigation must be based on previous knowledge in the studied field. The previous knowledge may be derived from other studies in the relevant area or extant theoretical knowledge (Raphaeli, 2011).

Life is subjective, yet quantitative research tries to provide an objective view of it. This is the significance of quantitative research since it tries to reflect reality as it is objectively. Objectivity is required for the quantitative research process but is not required with regard to the type of topic to be studied. Quantitative research is not only interested in objective phenomena but also in subjective phenomena such as people's attitudes and perceptions concerning different subjects (Raphaeli, 2011).

An additional stage in quantitative research where the researcher needs to maintain objectivity is the stage of data analysis. The data may be objective data that can be seen and measured, or subjective data relating to people's opinions and attitudes towards the studied subject. In order to maintain objectivity during data analysis, the researcher should analyze and interpret the data without any influence from his own attitudes and opinions. The interpretation of the research findings must not depend on the researcher, and it is important to take care that his opinions are not part of the research. The research conclusions will be objective if they have been the same conclusions when another researcher conducted the same research. In the analysis of quantitative data, there is a smaller probability, in contrast to other types of research, that the researcher will influence their analysis, because the data analysis is conducted with uniform and accepted statistical methods and does not include the expression of the researcher's attitudes and opinions (Cohen, Manion & Morrison, 2007).

To summarize: in quantitative research, the researcher cannot be a participant in the research, the researcher observes the phenomena from outside under the understanding that the phenomenon that is being investigated stands independently by itself, and its existence does not rely on the researcher or any other outside observer. The goal of the researcher is to explain, predict and describe the studied reality in the most objective manner and so the researcher must not have any preconceptions regarding the area of inquiry. If they do have such preconceptions, they should be aware of them to the extent that they will be able to neutralize their effect. The quantitative study is performed according to clear, accepted and agreed rules, whereby the results do not depend on the researcher, their culture or gender, so that it is possible to replicate the same research findings in the future (Cohen, Manion & Morrison, 2007; Muijs, 2010; Raphaeli, 2011).

In the present study, the chosen paradigm was a mixed-methods paradigm including both qualitative and quantitative research. The quantitative part of the research aimed to identify and investigate the ways in which the MDA was implemented in the kindergartens, in other words, to examine ways to implement theory that was developed in the qualitative part of the research, so that the quantitative data provided greater reliability and generalizability for the study.

II.6 Research tools

The research employed three research tools:

- Structured participatory observations (some of which were documented in writing while others were video-filmed and transcribed). The researcher used these observations to learn about the viewpoints of the participants, who in this research were kindergarten children, and to understand the reciprocal relations between the children (Mack et al.,

2005) and their use of social-communication skills (see Appendices 1 and 2).

- Semi-structured interviews were administered to a small number of kindergarten teachers. These interviews were administered in order to examine how the MDA was implemented in the kindergartens. The semi-structured interviews enabled the researcher to examine the extent to which the interviewee's beliefs and facts related to the research categories (Silverman, 2006). (See Appendix 3).
- Closed-ended questionnaires were administered to a large number of kindergarten teachers in line with the research goal. The closed-ended questionnaire enabled the researcher to conduct statistical analysis of the studied phenomenon (Shkedi, 2011) and helped to ensure optimal reliability of the data (Maykut & Morehouse, 1994; Shkedi, 2003). (See Appendix 4)

II.6.1 Video-films and participatory observations

The research tools used in this study included structured participatory observations (some of which were documented in writing while others were video-filmed and transcribed) of the kindergarten activities by the researcher. Observations are a humanistic approach method and employ qualitative field study techniques.

- Observations are used to identify daily behavior patterns, as they are seen from the viewpoint of the research participants and researcher (Sabar Ben-Yehoshua, 2002; Shkedi, 2003).

There are two principal types of observations:

(1) Non-participatory observation in which the researcher-observer remains outside and observes the phenomenon from outside-in, obtaining general evidence concerning the observed events, while discerning particular details.

(2) A participatory observation is one in which the observer takes

part in the observed activity, becoming one of the studied groups (Ashkenazi, 1986). This type of observation necessitates the researcher's presence over an extensive period of time in the studied environment in order to achieve maximal participation in the events (Shkedi, 2003).

"Participant observation is a qualitative method, whose objective is to help researchers learn about the perspectives held by studied populations. ... qualitative researchers ...presume that there will be multiple perspectives within any given community [and] ... are interested in knowing what those diverse perspectives are and in understanding the interplay between them" (Mack et al., 2005, p. 13).

The position of the researcher in a participatory observation significantly influences the success of the research. Participatory observation is actually a compromise, aiming to hide the presence of the observer, yet not completely remove it. In other words, the researcher, who uses a participatory observation, needs to find a fine balance between demands stemming from his involvement in the society that he studies and requirements that he must meet as a researcher. He needs to assimilate within the studied population so that he can have freedom to investigate from inside (Ashkenazi, 1986). Participatory observation relates to all types of human behavior, but primarily focuses on several types of personal and social behaviors: (1) verbal behavior - verbal acts with analyzable content; (2) non-verbal behavior, such as tone of speech that could point up important information for the researcher; (3) reciprocal activity that helps to map the behavior. For example, who talks or acts with whom? What do they do when they are together? What do they use? These different types of human behavior can occur simultaneously (Ashkenazi, 1986).

When the researcher wants to gain a profound understanding of social interaction (Shkedi, 2003) it should be observed close up in all its possible situations and forms (Woods, 1996). Participatory observation complies with this goal and is suitable for studies that investigate small groups, which are part of larger groups (Ashkenazi, 1986). In the present study, the studied kindergarten is a small group, which is part of the larger group of all kindergartens.

When conducting a participatory observation, it is important to be aware of its advantages and disadvantages. Disadvantages of this observation method are expressed in several dimensions: (1) a participatory observation necessitates investment of much time by the researcher; (2) the researcher must be accepted by the studied group in order to be able to study them from inside; (3) to a certain extent, it is the studied population that dictates the timetable of the research and of the researcher. Contrastingly, the obvious advantage of this research tool is its strong validity, since the information concerning the participants is accessible to the researcher in an overt and authentic manner because the research is conducted within the studied society (Ashkenazi, 1986).

The video-films used in this study allowed the researcher to attain additional understandings at each stage of the data-analysis. Renewed viewing of the video-filmed observation allows the researcher to distance himself from the data, providing new understanding regarding the studied phenomenon (Geertz, 1973). Additionally, videotaping can capture a strong description of the studied situation, which other research tools such as still photographs or written reports on observations cannot provide (Ryle, 1971). In fact, "every... videotape is a piece of objective data that can be examined without change at many levels for many different types of analyses" (Goldstein, 1964, p.44).

As already noted, video-films provide valid, reliable and trustworthy data and their reliability is easily tested (Lincoln & Guba, 1986). However, obvious disadvantages are: (1) the process of transcribing video-films makes the research more expensive and extends the time for its performance (Pidgeon & Henwood, 1996) and (2) ethical issues are involved in the use of video-films relating to ownership, exposure and access to the data, that may be badly exploited (Rosenstein, 2002). This issue is discussed in greater detail in the section on research ethics below.

As can be seen from the above-said, on the one hand, the use of video-films in any research requires care because of the overabundance of data it provides; however, the research data include voices and visual material and are not limited to the written words (Hockings, 1995).

In part of the present research, the researcher chose to conduct structured participatory observations, some of which were documented in writing, while others were video-taped and transcribed. This allowed her to trace and understand the studied phenomena and increased the reliability, validity and depth of her examination of the interaction and social-communication skills of the kindergarten children, who were learning according to the MDA. The researcher filmed some of her observations of the children's activities in the kindergarten. She watched the videotapes and analyzed them, selecting scenes suitable for the research and transcribing them. She then conducted further structured observations on particular activities. The filming and observations were conducted personally by the researcher, who decided which type of activities would be observed and filmed to adequately represent social and communication situations. The duration of the observations and filming were determined according to the length of the observed activity, from its beginning to its end. The categories chosen for observation were derived from the children's initiatives and related to interpersonal social-communication relations emerging from dialogue. The children's interpersonal communication relates to many different facets of the kindergarten. The films and observations dealt with interpersonal communication at various sites in the kindergarten.

The categories filmed and/or observed included:

- Interpersonal meetings between the child and teacher,
- Children's discourse while dealing with social dilemmas,
- Meetings and activities guided by the children,
- Philosophical discourse
- Feedback that the children gave one another.

The total number of hours of observations and films greatly exceeded the number of hours that were included in the research. As part of the initial analysis, the researcher chose observations and films for inclusion in the research that most clearly represented the multi-dialogical kindergarten as a place that offers the opportunity for interpersonal communication between the children. The researcher explained the reasons for the observations and filming to the participants. Since the participants were children, they were told by the researcher that they were being filmed in order to learn from them. The videotapes of the dialogical kindergarten were not edited. Although videotaping is an accepted technique for research recording, digital films present ethical dilemmas for any research (Flick, 2009), especially education research where the participants are children. Using editing software it is possible to delete sections of the filmed observations, which might distort the research findings. The researcher did not use editing software in order to transcribe the films and used them in their entirety, exactly as they were filmed.

II.6.2 The semi-structured interviews

In qualitative research the interview relies on direct reciprocal relations between the researcher and the interviewees, so that there is a reciprocal influence between the participants and the researcher (Shkedi, 2011).

Semi-structured interviews are interviews in which the researcher prepares a list of questions that they would like to investigate and yet the interviewees are allowed flexibility and much space within which to manage their responses. The questions are derived from the research categories that the researcher wishes to explore and interviewees do not need to respond to them in the order in which they are presented. There are questions asked in response to the interviewees' answers, even though they were not prepared ahead of time and the entire process of the interview is flexible both from the side of the interviewer and from the side of the interviewee. A semi-structured interview will be conducted in order to pursue "...what the interviewee views as important in explaining and understanding events, patterns, and forms of behavior" (Bryman, 2001, p.314).

A semi-structured interview is conducted as a conversation between the interviewer and the interviewee whereby the interviewer asks questions and the interviewee has a space to answer the question in an open and free manner. The reaction of the interviewer to the interviewee's response is expressed by his ability to identify what in the answer is relevant and appropriate for follow-up by him in relation to the research aim. The researcher should continually be conscious of the need to broaden and deepen data relating to the research categories through the interviewee's answers. Although the predetermined questions focus on the research categories, the interviewees can digress to talk about unexpected areas and relate to additional categories that were not predetermined. In other words, in a semi-structured interview the researchers will be open to changes, even if to a limited extent, from the set of questions and categories that they had prepared beforehand (Shkedi, 2011). There are three main aims for conducting an interview in a research: (1) the interview serves as an important means for collection of data relating to attitudes, preferences, beliefs, values, and information. (2) An interview is a good means to test research hypotheses and assumptions. (3) Data from an interview can reinforce the validity of data collected from other data-collection methods used in the research and provide greater depth in understanding the interviewees' motivations (Bryman, 2004).

In the present study, the researcher chose to use a semi-structured interview as part of her research tools in order to investigate the implementation of the MDA in the kindergartens, as this was seen by the responding kindergarten teachers. On the one hand, the teachers provided deep answers and thinking and expressed the spirit of their opinions, answering flexibly, giving their own views and understanding concerning the way in which the approach was implemented in their kindergartens, yet on the other hand, the researcher was able to use the data from this research tool including the teachers' quotations and deep answers as foundations for the construction of the closed-ended questionnaire. The following interview guide was designed by the researcher to elicit data to respond to the research questions and aims, and then piloted and validated by an expert in this field.

Semi-structured interview guide used in this research©

1. Do you know what the MDA for kindergartens is?
2. Please explain what this approach is?
3. Please explain what you understand the approach to be?
4. What, in your opinion, are the disadvantages of the traditional "dialogical" approach for the development of social-communication skills and learning? What are the disadvantages regarding interpersonal relations between the children?
5. What, in your opinion, are the advantages of the MDA for the development of social-communication skills and learning? What are the advantages with regard to interpersonal relations between the children?
6. To what extent would you be willing to implement this approach and why?
7. What, in your opinion, is required in order to implement this approach?
8. What, in your opinion, are the difficulties involved in implementing this approach?
9. How are the subjects studied in your kindergarten chosen?
10. Do you use reflective processes in your work? If so, how do you use them? What do you gain by using reflection?
11. Which types of dialogs take place in your kindergarten, and how are they organized?

II.6.3 The closed-ended questionnaire

The closed-ended questionnaire constitutes a quantitative paradigm analytical research tool. It is characterized by a structure based on criteria, which are outside the phenomenon that it investigates and relies on the researcher's analytical skills (Shkedi, 2011). A closed-ended questionnaire is given to a large number of respondents. It is analyzed with the assistance of statistics or mathematics and its goal is to be as objective and as faithful as possible to the reality it examines (Maykut & Morehouse, 1994; Shkedi, 2003).

A closed- response is recorded in predetermined categories selected by respondents or the interviewer as appropriate. These involve a wide range of questions, including those that ask respondents to check the box or circle the response that is most appropriate (Bradburn, Sudman & Wansink, 2004, pp. 156-157).

The advantage of this sort of questionnaire is expressed in several dimensions (1) strong reliability since it is given to a large number of respondents; (2) it is easy to answer since the respondents are simply asked to mark the most appropriate answer out of several possibilities; (3) data is lucid because the answers are clear and closed and so it is easy to analyze statistically, mathematically and analytically. Contrastingly, several disadvantages can also be noted (1) it is difficult to construct this type of questionnaire in order to accurately reflect the issues that the researcher wants to investigate; (2) the respondents are considered passive. They choose an answer from given possibilities. This passivity produces low validity for this research tool. Moreover, respondents can respond to complex questions passively without thinking too much about their answers or without organizing their thoughts and this may produce distortions in their answers (ibid.). In the present study, the researcher chose to use a closed-ended questionnaire, since it has a high level of reliability, as one of her research tools in order to examine the ways in which the MDA is implemented in kindergartens. The closed-ended questionnaire was constructed on the basis of the content analysis of data from the semi-structured interviews.

Semi-structured interviews administered to a smaller group of kindergarten teachers examined how they implemented the MDA in their kindergartens. In other words, the researcher's decision to use semi-structured interviews and also closed-ended questionnaires stemmed from the desire to provide strong reliability (with the closed-ended questionnaire) and validity (with the semi-structured interviews) for the research.

II.7 Data-analysis methods

Data analysis included both content analysis and statistical analysis. The filmed and transcribed records of the observations and responses to the semi-structured interviews all underwent qualitative content analysis and the data were sorted into categories (Kassen & Krumer-Nevo, 2010; Shkedi, 2003). In contrast, the closed-ended questionnaire was analyzed statistically through the use of variance tests and t-tests.

II.7.1 Qualitative content analysis

Qualitative content analysis by categories was applied in the present study to the filmed and transcribed records of the structured participatory observations and to the responses to the semi-structured interviews (Kassen & Krumer-Nevo, 2010; Shkedi, 2003).

Data analysis in qualitative research is an analytical, usually not statistical, process with intuitive elements or characteristics, whose goal is to provide meaning, interpretation and generalization for the studied phenomenon (Gibton, 2002, p. 195).

Analysis constitutes the heart of qualitative research, and its goals are expressed in three dimensions: (1) to allow the researcher to move from documentation of the data to science; (2) to allow the researcher to direct and decide on the continuation and procedure of the research; (3) to enable the researcher to find connections between the discovered findings and theory (Gibton, 2002).

Content data-analysis is a process in which the collected information is organized and structured in order to understand and interpret its meanings (Dey, 1993). In this process "the researcher is always faced with an analytical task of organizing and finding meaning in what seems at first glance to be incomprehensible" (Pidgeon, 1996, p. 77). Content analysis necessitates the division of the data into parts and reorganization of these parts, where each part is actually a "unit of meaning" (Shkedi, 2003).

Division into categories constitutes the foundation for content analysis and is based on a sorting process (Shkedi, 2003). Categories are conceptual units that reflect the structure and content of the phenomenon that they investigate; each category constitutes a concept related to additional concepts. The main function of the categories is to collect, analyze and organize the research data, and they contribute to the researcher's work by assisting him in distinguishing the meaning of the data and in sorting it. The main work of this sort of analysis is choosing bits of information and assigning them to a category (Shkedi, 2011); because it seems that they belong to the same phenomenon. There are two aspects of a category: internal and external. The internal aspect relates to the fact that each category has meaning relating to the data it contains. In contrast, the external aspect relates to the fact that each category is meaningful with regard to other categories and with regard to the conceptual perspective of the researcher that constitutes an important component in data analysis. The researcher's conceptual perspective is an additional central component of this type of analysis and while the researcher attempts to observe and understand the data, he should remain aware of his own viewpoint throughout the research process, an awareness that relies on understandings from the relevant academic literature, the researcher's areas of interest and personal background (Shkedi, 2003).

When data are analyzed through content analysis, the advantages and disadvantages of this method should be considered. One advantage is the ability of this method to analyze the studied phenomenon in depth and with different and varied emphases, so that the research has a high level of validity. Yet this means that the researcher must invest much time and effort in this type of analysis (Ibid.). It also means that it is impossible to accurately replicate the data from one research to another so that such analysis has a low level of reliability, a serious disadvantage of content analysis (Merrick, 1999; Schofield, 1989).

In the qualitative part of the present study, the data were processed using content analysis according to the qualitative method. The researcher chose this type of analysis in order to reinforce and provide greater depth and validity to the research data. The analysis of the observations and transcribed video-film and semi-structured interviews used categorical analysis through a sorting process was used to combine data belonging to the same phenomenon (Shkedi, 2003), and to create units of meaning which consisted of statements from the analyzed content.

At the first stage, the researcher conducted the initial analysis by selecting statements relating to the research question, dividing them according to criteria and providing names for the initial categories. At the second stage, the researcher conducted mapping analysis, discovering the connections between the categories and creating a new set of categories. Following the mapping, a new order of categories was formed that the researcher analyzed, and aided by this analysis the researcher reached two types of insights: (1) insights aiding the construction of the closed-ended questionnaire as a research tool for the quantitative part of the research; (2) insights relating to the research question. The categories that were traced during the observation of the multi-dialogical kindergarten were: attention and dialogue, negotiation, participation in planning and guidance, peer learning, discourse, ability to give and receive feedback, consideration and ability to see the 'other' and ability to demonstrate initiative and leadership.

A colleague and expert in this field read and validated the qualitative data analysis.

II.7.2 Statistical analysis

Statistics is a field within mathematics that involves the summary and analysis of data. The field of statistics can be divided into two general areas, descriptive statistics and inferential statistics. Descriptive statistics is a branch of statistics in which data are only used for descriptive purposes and are not employed to make predictions. Thus, descriptive statistics consists of methods and procedures for presenting and summarizing data. The procedures most commonly employed in descriptive statistics are the use of tables and graphs, and the computation of measures of central tendency and variability (Sheskin, 2003, p. 1).

Statistics are most appropriate for the measurement of main tendencies in research and also when multiple research cases are investigated, when conclusions can be drawn by comparing the data from each case.

Statistics are used for research descriptions that attempt to describe frequency, with percentages or absolute numbers and thus increase the objectivity of the research, enhancing its quality (Shkedi, 2003).

Statistical data analysis is based on objectivity that is achieved in two ways: (1) trials that are reported in such a way that they can be accessed by others; (2) results of the research reported through variables that have theoretical meaning, measured in ways that are justified by relevant theories (Kirk & Miller, 1986, pp. 13-14).

This objectivity is both an advantage and a disadvantage. Its advantage stems from the fact that it forms a reliable basis for the research and its generalization, while its disadvantage is due to the fact that it lowers the validity of the research since the responses are passive. In the present study, the researcher chose to use statistical analysis that emphasizes numerical expression (Shkedi, 2011) in order to provide a high level of objectivity, reliability and generalizability to the research.

II.8 Research quality: Triangulation, validity, reliability and generalizability

So that an 'investigation' can be elevated to the level of 'research' it must enlist external criteria to assist in achieving a controlled thinking process (Shkedi, 2011). These are the criteria of validity, reliability, generalizability and triangulation (Shkedi, 2003). These criteria are used to examine the research processes and results throughout the research, and also to make the research process transparent (Merrick, 1999; Shkedi, 2011).

Thus, the two important concepts involved in assessing an analytical thinking process of examination and control in research are 'objectivity' that relates to quantitative research, and 'perspective' that is the equivalent concept for qualitative research (Shkedi, 2003, 2011). The objectivity of quantitative research is factual and true. Perspective in qualitative research is a point of consideration for the determination of the research's meaning and quality, and is based on measurements of validity, reliability and generalizability.

Generalizability, validity and reliability can only be meaningful in a qualitative constructivist study in the context of the researcher's declared perspective (Shkedi, 2003, p. 230).

II.8.1 Validity

To test a research study's validity requires consideration of the concepts of deductive and inductive reasoning. Deductive reasoning occurs when a person draws conclusions from general information for a particular case, while inductive reasoning occurs when conclusions are drawn from the particular case for the general situation. Validation occurs when the examination moves to and fro between deduction and induction, between the research trials and reflection upon them, between the research data and the researcher's perspective, between the researcher's perspective and his conclusions (Shkedi, 2003). Conclusions and revelations "must be confirmed by returning to the empirical world that is studied and examining the extent to which the emerging analysis is suitable for the phenomenon and explains what was observed" (Patton, 1980, p. 47).

The advantages and disadvantages of validation are expressed in the question, "does the researcher see what he thinks that he sees" (Kirk & Miller, 1986, p.21). The advantage is that it is possible to defend the validity of the research results when they are conceptually and empirically grounded (Dey, 1993), while the disadvantage stems from the possibility that confusion may be created in qualitative research, since the research findings may be validated or not be validated because it is possible to analyze the same phenomenon in many different ways (Shkedi, 2003). It is noted that due to meticulous and deep data collection, the validity of qualitative research is strong, while the validity of quantitative research is weak. The strong validity of a research serves and contributes much to its quality (Shkedi, 2003). In the present research, the qualitative part of the research aimed to provide the research with strong validity and thus contributed to its quality.

II.8.2 Reliability

Research is reliable when it is possible to replicate the research and arrive at the same results. In other words, if a particular research is reliable, other researchers repeating the same processes used in the research will attain the same results (Shkedi, 2003). Thus, "reliability is the extent to which a research process produces the same answers each time and in every place that it is performed" (Shkedi, 2003, p. 234). Reliability is an advantage of quantitative research and unattainable in qualitative research, since it is usually impossible to expect that different researchers in similar or identical situations will be able to replicate a qualitative research process (Merrick, 1999; Schofield, 1989). In order to increase the reliability of a qualitative study, empirical support should be presented to inform the judgment of the research arguments. Moreover, data collection and analysis should be deepened by creating a data bank and maintaining documentation that can serve for analysis of the research, for purposes of supervision and examination of the data, and by presenting detailed evidence in the final report on the research (Shkedi, 2003). In the present study, the quantitative part aimed to provide strong reliability for the research and thus to contribute to its quality.

II.8.3 Generalizability

The generalizability of a research is also known as its external validity. Generalizability means that the results of the research can be applied to other contexts such as different situations, populations and times (Shkedi, 2003). Thus, quantitative research has an advantage since it is possible to generalize findings from one quantitative research situation to another. However, low generalizability constitutes the disadvantage of qualitative research, since the "challenge involved in generalizing qualitative findings on different people and environments than those in which the research was conducted is very difficult" (Shkedi, 2003, p. 236), and according to other scholars, it is even impossible (Firestone, 1993). This means that in a qualitative research, it is the reader who decides if he can find a basis for generalization from one case to another and which aspects of the research can be generalized to another context (Firestone, 1993; Peshkin, 1993). The qualitative researcher is therefore obliged to support the research process with a rich, detailed description in the research report, knowing that a high level of reliability contributes much to the research's quality (Shkedi, 2003).

II.8.4 Triangulation

Triangulation is a means of checking the data against [data collected from] two or more other methods of data collection, such as interviews, documents, or other observations of the same event (Rosenstein, 2002, p.26).

In the present research, the quantitative study aimed to provide the research with a high level of generalizability and thus to contribute to its quality. Triangulation contributes much to the quality of a research. It constitutes a central concept in the establishment and understanding of the use of a combination of methods in a research. Triangulation of data from different sources of information and from different data-collection methods can reinforce the validity of the research (Merriam, 1998; Shkedi, 2011; Stake, 2005). The obvious advantage of the use of triangulation is that it provides an additional process to validate the research, allowing the researcher to increase the validity of the findings irrespective of the method used to collect the data, and thus to reinforce the research project in its entirety (Denzin & Lincoln, 2000; Merriam, 1998; Shkedi, 2003). On the other hand, despite the importance of triangulation, its disadvantage is expressed in the researcher's dilemma, regarding the positioning of the boundary between the desire and the need to enrich the research through the use of multiple methods and the need to suit the methods to the type of research. Consequently, the researcher needs to consider reservations and limitations in order not to use a research method that is unsuitable for the type of research (Shkedi, 2011).

In the present study, the researcher chose to employ triangulation in a mixed-methods research; this strategy was based on the use of qualitative study based on the language of words, together with a quantitative research based on the language of numbers and mathematical calculations (ibid.). Triangulation reinforces the validity of the data (Shkedi, 2003). The present study compared data from participatory observations, video-films, semi-structured interviews, and closed-ended questionnaires together to present a systematic and careful methodology, and thus increased the level of triangulation (Shkedi, 2011).

II.9 The researcher's position

The researcher's position in the research is determined by the type of research that he is conducting. A quantitative researcher remains outside the research or above it, while a qualitative researcher is "incorporated within the research" (Woods, 1996, p. 51), as an integral part of it, but also separates himself from the situation that he is studying in order to rethink its meaning (Shkedi, 2003). This involvement stems from the qualitative researcher's understanding that "in order to understand the world you need to become part of it and at the same time to remain separate from it, belonging and distinguished" (Patton, 1980, p. 121). Humans understand the world by relying on two types of knowledge: overt and covert (Polanyi, 1967). Overt knowledge can be drafted in words, in mathematical equations and in graphs. It can be accurately described and it is possible to reflect on it (Shkedi, 2003). However, covert knowledge constitutes an important and integral part of human knowledge; it is fundamental, primary, is not expressed in words and precedes overt knowledge. This knowledge is "acquired [by the researcher] through assimilation in the studied environment. As someone who lives within the studied situation, he learns to notice what exists beyond eye-view; meaning that he learns to distance himself from the object and to come closer to the meaning of the object" (Maykut & Morehouse, 1994, pp. 31-32). Covert knowledge is the foundation for the insights and hypotheses of qualitative researchers (Lincoln & Guba, 1985), which turn covert knowledge into overt knowledge during a research process (Shkedi, 2003).

Choosing to be an involved researcher offers both advantages and disadvantages for the research. The advantage is the ability of the researcher to reach covert knowledge and thus to increase the research's validity, while the involvement of the researcher is also a disadvantage since it may reduce the objectivity of the research and thus decreases its quality (Shkedi, 2003). In the present study, which is a mixed-method research, the researcher was involved in the qualitative part of the research but was not involved in its quantitative part. The research emphasizes the qualitative study, in which the researcher was an involved researcher, meaning that she bonded with the respondents in order to understand their viewpoint out of empathy towards them, being with and within them (Maykut & Morehouse, 1994; Shkedi, 2003). The researcher's involvement was expressed, in addition to her role as researcher and manager of the research, by her role as the children's kindergarten teacher. She is also a lecturer and instructs courses for kindergarten teachers on the use of the MDA in the kindergarten and acts as pedagogic mentor and lecturer in a teacher training college in Israel that educates student-teachers for work in kindergartens. Due to her broad professional status, that relates to varied populations, the researcher has several different viewpoints regarding the field of kindergarten education in general and the field of the MDA, which she developed, in particular. Nevertheless, she is aware of the disadvantages of this strong involvement and the consequent difficulty to which she was exposed, so that during the research she needed to find the golden mean between her integration, empathy and involvement with the respondents on the one hand and the need for distance and critical thinking on the other hand (Shkedi, 2003). Her involvement in this study was essential for its performance. However, she knew that she needed to be reflective and to do this she needed to stop and think at each stage of the research, to remember to conduct a dialog with herself, to ensure that she processed situations that occurred during the research process and to be able to stand aside and re-examine understandings that had been learned (Maykut & Morehouse, 1994; Woods, 1996).

II.10 Ethics

The purpose of research ethics is to defend the personal rights of the respondents (Dushenik & Sabar Ben-Yehoshua, 2002). Ethics constitutes an important component of any research and stipulates clear rules. Although all researchers are obliged to comply with ethics, there are studies in which it is easier to comply with ethical rules and situations in which research ethics constitute a difficulty for the research process. The reason is that in quantitative research, ethical principles constitute an external component process (Guba & Lincoln, 1994), which makes them far easier to maintain, while in a qualitative research ethical principles are part of the research process and this makes compliance with their requirements more difficult (Dushenik & Sabar Ben-Yehoshua, 2002). Qualitative research is based on "the ethics of research concerning mutual respect, trust, reciprocity and collaboration between the researcher and the respondents and becomes ... a substantive part of the research goal, an internal component inseparable from the scientific component – the research methodology" (Dushenik & Sabar Ben-Yehoshua, 2002, p. 347). Yet, even if the qualitative researcher is aware of and sensitive to the ethical issues in their research, when he goes out into the research field, he may encounter a reality that engenders new ethical issues. In general, the nature of ethical issues is often only revealed during data-collection, data-analysis and interpretation, and when publishing the research (Dushenik & Sabar Ben-Yehoshua, 2002), which means that "ethics of qualitative research involves the search for principles, commitment and criteria, which should guide and characterize the proper behavior of the qualitative researcher" (ibid., p. 345).

The basic assumption of qualitative research that there is no one external truth that is correct generates both advantages and difficulties. Certain areas of the research can become vague and present ethical difficulties, yet despite all the ethical difficulties, the development of a qualitative research may afford the possibility of doing something that is socially beneficial. Ethical consideration of the respondents and awareness of the need to maintain their rights in qualitative research grew out of the fear that the research process might harm them and also out of awareness that it is important to respect their autonomy (Dushenik & Sabar Ben-Yehoshua, 2002).

With regard to compliance with ethical requirements in the present research, several ethical issues arose that the researcher, who is also the kindergarten teacher in the kindergarten where the research took place, addressed: (1) the fact that she was not only the researcher but also the kindergarten teacher responsible for the studied kindergarten; (2) the fact that the research population consisted of infant children (3) the use of digital videotaping (4) the need for informed consent of the other kindergarten teachers who participated in the research.

Dealing with ethical issues is the role of the researcher. The researcher entered the research field with two roles: teacher and researcher, so she was able to conduct a participatory observer research. The research also investigated participants from the kindergarten for which she was responsible, which might decrease the objectivity of the research. Interpretation of the situations in the research was conducted by the researcher: she studied the documentation (of her observations), reflected on the filmed activities and tried to understand whether these filmed situations complied with the MDA to education. The researcher-teacher chose the activities that had been filmed, the clips that were selected for analysis and interpreted and analyzed them too. Out of 70 hours of filming, a sample of situations was chosen that encompassed all aspects of work in the multi-dialogical kindergarten, for example, the individual child-teacher meeting, children guiding activities, meetings involving feedback, meetings involving negotiation, discourse and problem-solving between children, and meetings in which the children conducted philosophical discourse. This was an attempt to cover all the characteristic activities of work in a multi-dialogical kindergarten.

Another ethical issue arises due to the children's young age. The literature relating to ethical issues discusses two types of observation: observations in which the participants know they are being observed and give their consent to be observed, and observations where the participants do not know they are being observed and so they do not consent (Cohen, Manion & Morrison, 2007), meaning they do not give their informed consent to participate in the research (Dushenik & Sabar Ben-Yehoshua, 2002). Informed consent means that each research participant estimates whether it is worthwhile for them to participate and decides whether or not to consent of their own free will (Howe & Dougherty, 1993) after they have received information concerning the research and its purpose and the meaning of their participation. In the present study, the researcher and participants were not equal in status and power. Since the research investigated infants, it was impossible to ask for their consent to participate in the research, and they participated without any choice on their part. Following a conversation between the researcher and the children's parents in which she explained the purpose of the research and the children's participation, the parents, who are the children's guardians, were asked to give their signed consent to the children being video-filmed (see Appendix 5) and oral permission for the children's participation in the research, under the understanding that the research could contribute to educational practice. All the parents consented to the performance, filming and transcription of the observations.

The third ethical issue was engendered by the videotaping (Flick, 2009). Filming observations and activities engendered three complicated ethical dilemmas: (1) accessibility of the data: the videotaped data are open to abuse far more than other data, for example, because of the possibility of uploading them onto the Internet. (2) Exposure: videotaping captures the face, expressions and interpersonal relations, and in order to comply with ethics with regard to the participants' privacy, the faces of those filmed in the actions should be blurred. (3) Ownership: ownership is a relevant ethical issue in any research and especially one which employs video-films. Ethical consideration questions whether the ownership of the films belongs to the researcher or those who are studied? Can the researcher present these films at conferences, in lectures to students or wherever they wish? (Rosenstein, 2002). In the present research, the researcher promised the parents of the children, who would be filmed, that she would not transmit the films to any other entity, publish, distribute or upload on the Internet any of the observations and activities that were filmed. On the issues of exposure and ownership of the films, the researcher blurred the faces of those filmed on the films and received a written signed agreement from the parents (see Appendix 5), who was the children's guardians stipulating that only she could present the filmed material at academic conferences, out of the understanding that these films could be used to contribute to educational learning and practice. However, the parents did not give their consent either in writing or orally to the uploading of the films on the Internet or their transfer to any other entity or use by any other person apart from the researcher. The researcher understood that if she did any of these acts, it would be illegal. Thus, the video-films were transcribed and appeared in this form in the research. The filmed material is contained on a disc kept by the researcher and will not be transmitted to anyone and will not be uploaded onto the Internet. The names of the children were not used in the transcripts and each child was given a fictive name.

The fourth ethical issue related to the consent of the other kindergarten teachers to participate in the research and consent for its publication. The teachers gave their informed consent to participate in the research, after being given the opportunity to decide whether their participation would be worthwhile and to the consent of their own free will (Dushenik & Sabar Ben-Yehoshua, 2002; Howe & Dougherty, 1993). Moreover, they signed a written form (see Appendix 6) consenting to participate in a research intended to investigate "development of kindergarten children's social-communication skills in a kindergarten working according to the MDA". They did this, knowing that they were entitled to leave at any stage of the research and understanding that the researcher had promised them full anonymity and confidentiality at all the research stages and in any publication of the research.

With regard to the work in the research field, this was based on close interpersonal relations, intimacy and negotiations between the participants and the researcher during the qualitative part of the research. These elements created collaboration, reciprocity and mutual respect between the two sides (Dushenik & Sabar ben-Yehoshua, 2002). Despite the researcher's sensitivity to ethical aspects of her work, when she went out into the research field, she encountered a complicated reality in terms of ethics, and she had to cope with ethical issues stemming from the close relations between her and the research participants.

Chapter 3

Findings

III.1 Preview

This chapter presents both qualitative and quantitative findings as they emerged from the collected data.

III.2 Qualitative Findings

Note: All names appearing in the presentation of the findings are fictive names; the children's ages in years appear in brackets after their names.

The content analysis that was employed to analyze the data yielded six themes with categories belonging to each different theme. The identification of the themes and categories that emerged from the study was guided by the conceptual framework that underpinned this research in an attempt to respond to the research aims and research questions. In other words, since the aim of this study was to explore the communicative-social patterns in a multi-dialogical kindergarten based on data collected through the various research tools, then the following themes and categories are presented as the findings emerging from the qualitative study. Table III.1 below presents the themes and categories.

Table III.1: Themes and categories that emerged from the collected data regarding the implementation of the MDA in a kindergarten

Theme	Categories relating to the implementation of the MDA in a kindergarten
1. Listening and dialogue	1. The teacher's attentiveness 2. Attentive beyond words 3. Attentiveness between the children 4. Active attentiveness 5. Observation in attentiveness
2. Resources and difficulties involved in the implementation of the MDA	1. A change in the teacher's perspective 2. Alteration of the teacher's perception of control 3. The teacher's genuine attentiveness 4. Organization and management of time 5. Courses and mentoring on the subject 6. Flexibility and learning together with the child
3. Learning processes in a multi-dialogical kindergarten	1. The source of the content dealt with in the kindergarten 2. Construction of an activity and learning curriculum in the kindergarten 3. Learning from the children's field of interest 4. The teacher's role in learning according to the MDA 5. Implications of learning according to the MDA 6. Peer study 7. Development of independent thinking 8. The child's deepening of knowledge and investigation in their field of interest
4. Feedback and reflection	1. The children's ability to give and take feedback 2. The role of the teacher in feedback 3. Implications of the feedback for the children 4. Reflection
5. Dialog styles in a multi-dialogical kindergarten	1. Dialog and partnership between the teacher and students 2. Dialog as the kindergarten language 3. Brain-storming 4. Personal meetings between the teacher and the child 5. Children as guides 6. Discourse in general and philosophical discourse in particular 7. Mediation and documentation
6. Social communication patterns in the multi-dialogical kindergarten	1. Life skills 2. Consideration, tolerance and recognizing the 'other' 3. Ability to initiate and lead 4. The child as an active member of society 5. Cooperation between children 6. Empowerment

The themes and categories are presented in this section by the order of their appearance, with samples of representative answers collected from the interviews.

Table III.2: Listening and Dialog

Theme no. 1	Listening and dialog	Samples of representative answers
Categories	1. The teacher's attentiveness	"Out of this attentiveness, ideas grow" (Karen)
	2. Attentive beyond words	"The children don't only listen to the words, they pay more attention to the nuances" (Michal)
	3. Attentiveness between the children	"According to this approach, the children learn and exercise paying attention to one another" (Liron)
	4. Active attentiveness	Teacher: "How many children will be in the game?" Dalia (5.2) "Can I guide some children?" Teacher: "Yes" Dalia (5.2): "In the game?" Teacher: "Yes" Dalia (5.2) "The whole kindergarten" (Participatory Observation 4, Situation B)
	5. Observation in attentiveness	In the kindergarten yard, rainwater stands in puddles and in some dishes. The children are playing in the yard. Ohad (5.6) takes a hosepipe that he found and puts it into a puddle, drawing the water from the puddle with the help of the pipe, and blows the water onto the garden beside him. Teacher: "Ohad what are you doing" Ohad (5.6) Taking water from the puddle and watering the garden". (Film A, Situation 8).

Category 1 – The kindergarten teacher's attentiveness

Analysis of the qualitative data collected from the interviews with the kindergarten teachers indicates that according to their perceptions, the teacher's attentiveness forms the foundation for the MDA. This is evident in the words of Noam who said that "as I understand this approach, it is based on attentiveness." Judith added: "The approach is derived primarily from as much full attentiveness to the child, as is possible, when we really listen to the child. We pay attention to things that if we just listened, we would not notice at all". Michal noted that her ways of attentiveness had altered. "Today, I am attentive to the children in a different way than my previous attention before I worked according to this approach … I feel that I need to bring my whole self into this discourse with the child". Judith emphasizes that: "Out of this attentiveness, ideas grow, and initiatives grow from the child." The teacher's attentiveness helps the children to implement their ideas in practice, as can be seen in Film 2, which describes a meeting between a teacher and children to plan the performance of activities that the children initiated:

Teacher: “So what are we talking about today?”

Dor (5.1): “About the football pitch”

Teacher: “And can you tell me what you want to do in the activity?”

Ran (4.5): “We’ll draw the pitch with markers …”

Teacher: “And how do you want to lead the activity? How many children will participate?”

It seems that the multi-dialogical kindergarten is characterized by the teacher’s strong need for attentiveness, which she learns as the foundation for the approach and as part of the social communication patterns that characterize a kindergarten working according to the MDA.

Category 2 – Attentive beyond words

The qualitative analysis of the data from the teachers’ interviews indicated that the teachers’ perceptions of attentiveness according to the MDA go far beyond mere listening to words. As explained by Michal: “The children don’t only listen to the words, they pay more attention to the nuances. They are more attentive to body language because attentiveness is not only lingual listening, it’s communicative listening". Support for this perception can be seen in Participatory Observation 8, which describes a situation where two children are conversing without words when they want to understand each other’s drawings in greater depth: “Nave (4.8) looks at Yarden (5.6) and they both exchange drawings. Nave gives the drawing he is holding to Yarden and Yarden gives the drawing that he had to Nave”.

Irit adds another layer to the statement that attention is beyond words, explaining that “according to the MDA children learn how to be attentive”. This has implications regarding the operation of the kindergarten since they “discover and learn that attention is given to their desires and then they bring a tremendous amount of their own content,” added Michal. According to Noam, they do this because they “feel significant because they are being listened to, [someone is] paying attention to their opinions and knowledge”. Paying attention beyond words testified Ora "is very helpful for me because I learn about the child through their strengths." Thus too, Irit said that "attentiveness really allows us to identify and strengthen the channel that is strongest in each child." Michal summarized attentiveness as "paying attention to small things, to small details … attention that encourages the child and his activity. Attentiveness like this is not only attention; it's attentiveness that makes things happen. There will be development … a different type of attention than that with which we [as teachers] are familiar".

It seems that one of the characteristics of the multi-dialogical kindergarten is attentiveness that goes beyond the spoken words. The kindergarten teachers learn to assimilate this attentiveness for themselves and their staff as part of the social communication patterns of the kindergarten that operates according to the MDA, and thus they help the children's initiatives to grow/ OR nurture the children's initiatives out of the children's strengths.

Category 3 – Attentiveness between children

Analysis of the qualitative data from the kindergarten teachers' interviews indicates that they noted that there was attentiveness between the children in the kindergarten that operated according to the MDA as Irit noted: "I think that the MDA encourages attentiveness between the children" while Hana said: "According to this approach, the children learn to listen to one another." The attentiveness between the children, said Irit, "is something that we educate the children to do according to the MDA: to be attentive to others," and Gali adds that this is out of an understanding that "one of the reasons that this approach exists is perhaps the aspiration to form a society where people are able to listen carefully to each other." Michal said: "The way to educate for attentiveness depends on the model that the teacher provides; because I [the teacher] learned to be attentive and I am the model for them, they also are more attentive." Moreover, Liron added: "According to this approach, children learn and practice how to listen to one another." According to Carmel, one of the ways to engender attentiveness between children is that "in a multi-dialogical kindergarten group, activities between the children are given a platform, so this also necessitates that the children will listen to one another."

This evidence from the teachers is supported by analysis of the films, for example, in Film 5 in which the children were talking between themselves about God:

Afiq (5.2) "Do you there is someone living in the sky?"

Dalia (5.0) "Yes really, is there a god in the sky or not?"

Ronen (5.0) "I think that there is."

Dan (4.5) "That's right, me too."

Dalia (5.0) "If there's no god, so who gave birth to our parents?"

Noia (4.8) "Er, that's right … but it's our grandparents that gave birth to our parents."

Yuval (5.1) "And who gave birth to our grandparents?"

Yahav (5.2) "… God …"

Dan (5.5) "Then who created the world? … only God could."

Dalia (5.0) "I think that's not how it is, it's not God and I think there is no god living up there in the sky."

Avia (3.8) "But I once saw God."

Dalia (5.0) "It's impossible to see God."

Afiq (5.2) "But God can see us."

The above analysis indicates that the multi-dialogical kindergarten is characterized by the fact that the children are attentive to each other and that the teachers enable them to do this as part of the MDA and as part of the social-communication patterns developed in the kindergarten.

Category 4: Active Listening

Analysis of the qualitative data from the filmed and documented participatory observations of the children's activities indicates that both the kindergarten teachers and the children in the multi-dialogical kindergarten adopt the practice of active listening. "Active listening" is a mental activity necessitating much concentration from the listener. One of the expressions of this type of listening is that the listener ascertains that he understands the speaker correctly. This practice was seen clearly in Participatory Observation 4 during one of the preparatory meetings for activities between the teacher and one of the girls:

Teacher: "How many children will be in the game?"

Dalia (5.2) "Can I guide some children?"

Teacher: "Yes"

Dalia (5.2): "In the game?"

Teacher: "Yes"

Dalia (5.2) "The whole kindergarten."

The teacher asked (the girl) Dalia (5.2) how many children would participate in the game that she was planning. Dalia (5.2) did not give a number as an answer. Instead, she chose to exercise active listening and answered with clarifying questions to see whether she had understood what the teacher said correctly. Thus, too in Film 6, which was filmed during part of a meeting in the kindergarten, it was possible to see how the girl Carin (5.0) practiced active listening when conversing with the teacher, and before giving an answer, she ensured that she has correctly understood the teacher's words:

Teacher: "Carin, do you agree to us seeing the drawing that you sketched on the question that I asked?"

Carin: "The drawing that I sketched shows how migrating birds are not tired when they fly?"

Teacher: "Correct".

The teacher uses active listening in her contacts with the children. Active listening allows the children to voice their ideas and theories, as was evident from Film 12. This was filmed on the kindergarten children's walking tour before the rain began:

Ronit (5.6) says to the teacher: "We are waiting very quietly … until the rain comes. And if we are quiet, the rain will come. If we suddenly make a loud noise when the rain comes, then the rain will stop".

Teacher: "Is the rain connected to being quiet?"

Ronit: "Yes".

Teacher: "How?"

Ronit: "Because it dripped drops on us"

Carin (4.2): "Yes, it dripped".

Teacher: “And is that because of the quietness?”

Carin: “Yes”.

It seems that the multi-dialogical kindergarten is characterized by the ability of the teacher and also of the children to assimilate a social- communication practice of active listening, a practice which they exercise as part of the social-communication patterns that develop in the kindergarten.

Category 5 – Observation as attentiveness

Analysis of the qualitative data from the transcribed video-films of the observations that recorded the children's activities in the multi-dialogical kindergarten indicates that one of the ways for the teacher to pay attention is expressed in observing the children's activities and being able to identify their areas of interest in any place and time. Evidence of this can be seen in the analysis of Film 11 in which the children are seen playing in the playground and suddenly they find a dead bird lying on the ground. They stand around it and talk, the teacher comes closer and listens to what they are saying:

Gali (3.9): “Look, a dead bird”.

Carin (4.5) looking at the teacher: “So why did this bird die?”

Teacher: “Why?”

Carin (4.5): “Perhaps …”.

In this situation the teacher identified that the dead bird interested the children. Thus too, Film 12 shows how from her observation the teacher identifies an area that interests the children. The film describes the children's autumn trip. The weather was cold with a slight wind blowing; the sounds of thunder could be heard. The children stopped for a break in natural surroundings. Some of them ran around and played. Four girls sat in a circle quietly. The teacher came closer to the four girls:

Teacher: “What are you doing?”

Ronit (5.6): “We are waiting very quietly, Gil (3.1), Liran (3.4), Carin (4.2) and me until the rain comes. And if we are quiet, the rain will come. If we suddenly make a loud noise when the rain comes, the rain will stop”.

In this way the teacher was able to identify that the girls were interested in how the rain came down? Additional support for the teacher's use of observation to be attentive to the children's activities can be seen from analysis of Film 8 that describes a situation that occurred in the kindergarten playground where rainwater had collected in puddles and in some dishes. Ohad (5.6) took a hosepipe that he found and put it into a puddle, drawing water from the puddle with the help of the hosepipe and blowing the water out into the garden that was beside him:

Teacher: "Ohad, what are you doing?"

Ohad (5.6): "Taking water from the puddle and watering the garden".

Teacher: "Can you show me exactly how you are doing that?"

From her observation, the teacher identifies scientific areas that Ohad has discovered by chance and goes deeper into what he is doing.

It seems that the multi-dialogical kindergarten is characterized by the kindergarten teacher's attentiveness that is also expressed in her observations of the children that she uses to identify their areas of interest. The teacher learns to apply these observations in any place and time during the day and uses them as a foundation for the development of social-communication patterns in the kindergarten, which works according to the MDA.

In the comparison between the MDA and the traditional approach, the following findings emerged from the analysis of this theme in the transcripts of the interviews with the teachers:

1. The teacher's attentiveness - it was found that teachers working according to the traditional approach paid less attention to the children than the teachers using the MDA as testified by Dina: "It is difficult for me as the teacher to stop talking all the time and to begin to be really attentive".
2. Listening beyond the words – it was found that although teachers working according to the traditional approach sometimes listen to what the child is saying, in the MDA the teacher succeeds in listening to what is concealed behind the spoken words. This is evident from the words of

Michal: "When I worked according to the traditional approach, I did not know how to really pay attention, I did not know how to listen beyond the words spoken by the children".

3. Attentiveness between the children – in the traditional approach there are less opportunities for the children to pay attention to one another than there are in the MDA. This was voiced by Liron: "In the traditional approach the teacher is at the center, she determines who will speak and when, what they will deal with and what they will learn. There is a price for this expressed by the fact that the children do not really have to learn and to train in how to pay attention to each other".
4. Active listening – It becomes clear that in the traditional approach there is almost no expression of active listening in contrast to the MDA. Michal explained: "It's difficult to explain it, but it's definitely another type of listening. The teacher who works according to the traditional approach, which I once used, listens less and talks more. She does not use active listening based on the children's words".
5. Observation through attentiveness – it was found that teachers working according to the MDA assimilate a type of planned observation of the children as part of their attentiveness and their work program for the kindergarten, in contrast to teachers working according to the traditional approach. This was explained by Frieda: "As a teacher I am so busy trying to survive or to cope with other things, and so I am less open emotionally to pay attention and observe the children as they do when using the MDA".

Table III.3: Resources and difficulties involved in the implementation of the MDA

Theme No.2	Resources and difficulties involved in the implementation of the MDA	Samples of representative answers
Categories	1. A change in the teacher's perspective	"The transition to work according to the MDA is a very complex and really deep revolution in my approach and work method as a kindergarten teacher" (Ora)
	2. The teacher's perception of control	"I have to lower the level of control that I usually have in a discussion or over what happens and the program and not to be afraid of things that the children bring" (Dina).
	3. The teacher's genuine attentiveness	"Implementing the MDA primarily necessitates that the teacher works on her attention to the children" (Liron).
	4. Organization and management of time	"The teacher needs to learn everything in relation to time management and planning in order to work according to this approach" (Karen).
	5. Courses and mentoring on the subject	"The whole matter of the courses, mentoring and learning on the MDA that we experienced was very significant" (Irit)
	6. Flexibility and learning together with the child	"The method means that I as the teacher have to learn new subject together with the children that are derived from their areas of interest and not necessarily from mine" (Judith).

Category 1: A change in the teacher's perspective

Analysis of the qualitative data from the interviews with the teachers indicated that the implementation of the MDA in the kindergarten depended on an alteration in the teacher's educational perspective. Evidence of this can be found in the words of the teacher Ora: "The transition to work according to the multi-dimensional approach necessitates a very complex and really deep revolution in my approach and work method as a kindergarten teacher", while Liron noted, "you need to change your thinking in order to succeed in implementing this approach," and Anat explained that "as a kindergarten teacher, you need to undergo a process with yourself in order to implement this approach, to be in contact with yourself". This led Michal to conclude that "the MDA challenges me day by day, hour by hour in the kindergarten", while Noam indicated that "in order to implement this approach, as a teacher I needed to overcome my fear of experimenting … not to be afraid to make mistakes, not to fear something new". As a result of her altered perspective, Judith noted that she understood "that my educational perception really puts the emphasis on important things and does not put me as the teacher in the center". Karen added: "[My] change in perception and transition to the MDA has made me a better teacher; a teacher than understands more, and pays more attention and not only to the children, also to the entire staff and to the parents around us, to the kindergarten community as a whole and it seems to me that this has an impact".

The kindergarten teachers' alteration in educational perspective is an essential condition for the implementation of the MDA in the kindergarten that the teachers undergo gradually and profoundly with a deep connection to their inner world and as part of their communication with their selves

Category 2 – The teacher's perception of control

Analysis of the qualitative data from the interviews with the teachers indicated that in order to work according to the MDA in the kindergarten, the teacher must give up complete control over discussion and the kindergarten contents and pay attention to subjects that interest the children. Evidence of this can be found in Dina's words: "I have to lower the level of control that I usually have in a discussion or over what happens and the program and not to be afraid of things that the children bring". She added that: "The main difficulty is not putting yourself in the center as the teacher".

Carmel explained that the difficulty involved in giving up the teacher's complete control had other implications: "In this approach there are things that make it impossible to plan ahead. You (the teacher) need to go one step after another to see what is happening now and how you can proceed with this to the next stage. It's a difficulty for the teacher." So in order to succeed, as Frieda explained: "I have to work to change from being a teacher that is the only source of knowledge and accept that the children may also take me in another direction". And Bilha added that in order to work according to this approach, "the teacher should not be afraid of the process that leads to places that she has not thought about; rather she should simply be there, and give a place to others; and this requires a lot of work on oneself for those who deal with this". This work on oneself depends on "the teacher's ability to understand what it means to release control. She has to operate from a more adult position, more mature, softer; as a more professional teacher", added Anat.

A teacher working according to the MDA learns through a process of inner work on herself, relinquishing total control over the contents that are raised in the kindergarten and over the discourse that is conducted there, and when she waivers this control, she becomes available to really be attentive to the children, as part of her communicative patterns with them.

Category 3 - The teacher's genuine attentiveness

Analysis of the qualitative data from the interviews with the teachers indicates that the teachers have difficulty listening with real focused attention to the children, as was noted by Liron: "Implementing the MDA, the teacher needs to work on her attention to the children". Dina added: "It's very difficult for the teacher to stop talking all the time and start really paying attention, but that is what you have to do in order to begin to implement this approach". Karen reinforces this viewpoint: "It is difficult to continually pay attention; it's easier to come with a predetermined program that's completely closed". In the transition to real attentiveness "suddenly it's not only what I as the teacher decide and not only what I want, suddenly I need to genuinely pay attention to what the children are saying, what the children want" emphasized Irit and "it is difficult to learn how to pay attention and to know how to embrace the child's initiative and empower it. [It is difficult because] we the teachers are not always open to paying attention," said Judith. Moreover, in order to learn how to apply genuine attentiveness to the children, the teacher needs "to come to the kindergarten without any orderly program of my own in order to mark it with a 'v'" said Karen, and Michal noted "not only to do what is demanded of me" but also as Karen added to devote "a huge amount of attention and listening to what emerges from the world of the child and helping to empower it".

The teacher needs to develop awareness towards the children and learn how to apply concentrated and genuine attentiveness to the child as the attentiveness that is needed by the teacher. This is not simple to perform and experience and often constitutes a difficulty for the teacher. Implementation of the MDA in the kindergarten depends on this type of attentiveness, attentiveness from which children's initiatives emerge as part of the social-communication patterns that develop in a multi-dialogical kindergarten.

Category 4 – Organization and management of time

Analysis of the qualitative data from the interviews with the teachers indicates that in order to implement the MDA in the kindergarten, the teacher has to learn how to organize, plan and manage time correctly. This was clearly stated by Karen: "the teacher needs to learn everything relating to time management and planning in order to work according to this approach". Proper time planning constitutes a difficulty as noted by Anat: "We have a technical difficulty relating to the teacher's proper time management". In this context, Judith added: "Work according to this approach actually requires immense organization by the adult". Her words were supported by Michal who testified that "my main difficulty is being more focused, more organized". Since the work in the multi-dialogical kindergarten "engenders [the voicing of] a lot of desires from the children …the teacher needs to know how to organize all the desires that are voiced, how to give expression to everything and that's difficult" added Gali. This means that "often when beginning to work according to this approach, there is a sense that you as the teacher have to create extra time," said Karen. Judith explained that "I have to follow-up on the children, to see that I am succeeding in reaching each child, each in their own unique manner", and so, Karen added, "when I understood how to work properly, with correct time planning and a daily schedule, then the implementation of the MDA became part of our day, as a routine".

The effective management and organization of time constitute an important component in the implementation of the MDA in a kindergarten. The teacher learns this when she wants to respond to the children's needs and initiatives that she has previously identified through her attention to them. This is part of the development of social-communication patterns in the kindergarten.

Category 5 - Courses and mentoring on the subject

Analysis of the qualitative data from the interviews with the teachers indicates that in order to implement the MDA in the kindergarten, the teacher needs to receive courses, mentoring and modeling by an instructor on this course and to participate in a support group of other teachers working according to this approach. In order to implement this approach the teacher needs courses: this need was voiced by Anat, "in order to work according to the MDA we need to learn about it and have a mentor". Irit added: "The course, mentoring and learning of the approach were all extremely significant". Judith explained what she needed: "I need a place where I can ask questions in order to develop, and I found that in the course". Another thing that the teacher needs to implement the approach is a support group. This was clear from the words of Ora, who said that she needed: "a learning and support group on the MDA, because it was difficult to use the approach alone. You need continuous professional support". This view was supported by Liron, who said: "I think that peer study in a guided group was also very necessary". When they began to implement the approach in the kindergarten, Karen noted, "what I needed in addition was the cooperation and support of the other kindergarten teachers who took the course, who were members of this group, where they all gave and shared their insights". Another thing that the teachers needed to implement the approach was coaching and modeling. This was expressed by Carmel: "I need guidance on this subject, coaching that will show how it is done in practice, how it is done in the kindergarten".

In order to implement the MDA in a kindergarten the teacher needs professional courses on the MDA, a support group with other teachers practicing the approach in kindergartens and

mentoring by a professional mentor on this approach that is characterized by social-communication patterns of queries, support and modeling.

Category 6 – Flexibility and learning together with the child

Analysis of the qualitative data from the interviews with the teachers indicates that the teacher's flexibility and her learning together with the child constitute important elements of the implementation of the MDA in a kindergarten. This was expressed by Judith: "It demands that I as the teacher should learn new subjects together with the children that emerge from their fields of interest and not necessarily from mine". This learning shared with the children means that "I feel that I have learnt a lot about what is interesting for the children, a lot about the personal position of each child, a lot about how to give time for learning," said Liron. In order to achieve learning together with the children, Noam said: "The teacher must continually have her finger on the pulse, reading the environment and the children's fields of interest correctly…you always have to be flexible and to adapt yourself to the children's environment". Judith noted that this meant that "I succeed in building the learning foundation that I need to provide in the kindergarten in line with the child's initiative and areas of interest"

In the kindergarten that works according to the MDA, the teacher learns together with the children and out of her attention to their fields of interest as part of her communicative patterns that she uses with them. In order to do so she must be flexible in her reactions to the children's initiatives and to the subjects that they broach out of their interest, so that this flexibility is part of the social patterns that she practices with the children.

In the comparison between the MDA and the traditional approach from the transcripts of the interviews with the teachers, the following findings emerged from the analysis of this theme:

1. Alteration of the teacher's perception – in order to transition from work according to the traditional approach to work according to the MDA the kindergarten teacher needs to

alter her/his perception concerning the substance of her/his profession as Anat noted: “And perhaps if they would have taught the MDA when we were still studying to be kindergarten teachers we would have assimilated it [work according to the MDA] far more naturally”.

2. The teacher’s perception of control – in the traditional approach, the teacher’s perception of control is far stronger than the perception of control held by the teachers working according to the MDA. This was explained by Noam: “I think that from a professional viewpoint it is far easier to work with a group of children according to the frontal highly structured model, as is accepted according to the traditional approach. It is far simpler for the teacher because they control everything; they know exactly what to do and what to teach”. Contrastingly, Irit noted: “In the MDA the teacher needs to relinquish a bit of the control in order to give more room to the children”.
3. The teacher’s genuine attentiveness – there is a difference in the quality of attentiveness between teachers working according to the traditional approach and teachers working according to the MDA. This was clear from the words of Dina: “I need to learn how to listen, to develop the ability for real attentiveness as a teacher, far more than when I listen according to the traditional approach. It’s not the same sort of attentiveness. In the MDA it’s genuine attentiveness; in the traditional approach we pay attention in order to do more and more things”.
4. Organization and time management - there is a difference in the manner of organization and time management between the MDA and the traditional approach as testified by Dina: “In the traditional approach the daily agenda and the activities are clearly determined and the teacher works according to a predetermined and highly structured program”. The MDA is based on “many desires and ideas that come from the children,” added Gali and so as Anat

noted, "there is a technical difficulty involved in the teacher's proper management of time".

5. Training and guidance on the subject – all the teachers, both traditional and MDA thought that without courses and guidance it would not be possible to implement the MDA in the kindergarten. Anat said: "In order to work according to the MDA I need studies and mentoring".
6. Flexibility and learning together with the child – a difference was found in the extent of flexibility needed by the teacher working according to the MDA in contrast to the teacher working according to the traditional approach. Anat explained that "according to the traditional approach the teacher often works in a set mold, in the MDA there are no templates, there is far more flexibility in the teacher's learning with the child".

Table III.4: Learning processes in a multi-dialogical kindergarten

Theme no. 3	Learning processes in a multi-dialogical kindergarten	Samples of representative answers
Categories	1. The source of the content dealt with in the kindergarten	"The subjects studied in the kindergarten are determined by me and also by the children" (Irit).
	2. Construction of an activity and learning curriculum in the kindergarten	"You need to really know the children in depth and to construct a curriculum according to their fields of interest" (Noam).
	3. Learning from the children's field of interest	"The children are far more open-minded and have a desire to learn because the learning takes place in their fields of interest" (Noam).
	4. The teacher's role in learning according to the MDA	When the children speak the dialogical language and live the dialog, their ideas stream out and it's possible to run and develop it with them in very many directions, it encourages creativity, it arouses imagination" (Liron).
	5. Implications of learning according to the MDA	"Learning that poses problems, as in multi-dialogical education, develops thinking, it is not static, it does not provide answers, it does not provide solutions, it encourages creativity, it stirs the imagination" (Irit).
	6. Peer study	"The children often create interest groups revolving on a particular matter of interest, and this develops cooperation, friendships and peer study".
	7. Development of independent thinking	"It (learning according to the MDA) simply transforms the child into a thinker, so that the child learns autonomously, they know how to draw conclusions" (Frieda).
	8. The child's deepening of knowledge and investigation in their field of interest	Ziv (5.11): "Marie, that mask, that head – is it one of a real animal?" Marie (5.9): "Yes …" Yahel (5.1): "Marie, who are they fighting? You still haven't explained it to us?" Marie (5.9): "I'll now explain it to you …" (Film 10, Situation F).

Category 1 - The source for the program dealt with in the kindergarten

Analysis of the qualitative data from the interviews with the teachers indicates that the source of the contents dealt with in the multi-dialogical kindergarten is from the teacher and is primarily derived from the children's fields of interest. This was evident from the words of Irit: "The subjects learnt in the kindergarten are actually determined by me and also by the children. The children definitely bring things from their world of content and we use that to construct complete subjects". Hana supported Irit's words: "The contents that the children raise and want to discuss are equal in value at least to the contents that the teacher brings". Judith added: "When a child shows an interest in a subject, a whole world relating to that subject is opened up for us that we had not thought that we would broach and discuss in the kindergarten", and so "the children are full partners in planning contents ... they bring things from their own world of content and from that we build complete subjects" said Irit. Michal testified that "the children take an active part, they express their opinion, their desires, what they want to do; a lot of ideas that they are able to bring into expression". When the teacher brings content into the kindergarten she examines it with the children, as Ora explained: "On every subject I examine what the children know about that subject, what they would like to know and what I (the teacher) can bring to this subject and from there I continue to plan how to present the subject". Karen emphasized: "Even when I bring content to the kindergarten such as a festival, I ask the children what would interest them, what their need is and from there I begin to plan the festival".

The contents for the kindergarten that works according to the MDA are derived from the children's fields of interest combined with the contents that the teacher brings. Moreover, even when the teacher chooses to bring the contents, the planning and learning of the contents are organized after examining with the children what they know about the subject, what they are interested in knowing and learning about it and what they want to do about it, and all

this is part of the social-communication patterns emphasized in a kindergarten working according to the MDA.

Category 2 - Construction of a work and learning curriculum in the kindergarten

Analysis of the qualitative data from the interviews with the teachers showed that the work and learning curriculum in the kindergarten working according to the MDA is mainly determined in line with the children's fields of interest. Noam noted: "You have to get to know the children very deeply and to construct your work program according to their fields of interest". The planning of the learning comes "after I have identified the child's field of interest concerning the subject, I then continue to construct the program and in consideration of the child's interest, I add other contents relating to the learning of science, nature or mathematics or literacy. Everything is included through dialogical learning, and then the learning is far more significant for the child". It is not only the general program that is constructed according to the children's fields of interest but also every subject that is broached in the kindergarten. Judith explained: "My goal is to examine where the children are with regard to the subject, before I begin to plan it, so that it will be relevant for them. Liron summarizes by saying that "to create a work program for the kindergarten based on the children's fields of interest is far more complicated than constructing my own program and bringing it as it is".

The work and learning curriculum in a kindergarten working according to the MDA is determined in line with the children's fields of interest, based on the teacher's ability to identify these fields of interest through attentiveness to the children. The program is not predetermined to the last detail. The frame is fixed and determined according to the calendar, but what happens within it stems from the children's fields of interest and is part of the communication patterns emphasized by the teacher in the development of the program.

Category 3 - Learning from the children's field of interest

Analysis of the qualitative data from the interviews with the teachers indicates that when the MDA is used in a kindergarten,

the children learn about and go deeper into their fields of interest and so they have a strong curiosity to learn. This was evident in the words of Noam: "The children are far more open-minded and have a desire to learn because the learning takes place in their fields of interest". "Learning in this manner responds to the children's needs," Noam added, while Carmel noted that it was important that "the learning in the kindergarten should not only come from something that seems to fall from above, from the teacher," and Liron said: "I really pay attention and observe what is interesting for the children, and which contents will interest them". Anat added: "When the learning comes from the child, when the learning interests the child, when it is the need of the child, as happens in the MDA, then it will be much more significant". So that "learning out of interest, learning out of meaning, I think is far more correct, especially in our times when knowledge is so accessible," added Noam.

The multi-dialogical kindergarten is characterized by the fact that its contents are constructed in line with the children's fields of interest. The teacher identifies these fields out of her attentiveness towards the children and her observations of them. This learning is deep and meaningful learning and constitutes part of the social-communication patterns that develop in the multi-dialogical kindergarten.

Category 4 - The teacher's role in learning according to the MDA

Analysis of the qualitative data from the interviews with the teachers indicates that the role of the teacher in learning according to the MDA is expressed inattentiveness and in meaningful mediation for the child in their learning process. Evidence of this appears in the words of Liron: "When the children speak the dialogical language and live the dialog, their ideas flow from them and it is possible to run on and to develop in many different directions with them, through meaningful mediation". The teacher's attentiveness is part of her role in the children's learning process, as noted by Michal: "I try to be as attentive as possible, to look at the children, to observe them and I try to see how I can deal with things that come from them".

Judith adds: "Every activity and anything that the children initiate, I can adopt that, empower it and touch upon all the possible aspects". For this to happen the teacher has to have "a lot of amenability to things that interest the children and emerge from the children" said Liron. This is because "in the MDA you do not relate to the children as if they are *tabula rasa*, as if they have no opinion and significant knowledge. On the contrary, we use their knowledge as a basis for learning and investigation," added Noam. According to the MDA the teacher is not the one who delivers the knowledge," said Ora. Her role is expressed in her "ability to reach each child, to respond to the expectations and fields of interest of each and every one of them," noted Noam.

The data indicate that the role of the teacher, who works according to the MDA in the children's learning, is expressed by attentiveness to the children and identification of their fields of interest and in meaningful mediation for them. The teacher understands that she is not the sole source of knowledge and that the questions should come from the child's field of interest, understanding that the supply of the learning material is not the main thing. Instead, it is important to attain deep familiarity with the child's strengths with which the child begins her/his learning, and this is all part of the social-communication patterns that develop in the multi-dialogical kindergarten.

Category 5 - Implications of learning according to the MDA

Analysis of the qualitative data from the interviews with the teachers indicates that in the MDA the children learn to know their abilities; they learn in depth and gain expertise in the field of their interest, and they develop and exercise certain life skills. An additional consequence is that a variety of content(s) is discussed in the kindergarten. Irit noted: "Learning that poses problems, such as in multi-dialogical education, develops thinking, it is not static, it does not provide answers, it does not give solutions, it encourages creativity, and it stirs the imagination". "In this approach the child learns more because he/she wants to learn," said Gali. "I just think that they are learning to think big and are open-minded," added Karen. An additional consequence is that the children exercise life skills when they learn according to this approach. Bilha explained: "I think that learning out of a subject that interests the child alters the way in which the children relate to each other and also the discourse between them". "This approach reinforces the child's desire to be part of the learning, part of the group, part of the meaning that they construct" added Gali. Another consequence that stems from this type of learning is that there is a large variety of unique subjects and contents that are dealt with in the kindergarten. Hana noted: "When you pay attention to the subjects which interest the children, all sorts of original and special initiatives and subjects and contents appear, which would not appear at front stage in any other manner …The activities and learning, according to this approach, takes on a special character out of the children's ideas and so no day and no year and no group is similar to what happened before".

According to the findings, the implications of learning according to the MDA are expressed in the fact that the child learns to know their abilities as a result of learning that poses problems, the child learns in depth and develops expertise in their field of interest. They also learn life skills as part of the social-communication patterns that develop in the kindergarten. Additionally, it seems that there is a broad range of learning contents in the kindergarten working according to the MDA in comparison to the contents in a kindergarten working according to the traditional approach.

Category 6 - Peer study

Analysis of the qualitative data from the interviews indicates that when applied in the kindergarten, the MDA invites the children to become partners in peer study. This was evident in the words of Michal: "I think that there is a lot of peer study here". Liron added: "The children often create interest groups revolving on a particular matter of interest, and this develops cooperation, friendships and peer study". The path to peer study arises "because there is a lot of open-mindedness for matters that interest the children and that are raised by the children, and often what interests one child is also interesting for another. They teach each other and open different worlds for each other," said Noam. Analysis of the participatory observations supports Noam's testimony, for example, in Participatory Observation 8, where children were talking about the atmosphere:

Naveh (4.8): pointing to the painting that she received from Yarden, "that's the atmosphere and it's fallen down".

Yarden (5.6): "I have a question, what is the atmosphere?"

Naveh (4.8): "The atmosphere is …"

Yarden (5.6): "Space?"

Naveh (4.8): "No, atmosphere is a sort of circle in a spaceship. If you pass through it, then you reach space".

Yarden (5.6): "I understand".

In Film 8.1, it was also possible to see peer study between the children. In this film the children were speaking about physics with the help of a pipe, water and a bucket:

Ohad (5.6) "I shall explain how; here I have a pipe and water", points to the pipe and water.

Yahel (5.0) "Correct".

Ohad (5.6): "You bring your mouth close to the pipe and suck the water close to your mouth, and transfer it to the bucket".

Ronen (4.5): "But how does it work? You didn't say how it works".

Yahel (5.0): "Yes, I didn't understand how it works".

Ronen (4.5): "It works?"

Lear (4.9): "How?"

Ohad (5.6): "Come and see. I'll show you". Ohad demonstrates.

Yahel (5.0): "Wow!"

Ronen (4.9): "Ah, I think I understand; you draw the air up and then let out the water below".

The multi-dialogical kindergarten appears to offer the children opportunities for peer study, stemming from interest groups that are created due to their common fields of interest and shared investigation, and this is part of the social-communication patterns developed in the kindergarten working according to the MDA.

<u>**Category 7 - Development of independent thinking**</u>

Analysis of the qualitative data collected from the interviews with the teachers indicates that in the MDA, the children develop independent thinking. This is clearly seen in the words of Bilha: "Learning according to the MDA frees the child to think in an independent manner" while Frieda added: "[This is because] it simply transforms the child into a thinker, an independent learner, a child who knows how to draw conclusions". Ora stressed that "it opens people up, turning children into independent thinkers and independent people, people who are curious". Thus, it seems that "one of the things that stem from this approach, which is most profitable for a society that grows in this spirit, is that they learn to solve complex problems independently," added Judith.

Analysis of the participatory observations supports the teachers' impressions. For example, in Participatory Observation 8, where a child tells a group of his peers about his theory on the creation of the world and maintains his opinion:

Naveh (4.8): "In my opinion, God created the world and when all the things were already on the earth, God fell from a plane and died. I think that God created the earth and then all the tickets for the earth were sold out".

Yarden (5.6): "But how could there have once been tickets?"

Naveh (4.8): "Because that's my opinion".

Teacher (turning to Naveh): "Very good, you answer and use the words 'my opinion'".

In the films it was also possible to see the independent thinking that the children adopted as expressed for example in Film 11.1 where the children discovered a dead bird lying on the ground on a walking trip:

Yoram (5.3): "Perhaps the bird was playing, it flew and then received a blow and then it bled and it died on the ground."

Ravit (3.11): "Or it could be that the raven peeled off its head and scratched it then it died".

Carin (4.5): "I think that she doesn't have a wing, so that's why she fell".

It seems that the kindergarten, which works according to the

MDA, allows the children to think and draw conclusions independently and thus enables them to develop independent thinking as part of the social-communication patterns that develop there.

Category 8 - The child's deepening of knowledge and investigation in their field of interest

Analysis of the qualitative data that emerged from the films of the children's activities indicates that when using the MDA the children go deep into their fields of interest as part of the learning patterns characteristic of a kindergarten using this approach. Evidence of this appeared in Film 10 in which Marie (5.9) investigated the subject of the Indians and guided a group of children on this subject. Marie shared her knowledge with the children and the children saw her as having expertise in this field.

Marie (5.9) opens a file that she has prepared on the subject of the Indians. She shows it to the group and says: "Here these are Indians, they live in tepees, but they don't only live there, they sleep there, they eat there, they light bonfires and play on bamboo pipes, they eat buffalo, and they make combs from the buffalo's bones".

Dealing with this field of interest stimulates the children to ask the girl with the knowledge questions:

Ziv (5.11): "Marie, that mask, that head – is it one of a real animal?"

Marie (5.9): "Yes ..."

Yahel (5.1): "Marie, who are they fighting? You still haven't explained it to us?"

Marie (5.9): "I'll explain it to you now. They fight with trade and they fight about ...".

Yahel (5.1): "What are trades?"

Marie (5.9): "Trades are, for example, if you want me to give you something, then I give you [something] and you give it to me".

It seems that the kindergarten which works according to the MDA is characterized by the children's desire to develop their field of interest in depth, alongside their ability to explain themselves and to transmit knowledge that they have acquired to their peers. Moreover, the children relate to their friends as the source of

knowledge and ask them questions on different subjects as part of the social-communication patterns developed in the kindergarten.

In a comparison between the multi-dialogical and the traditional approaches in the analysis of this theme, it emerged from the interviews that there was a significant difference in the learning processes between the two approaches. This difference was expressed in several dimensions:

1. The source of the program dealt with in the kindergarten – "In the traditional approach the teacher is usually the one who brings the program that she has planned to deal with and what will happen is quite clearly predetermined more or less," noted Hana. In the MDA, "children are full participants in planning the kindergarten program," noted Irit.
2. Construction of a kindergarten work and learning program – all the teachers, both traditional and multi-dialogical, construct their program according to the calendar and festivals. Traditional teachers construct more closed programs than their multi-dialogical colleagues: "I determine the subjects according to the annual program, according to the season, festival, contents that are age-appropriate, things that I feel that it is important for them and to reinforce them in the group. I know that the multi-dialogical teachers leave far more room for subjects that arise from the children when they plan their work program", explained Frieda.
3. Learning out of the children's fields of interest – it was found that in the multi-dialogical kindergarten, as Irit explained: "The children bring things from their own world of content and we use that to construct complete subjects", while Anat testified that in a traditional kindergarten, "I determine the program mainly based on the learning programs".
4. The teacher's role in learning according to the MDA – a

difference was found between the two approaches with regard to this subject, as noted by Frieda: "In the MDA the adult is not the one who delivers the knowledge, in the traditional approach the adult answers all the questions and teaches and transmits the knowledge to the children. As a teacher I am almost the only source of knowledge for the children".

5. The implications of the learning for the child – a difference was found between the two approaches regarding this subject as testified by Karen: "Learning according to the traditional approach develops the child's learning in a monotonic-passive manner" while as Frieda noted, "in multi-dialogical education learning sets problems, it stimulates the child's creativity and imagination" so that the child "undergoes higher thinking processes of conclusion deduction" added Irit and Frieda.
6. Peer learning – it was found that those teaching according to the traditional approach teach by themselves and thus permit less peer learning between the children, as noted by Dina: "The teacher needs to be at the center and so she does not allow real peer learning between the children". In the MDA in contrast: "the children teach each other and open worlds such as these to one another, and then there is peer learning," noted Lior.
7. Development of independent thinking – differences were found between the two approaches regarding this subject as was obvious from Frieda's words: "In the traditional approach the learning is less independent and similar for everyone. The teacher teaches more and the child is less autonomous in their learning. In the MDA the teacher liberates the child from their chains, so he thinks for himself".
8. Children go deeply into the field of their interest and its investigation – a difference was found between the two approaches with regard to this subject as noted by Noam:

"In the traditional approach the children are considered to be *tabula rasa,* as if they had no significant opinion or knowledge. According to the MDA the children's knowledge is used as the foundation for learning and investigation [and so] there is deeper consideration from a learning aspect," added Michal.

Table III.5: Feedback and reflection

Theme no. 4	Feedback and reflection	Samples of representative answers
Categories	1. The children's ability to give and take feedback	"A child made an effort and planned an activity for his friends and guided them on it. I think it's important that they learn to tell him what they enjoyed and what they enjoyed less, so they learn to give feedback" (Irit).
	2. The role of the teacher in feedback	"I participate in the circle when a child guides an activity. I also give feedback" (Karen).
	3. Implications of the feedback for the children	"The children learn that feedback involves consideration of others and also self-evaluation for whatever you have done" (Michal).
	4. Reflection	"I see and hear everything through their feedback, and in this way I can reflect on my own work" (Judith).

Category 1 - The children's ability to give and take feedback

Analysis of the qualitative data from the interviews with the teachers indicates that the children exhibit the ability to give and receive feedback, skills that the teacher emphasizes in the MDA. This is described in the words of Irit: "A child made an effort and planned an activity for his friends and guided them on it. I think it's important that they learn to tell him what they enjoyed and what they enjoyed less, so they learn to give feedback". Liron said that "the children whose friend guides them in an activity give feedback, saying how they feel and what they have learnt from the activity or what was interesting for them in the activity that the child led". Judith added: "I see the strong satisfaction that the guiding children reap from the feedback, the empowerment that they receive from it, that happiness, also the desire to participate". Moreover, Hana said: "In the MDA, the children learn to express criticism or agreement with the other with respect and attentiveness, and they also do this through feedback that they learn to give and accept".

Analysis of the participatory observations and films reinforces the words of the teachers regarding the children's abilities in the multi-dialogical kindergarten to give and accept feedback through the expression of their feelings as can be seen in Participatory Observation 2:

Eden (5.3): "It was fun to be in the middle".

Roni (4.8): "It was funny to sing".

Dan (5.5): "It was hard for me to do difficult things with the drum".

Additional support was found in Film 10:

Guy (4.11): "I thought it was interesting when you showed us the bamboo pipes".

It seems that the children were able to give and accept feedback in the multi-dialogical education. They learn to do this through the expression of their feelings and learn how to tell their friends what is pleasant for them, what interests them, what they find difficult and what could help them, and this is part of the social-communication patterns that characterize the multi-dialogical kindergarten.

Category 2 - The role of the teacher in feedback

Analysis of the data from the interviews with the teachers shows that the teacher working according to the MDA teaches the children to give feedback to one another and even constitutes part of the circle of feedback together with the children. This was evident in the Karen's words: "In the activity that a child leads, I am part of the circle. I also give feedback". Irit adds: "It is very important for me to give feedback to the children as part of the group". Feedback of this kind presents a difficulty for the teacher: "Feedback with children and by the children is something that it is not easy to perform," noted Irit, and Ora supported her words: "Even for us as adults, it's not easy to give feedback". Despite the difficulty, "I try to help the children, to teach them to adopt this approach of giving feedback even outside the activities that they guide; so that they will have tools for life," noted Karen.

Teachers using the MDA saw feedback as a communication tool for life that they try to transmit to the children. The teacher consti-

tutes part of the feedback circle; her role is to teach the children to give feedback one to the other, while the feedback also deepens her familiarity with the children's world. In the feedback, the teacher emphasizes values, relationships and communication between the children as part of the social-communication patterns developed in the multi-dialogical kindergarten.

Category 3 - Implications of the feedback for the children

Analysis of the qualitative data from the interviews with the teachers shows that the feedback has consequences for the children in their communication and relationships with others, and in their coping with difficulties and strengths and in their ability to express their feelings. This is clear from the words of Michal: "I feel that feedback is a tool that it is important to pass on to the children because the children learn that feedback involves consideration of others and also self-evaluation for whatever you have done". Thus too, Film 8, which shows part of the feedback that the children gave to their peer who guided them in an activity, indicates how feedback develops the children's ability to understand and say what is difficult for them and what helps them with their difficulties:

Naveh (4.9): "In the activity I swallowed some water, but I didn't choke, and you (talking to the boy who guided the activity) helped me"

Marie (5.8): "It was difficult for me and I tried a lot. But in the end you (talking to the boy guiding the activity) explained again and again until I understood.

Participatory Observation 7, which viewed part of the feedback that the children gave to their friend who guided them in an activity, also showed how the feedback develops the children's ability to converse, to pay attention and to understand and say what they find difficult:

Danny (4.5): I did not enjoy the activity that you led at all".

Shir (5.0): "Why?"

Danny (4.5): "Because it was difficult for me to work with the stapler and the activity needed a stapler".

Shir (5.0): "It's a pity that you did not enjoy it".

Another consequence of the feedback for the children is the children's desire to go deeply into their studies, as can be seen from Film

10, which showed some of the feedback that the children gave to one of their friends who guided an activity:

Ziv (5.11) spoke to a girl that guided the activity: "What you did made me want to know more about the Indians".

Noam summarized this issue by saying, "for the children feedback enables them to feel they are significant, real partners".

It seems that the children's feedback is used to express their consideration of others, to cope with difficulties and strengths, and to point up their difficulties and find solutions for those difficulties. Other consequences of their feedback can be seen in the children's feeling that they play a significant part in the learning, and this is as part of the social-communication patterns that characterize the kindergarten working according to the MDA.

Category 4 – Reflection

Analysis of the qualitative data from the interviews with the teachers indicated that the teacher working according to the MDA ensures that both she and the children will perform reflection. Evidence of this is found in Judith's testimony: "I [the teacher] perform reflective processes together with the children". From the teacher's viewpoint reflection is expressed in their participation in the feedback circle with the children as noted by Noam. "In the feedback I have an opportunity, as the teacher, to really pay attention to what the children succeeded in learning from the other children's guidance. This constitutes reflection for me". Thus, "when I am part of the feedback, I am given an opportunity to see whether this approach is working," added Michal, "I see and hear everything through their feedback. This helps me to reflect on my own work," said Judith. Karen explained how she conducted reflective processes with the children: "At the end of the subject I ask the children about the joint planning that we did when the subject was raised, and together we see what we managed to consider and what we have still not considered".

It seems that the multi-dialogical kindergarten is characterized by reflective learning by both the teacher and the children. Reflection is performed by the teacher with regard to her work, the teacher teaches the children to reflect on their own activities that

they guide, and the teacher and children reflect on subjects and contents that they planned together and dealt with in the kindergarten, as part of the social-communication patterns that characterize a kindergarten working according to the MDA.

In the comparison between the multi-dialogical and the traditional approaches, it emerged from the analysis of this theme in the transcripts of the interviews with the teachers that the traditional teachers do not perform planned feedback and reflection with the children in the kindergarten so that the following categories: (1) the children's ability to give and accept feedback, (2) the role of the teacher in feedback, (3) implications of feedback for the children, cannot be compared between the two approaches. In contrast, in Category 4 that relates to reflection, it was found that all the teachers, whether they worked according to the MDA or traditional approach, performed reflection with themselves in the context of their work. Evidence of this was given by Dina: "Every day I go home and think about how the day had gone, what I had done, what I could have done in another way". It was also found that only the MDA teachers taught the children how to reflect as part of their learning program for the kindergarten. This was explained by Liron: "Together with the child, I often think why this particular activity did not succeed or did succeed or we think about what was good and what could have been done in another way, what we learned from this. This is actually the basis for the beginning of the child's ability to reflect".

Table III.6: Dialog styles in the multi-dialogical kindergarten

Theme no. 5	Dialog styles in a multi-dialogical kindergarten	Samples of representative answers
Categories	1. Dialog and partnership between the teacher and students	"The foundation for this approach is that the children and teacher share their ideas" (Carmel).
	2. Dialog as the kindergarten language	"The dialog in the multi-dialogical kindergarten is the language that the children have learnt to speak" (Anat)
	3. Brain-storming	"We think together, the children and I, what we shall do regarding the subject … and begin to do it helped by … our brain-storming" (Noam).
	4. Personal meetings between the teacher and the child	"I hold individual meetings with the children, the learning and emotional subjects grow out of those meetings" (Judith).
	5. Children as guides	"In the multi-dialogical kindergarten children know how to guide others, to present a subject, to say what they want to do, to summarize it" (Anat).
	6. Discourse in general and philosophical discourse in particular	"The children learn how to converse and they learn the rules of discussion and how to speak to one another and how to solve problems and how to pay attention" (Liron). "Children bring all sorts of theories, they raise all sorts of questions in the kindergarten … and we conduct a discussion on the question. It's actually philosophic questions that they raise" (Irit).
	7. Mediation and documentation	"My mediation helps me to examine together with the child how to develop their ideas, so that there will be peer study" (Noam). "I write everything that we have planned in our meeting regarding the activity, and the child draws a symbol beside it so that he/she can understand what is written and become an independent learner" (Karen).

Category 1 - Dialog and partnership between the teacher and students

Analysis of the qualitative data from the interviews with the teachers indicates that the dialog between the teacher and the children is conducted in full cooperation between them. This is evident in the words of Carmel: "The foundation for this approach is that the children and teacher transmit their ideas and their thoughts one to the other, they are constantly in communication". Liron expands and explains: "There is the teacher and there are the children and this approach brings them together, combining what the children want with what the teacher wants", so that "all the processes that occur in the kindergarten are created in cooperation with the children and of course under the guidance of the adult" added Noam. This indicates that "the daily operations are conducted in the form of a dialog between the teacher and the children and this dialog determines what will happen in the kindergarten," explained Edna, while Liron noted: "This approach is actually some sort of lifestyle for the kindergarten, a sort of partnership between the teacher, the staff and the children".

It seems that the dialog between the teacher and the children in the kindergarten working according to the MDA is expressed in a partnership and negotiations between them, in the shared construction and learning of contents and the life of the kindergarten, in which the children are active partners. This is all part of the lifestyle and part of the social communication patterns developing in the kindergarten according to this approach.

Category 2 - Dialog as the kindergarten language

Analysis of the qualitative data from the interviews with the teachers shows that dialog constitutes the language of the kindergarten that uses the MDA, as was explained by Anat: "The dialog in the multi-dialogical kindergarten is the language that the children have learnt to speak. Children do not see these dynamics in every kindergarten. Here the children know how to discuss things with each other". Judith added: "As the teacher I try to conduct dialog throughout the day in the kindergarten" so that "the children know that they can raise any subject that they want, they can ask anything they want to and they receive consideration, they receive a response" noted Michal. Moreover, "In the MDA not all the children have to participate in everything, each one has the choice to participate more in what they choose, and to participate less where it is less appropriate for them– this is the dialogical language as I see it," said Liron. Bilha noted: "I think that there are more opportunities for dialog and personal expression in this approach to our work, and so that communication is created between one and the other".

It appears that the multi-dialogical kindergarten is characterized by dialog that takes place throughout the day between the children themselves and between the children and the kindergarten staff. Dialog allows the children to choose many possibilities and constitutes the kindergarten's language. It takes time for the participants to assimilate this language, and it constitutes part of the social-communication patterns that develop in a kindergarten working according to this approach.

Category 3 - Brain-storming

Analysis of qualitative data from the interviews with the teachers shows that brainstorming conducted between the children and the teacher concerning the kindergarten contents is a work tool that is used by the teacher according to the MDA. This was explained by Ora: "The children and I have brainstorming sessions and think together about the topic that we shall discuss in the kindergarten", while Noam also noted: "We think together, the children and I, what we shall do regarding the subject … and begin to do it helped by shared thinking, our brain-storming". "The material that we write together in our brainstorming sessions constitutes the basis for my work program as the teacher, grounded in the said content," explained Judith. This is because "when I want to build the content for the kindergarten, I first of all need to know where the children are in regard to the content, what interests them, what they know and what they want to do regarding the subject. Brainstorming about the subject helps me with this," said Ora. Liron added: "I will not construct a learning curriculum that is imposed on the children because I know that if I do that, their learning will not be relevant for them", while

Michal noted: "Brainstorming about the subject between the children and I constitutes a dialogical work tool that I use to construct the content program for the kindergarten".

It seems that in the multi-dialogical kindergarten, brainstorming between the teacher and the children constitutes a dialogical work tool used by the teacher to construct a learning curriculum that will be relevant to the children's knowledge and fields of interest. This tool constitutes part of the social communication patterns that develop in a kindergarten using this approach.

Category 4 – Individual meetings between the teacher and the child

Analysis of the qualitative data from the interviews with the teachers indicates that a teacher working according to the MDA conducts individual meetings with the children as part of the dialog that she maintains with them. Judith explained: "I hold individual meetings with the children. The learning and emotional subjects grow out of those meetings". Ora added: "I find it important to show the child that we also take what he wants seriously, so I write it down in a journal when he is beside me, and I show him on which day and at what hour we can meet to discuss what interests him". The discussion in these individual meetings is usually very open as Noam explained: "I conduct a meeting with a child, and it can go in so many different directions". The initiative for these individual meetings may come from the children or from the teacher as Michal explained: "The personal meetings take place according to the children's initiatives or according to my needs", while Lior noted: "The children also know that they can come and ask for a personal meeting with me, it's the language of the kindergarten".

The individual meetings between the teacher and the child take place as part of the MDA and can be divided into two types of meeting: a personal meeting to voice or a personal session to plan an activity, as Judith explained: "There are individual meetings between the teacher and the child which act as emotional meetings: when the child wants to tell the teacher something when they experience something, I feel that he needs to meet with me, even if it's a short session". In addition, Liron noted that "There is an individual meeting between the teacher and a child when the child asks for the meeting in order to plan and guide an activity in the kindergarten". Ora explained: "My goal as the teacher, in a personal meeting with the child to plan an activity, is to pay attention to him and together with him to examine how we can develop his spark of an idea, in which directions it can be taken and how to present it to the other children in the group so that peer study can occur".

The individual meeting between the teacher and the child constitutes part of the teacher's attentiveness and work method according to the MDA. There are two types of individual meetings: a personal emotional meeting and a meeting to plan an activity. The initiative for these meetings comes from the children and the teacher as one. Individual meetings are part of the work and learning curriculum in the kindergarten working according to the MDA and constitute part of the social-communication patterns that develop there.

Category 5 - Children guiding activities

Analysis of the qualitative data from the interviews with the teachers shows that the children acquire social-communication skills when they learn how to guide a group as part of the dialog conducted in the kindergarten. Judith explained this succinctly: "children guide other children in the kindergarten", while Anat explained further: "In the multi-dialogical kindergarten children know how to guide others and to present a subject, to say what they want to do, to summarize it" (Anat). This guidance is based on the fact that, as Iris noted, "The children have many ideas", while Judith explained that "the children profit from their guiding of other children". This occurs when "The child with the help of the activity that he initiates and guides, transmits a message to his friends in different ways," noted Bilha. However, "If the child wants to lead a session for a small group on a subject that he likes, he must travel a long path until he gets there," said Ora. Michal gave an example of this: "A girl, who led an activity table, prepared the materials that she wanted to bring to the group, the day before the activity". For the children who want to lead an activity in a kindergarten working according to the MDA, "the guidance is actually a language that they learn," said Anat and "when they learn and teach the subject or activity to their friends in the kindergarten, it also means that they need to use learning and communication skills that they would not acquire in another way" added Bilha.

It appears that one of the types of dialog that exist in a multi-dialogical kindergarten is the guidance of their peers by the children themselves, skills that are learnt and acquired by the children as part of the social-communication patterns that develop in the kindergarten.

Category 6 - Discourse in general and philosophical discourse in particular

Analysis of the qualitative data from the participatory observations conducted in the multi-dialogical kindergarten revealed that the children in this kindergarten learn to conduct discourse and to discuss things between them independently, and they acquire the rules of discussion. The children manage to discuss a problem that worries them without the intervention of the teacher but in her presence. As a result, they learn the rules of discussion from their practice, under the teacher's guidance. The teacher mediates the children's discussion, allowing the children to internalize these rules.

The following example from Participatory Observation 1 relates to the children exercising the rules of discussion. Shani (5.1) turned to the teacher and asked her if all the kindergarten children could hold a discussion on a subject that worried her. The conversation went like this:

Teacher: "Children, Shani came to me … and she asked us to discuss something that concerned her on the subject of … if anyone has anything to say, they are invited to do so. I remind you of the rules – only one person can speak at a time".

Shani (5.1): "And we also don't interfere when someone is talking".

Nira (5.2): "And we don't need to raise our hands".

Social conflicts between children are resolved in the multi-dialogical kindergarten through negotiations between them. The children learn to help their friends to resolve disputes independently. An example appears in Participatory Observation 5 in which there is a game activity led by a girl for all the kindergarten children. They were asked to arrange themselves in a circle:

Yotam (4.0): "I don't want to hold Ofri's hand".

Ofri (4.2): "Yotam won't give me his hand".

Dalit (5.0) turning to Yotam: "Will it help you if Matan is next to you?"

Yotam (4.0) nods his head in agreement, Matan and Ofri change places in the circle.

Analysis of the qualitative data from the interviews with the teachers supports what was seen in the participatory observations. From this analysis it appears that "The children learn how to converse and they learn the rules of discussion and how to speak to one another and how to solve problems and how to pay attention," said Liron. Thus as Ora notes, they actually "acquire skills," and Noam adds that this means that the "inter-personal discussion and the general discussion is at a far higher level when using this [dialogical] approach". Michal indicates that "this MDA is actually one large discussion", whereby "the children are exposed to the concept of discussion, and they learn and know how to use it," adds Irit. Philosophical discussion is part of the discourse that is conducted in a kindergarten working according to the MDA. Philosophical discussion is a discussion that arises because "children bring all sorts of theories, they raise all sorts of questions in the kindergarten … and we conduct a discussion on the question. It's actually a philosophic question that they raise," explained Irit. "The fact that they know how to give answers to a question that they raise in such a philosophical discussion is something they learn from the MDA" added Judith.

The films also show that the children raise philosophical questions, discussing them independently and expressing philosophical thoughts derived from the questions, as can be seen in Film 5:

Afiq (5.2): "I wanted to ask if you think that someone lives in the sky?"

Ronen (4.5): "I think they do. God".

Dalia (5.0): "If there is no God then who gave birth to our parents?"

Noia (4.8); "Ah, that's right … but our grandparents gave birth to our parents…".

Dan (5.5): "So who created the world … only God can".

Dalia (5.0): "I think it's not like that, it's not God and I don't think there is any God who lives in the sky".

It seems that discussion in general, and in particular philosophical discussions are types of dialog that take place in kindergartens working according to the MDA. The children learn to assimilate clear rules as part of the social-communication patterns developing in the kindergarten.

Category 7 - Mediation and documentation

Analysis of the qualitative data from the interviews with the teachers showed that according to the teachers' perceptions, the teachers' mediation and their documentation of things together with the children form a basis for the implementation of the MDA in the kindergarten. This is evident from Noam's words: "My mediation helps me to examine together with the child how to develop their ideas, so that there will be peer study". While Karen noted: "In order to document these processes I write everything that we have planned in our meeting regarding the activity, and the child draws a symbol beside it so that he/she can understand what is written and be an independent learner".

Analysis of the films reinforces the analysis of the interviews of the teachers. The films show the teachers' mediation for the children and the shared documentation on an activity planning page that they compose together. This is shown clearly in Film 2, in which the teacher and two children meet for a session to plan an activity:

The teacher turns to the two children who are planning the activity with her and says:

"Let's write a plan of the activity. I will write what you are planning on the page and you will draw next to what I have written. In this way you will remember what to do, is that clear?"

The teacher writes and the children draw symbols next to what she has written.

Analysis of the qualitative data from the interviews with the teachers also showed, as Noam noted, that "in the documentation of the activity planning, after the children and I finish writing and documenting the activity, I check that all of us, the children and I, have understood what we wrote and drew".

The situation shown in Film 2 demonstrated and supported Noam's statement. It showed how the children and the teacher check the shared records that they have written up:

Teacher: "How nicely you have drawn this. Now we will go over each page

and see that we have understood what we have written".

The teacher points to what the children have drawn and they tell her what is written on the page.

Rani (5.5): "Three children".

Dean (4.11): "The football pitch".

Teacher: "Excellent, you understood everything, yes. Is tomorrow suitable for you to lead the activity?"

In the interview, Judith added: "One of my roles as a teacher is to pay attention and to observe what the children are doing, how they are playing and what interests them; and according to what I discover from that I begin to mediate to them".

In the films, it was also possible to see the teacher's mediation for the children out of her observations of their play. The following situation is taken from Film 8. In the kindergarten playground there is rainwater in puddles and in dishes. The children are playing in the playground. Ohad takes a hosepipe that he has found and puts it into a puddle. He draws water from the puddle with the pipe and blows the water out onto the garden beside him.

Teacher: "Ohad, if I give you a bowl with water and a bowl without water, can you transfer the water from bowl to bowl with the help of the hosepipe?"

Ohad (5.6): "Yes"

The teacher puts a bowl with rainwater and a second empty bowl next to Ohad. He transfers the water from bowl to bowl with the help of the hosepipe. Three children watch him.

It appears that the multi-dialogical kindergarten is characterized by the teacher's strong need to mediate for the children that stem from the attentiveness and observation that she learns to do. Moreover, the teacher and the children share their learning of the subject through documentation as part of the social-communication patterns that develop in the kindergarten.

In the comparison between the multi-dialogical and the traditional approaches, the following findings emerged from the analysis of this theme in the transcripts of the interviews with the teachers:

1. Dialog and partnership between the teacher and the children – in the traditional approach, "there is no real shared discussion between the children and the staff," said Gali, because "the teacher is the one who dictates things. She doesn't really bond with the children so that they are not full participants in decisions and processes that happen in the kindergarten" said Bilha. In contrast: "The MDA is a sort of partnership between the teacher and the children and the staff. There is the teacher and there are the children and the approach actually creates a connection between them, between what the children want and what the teacher wants," noted Liron.
2. Dialog as the kindergarten language – all the teachers, both the traditional and multi-dialogical teachers, testified that they allowed choice and dialog in the kindergarten: "I don't dictate to the children where they should go and what exactly they should do in the kindergarten at a given moment. They can choose," said Edna. Nevertheless: "real dialog is not like the dynamics of the children one sees in a traditional kindergarten. In the multi-dialogical kindergarten the children know how to conduct dialogs," said Anat. This is because "the type of dialog in this kindergarten is not at all defined and planned," explained Hana.

3-5. The teachers who employed the traditional approach did not relate to category 3 that dealt with brainstorming, to category 4 that dealt with personal meetings between the child and the teacher or to category 5 that dealt with the children's guidance of meetings, as a sort of dialog that exists in the kindergarten and so the responses for these categories could not be compared.

1. Discourse in general and philosophical discourse in particular – In the traditional approach: "The teacher manages the conversation through the raising of the children's hands, she asks the children questions concerning the content that they are dealing with and they answer after raising their hands" said Hana. In the multi-dialogical kindergarten: "The children are exposed to the concept of a conversation, they learn and know how to use it" explained Irit, so that "they learn how to speak with each other, how to solve problems and how to pay attention, and also how to broach questions that are actually philosophical questions," noted Liron.
2. All the teachers, whether traditional or multi-dialogical indicated that they perform mediation in the kindergarten. Traditional teachers indicated that their mediation is mainly expressed in resolving conflicts between the children. They also noted that they almost never documented things together with the children in the kindergarten. "When there was a conflict between children, I called them to clarify things. I gave the child the feeling that I had not yet heard his story and that it was possible that he was right," noted Frieda. "In the traditional approach I do not often record things. In the MDA the teacher also needs to pay attention and to document things … I don't know how to do that and I don't do it," said Edna

Table III.7: Social-communication patterns in the multi-dialogical kindergarten

Theme no. 6	Social-communication patterns in the multi-dialogical kindergarten	Samples of representative answers
Categories	1. Life skills	"The MDA teaches and develops life skills since it engenders and develops friendships and communication between the children" (Edna)
	2. Consideration, tolerance and recognizing the 'other'	"It [the MDA] gives a lot of responsibility to children to be aware of others, the feelings of others, the thoughts of others" (Anat).
	3. Ability to initiate and lead	"And there is something in this approach that promotes something very authentic in the children's upbringing, something that encourages them to initiate and to think" (Ora).
	4. The child as an active member of society	"My goal, as a teacher, is to teach the children to be people who can integrate within society and take an active part in it" (Karen).
	5. Cooperation between children	"This approach leads to more cooperation between the children" (Frieda).
	6. Empowerment	"Using this approach, the children are strengthened; they are very dominant, more socially empowered" (Karen).

Category 1 – Life skills

Analysis of the qualitative data from the interviews with the teachers indicates that the teachers perceive the MDA as a means to develop the child's life skills and social-communication patterns. This is evident in the words of Edna: "The MDA teaches and develops life skills since it engenders and develops friendships and communication between the children". Carmel added: "With regard to life skills, the MDA teaches tolerance, delayed satisfaction, polite speech, dialog, and in general how to conduct a dialog. It teaches the children about the subject of opinions, what my opinion is and what the opinion of the other is".

Noam noted: "The MDA requires interaction between the children at a very, very high level". While Dina added: "This approach is based on and works on the basis of tolerance, respect, containment, acceptance of the other, acceptance of diversity, knowing that there can be several opinions, and that I am not the only one and that even if I do not think like others, I respect what they say". Karen said: "When a child knows how to take the initiative, to express himself in a respectful manner, I know that I have succeeded as a teacher, and that is the goal of the MDA".

It seems that the MDA is characterized by emphasis on the development of life skills, respect, expression of feelings and acceptance of different opinions between the children as part of the social-communication patterns that develop in the kindergarten.

Category 2 - Consideration, tolerance and recognizing the 'other'

Analysis of the participatory observations conducted in the multi-dialogical kindergarten revealed that the children were exposed to and exercised patterns of consideration, tolerance and acceptance of others. An expression of this can be seen in Participatory Observation 6, in which the children did not interfere or intervene when a child with a speech disorder was talking, but they waited until he had finished speaking. In the situation detailed below we can see how Eden, the child with speech difficulties, gave feedback to a girl who was leading an activity session. It took him 10 seconds to say one word, and it was not possible to understand what he was saying. The children waited patiently for him to complete his words:

Eden (4.0): "Dalia, it was a funny ssseongg (the word was unclear and lasted for 10 seconds).

Teacher: "The song amused you?"

Eden: "Yes".

Another expression of the children's consideration can be seen in Participatory Observation 5, which shows the process of a game initiated and led by a girl for her friends in the kindergarten. She tried to remember who had participated in the game and who had not. She checked with the group which child had still not participated. The children helped her to remember:

Dalia (5.0) turning to the teacher: "Do you remember who had a turn already? I remember Ofri … Shahaf was in, Ben was too?"

The children continued to say who had been in the game and who had not. It was possible to see how the children were willingly considerate so that everyone could participate and made sure not to leave someone out.

Thus too in the interviews of the teachers it seems that "the children learn to pay attention to the child who is leading the activity and later to give them feedback and this very strongly encourages tolerance," noted Irit. Noam added: "I think that the MDA encourages lack of judgment", and added Irit: "It truly gives a place to listening to the opinions of other people, and to be open-minded". From a practical point of view, "in the MDA the children learn how to help each other," noted Irit, since "they learn to give words to their feelings, and their emotions and this eventually helps them to develop tolerance" noted Michal. Irit added: "This helps them to learn how to respect the pace and the desires of each person … this is an approach that encourages attentiveness and respect and tolerance". "It (the MDA) gives a lot of responsibility to children to be aware of others, the feelings of others, the thoughts of others," said Anat, something that "helps people to grow and develop to respect others and be tolerant," added Ora.

It seems from the analysis of the teachers' interviews and the participatory observations that in the multi-dialogical kindergarten the children are exposed to, learn and exercise the ability to respect others, to be tolerant, accept diversity and develop sensitivity to and help one another as part of the social-communication patterns developed in the kindergarten.

Category 3 - Ability to initiate and lead

Analysis of data from the participatory observations in the multi-dialogical kindergarten reveals that the children in this kindergarten are exposed to and practice initiative and leadership. This was evident in Participatory Observation 2, in which a child called Eran (5.3) initiated, planned and led an activity with a drum for a group of three children. At the beginning of the activity he explained what it was necessary to do:

Eran (5.3): I have brought some real drums from home and I want to teach you how to play them …each of you has two turns, twice, you can try them … Tomi, try to do what I do like this, now, on the drum … you have another opportunity so try to follow after me".

Film 9 also shows the children's ability to lead a group. The film was taken during a session led by a girl, Orel (5.6), for all the kindergarten's children:

Orel (5.6): "Stand up, everyone. Now we will dance an Ethiopian dance and when I pick up the card, then you have to do what is drawn on the card. I will demonstrate it for you."

Orel raises her shoulders.

Orel (5.6): "Do what I am doing" The children do the same as her.

Thus too, analysis of the qualitative data from the interviews with the teachers showed that the children practice the ability to show initiative and leadership. This was seen in the words of Ora: "The MDA develops and helps children to grow …And there is something in this approach that promotes something very authentic in the children's upbringing, something that encourages them to initiate and to think independently". The children's initiative and leadership are expressed in various areas including in feedback that is part of the activities, as noted by Michal: "After the children worked on the table that the girl initiated and led, she called the children and told them … 'it's very important for me to receive your feedback'. Before this, she organized a circle of chairs. At the end of the activity, she by herself collected the children who had participated and asked them to sit down in the circle and give her feedback on the activity. She managed the feedback under her own initiative. She asked me [the teacher] to also give her feedback. She told the children how she felt and what she had gained from the activity".

Analysis of the qualitative data from interviews with the teachers and the participatory observations conducted in the multi-dialogical kindergarten reveal that the children are exposed to, learn and practice the ability to initiate and to lead others in a group. This is expressed in their ability to stand up and guide others and to speak before a group and to gain their attention, in their ability to lead feedback and their ability to see the whole

group and to lead it as part of the social-communication patterns that develop in the kindergarten.

Category 4 - The child as an active member of society

Analysis of the films taken in the multi-dialogical kindergarten reveals that the children play active parts in their lives and studies. Evidence of this can be seen in Film 11, in which the children encountered a dead bird lying on the ground:

Nitsan (3.9): "Perhaps we should make her [the bird] a grave?"

Teacher: "A grave. Would you like to bury her?"

Nitsan (3.9), Yael (3.8) and Ravit (3.11): "Yes".

The children gather stones in order to prepare a grave for the bird.

Following this scene in the film, after they buried the bird, the children were active and suggested ideas:

Carin (4.5): turning to the other children: "where exactly did you bury her?"

Nitsan (3.9): "Here" points.

Carin (4.5): "I've got an idea; let's put a pine cone on the grave so that we remember where the grave is".

Yahav (4.9): "Let's put it here", points to the grave.

Carin (4.5) puts a pine cone on the grave. The children watch.

Additional support for the fact that the children are active in their studies and socially can be seen in the analysis of the qualitative data from the interviews with the teachers, which shows that according to the teachers' perceptions, children who attend the multi-dialogical kindergarten grow to be active members of the society in which they participate. This is evident from the words of Karen: "My goal, as a teacher, is to teach the children to be people who can integrate within society and take an active part in it, the MDA leads to that" (Karen). Dina added that "this approach guides and trains the children to be active so that it creates respect and containment and tolerance in future society, what is missing at present in our society".

Analysis of the interviews with the teachers and the films taken in the multi-dialogical kindergarten show that the multi-dialogical kindergarten allows the children to become active participants in learning and in the kindergarten society. Thus, they actually prac-

tice this ability and this can influence their citizenship when they grow up to become citizens of society. This is one of the social-communication patterns developed in the kindergarten.

Category 5 - Cooperation between children

Analysis of the qualitative data from the films taken in the multi-dialogical kindergarten reveals that the children inevitably collaborate as a result of the reality in the kindergarten working according to this approach. This can be seen in Film 8, in which the children are seen collaborating with a child who guides an activity and also cooperating one with another. In the film Ohad (5.6) guided a group of children on a scientific discovery that he had revealed; the transfer of water from one bucket to another with the help of a hosepipe:

Ohad (5.6) blows water from the hosepipe into the bucket: "But you need to be careful not to spray it when you are blowing the water into the bucket. Look, you put the pipe into your mouth and also into the bucket; you take it out with the water and then spit it out".

Yahel (5.0): "Can I try?"

Ohad (5.6): "Yes".

Yahel (5.0): "So give it to me". Putting her hand out towards the pipe.

Ohad (5.6): "O.K.", gives the hosepipe to Yahel. He looks at everyone: "First Yahel because he knows, I guided him before you".

Ronen (4.5): turning to Ohad: "Can I also do it?"

Ohad (5.6) replies to Ronen: "Not now because I can only guide two children at a time".

In Film 11, the children can be seen exhibiting their ability to work together, to listen to one another and to collaborate. The film was taken during a walking trip when the children encountered a dead bird lying on the ground and collaborated without any adult help so that none of them would tread on her:

Carin (4.5): turning the children beside her: "Move away, it's a bird, she's dead".

Yoram (5.3): "Who brought her?"

Ravit (3.11): "I don't know". Other children draw closer.

Gili (3.9): talking to the children who drew closer: "No one should tread here".

Additional support for the children's learning to collaborate through the work according to the MDA can be found in the analysis of the qualitative data from the interviews with the teachers. This was clearly seen in Frieda's remarks: "This approach leads to more cooperation between the children" (Frieda). "The approach engenders more collaboration between the children [since] it creates a very strong bond between the children, giving them opportunities for interpersonal interactions, collaboration and positive communication between the children," added Noam. Irit noted: "I see that in the MDA, the children learn how to collaborate," and Frieda added: "They learn to respect the opinions of others and then they can collaborate one with the other". Michal remarked that "you can see all sorts of social combinations and collaborations that as a teacher I never thought that I would see if we did not employ this approach that engenders this"; and Ora noted: "I feel that this strengthens friendships and creates new relationships that emerge from the communication and collaboration that this approach offers to the children".

The multi-dialogical kindergarten offers many opportunities for the children to collaborate as part of its learning processes and as part of the social- communication processes that develop in the kindergarten.

Category 6 – Empowerment

Analysis of the films taken in the multi-dialogical kindergarten indicates that a consequence of the use of the MDA is the empowerment of the children. The children are empowered by the teacher and learn to empower each other and to thank one another. Evidence of this is found in Film 9, in which children empower their friend Orel (5.6), who guided them in an activity, and they also expressed their feelings:

Shir (4.5): "Orel, you danced very, very well in the activity that you did for us".

Yahel (5.0): "Yes, that's right and you also invested a lot in that meeting that you made for us".

Gal (5.8): "I loved how you explained the pictures to us and I also loved how we danced".

Film 8 shows the ability of the children to thank others, to give compliments and to empower their friends by expressing their feelings. The film is part of the feedback that is given to the child, Ohad (5.6), who guided his friends on a scientific discovery that he had found:

Ronen (4.5): "Ohad, it was nice that you did that. It was interesting".

Yahel (5.0): "Ohad, thank you. I liked doing that, transferring the water with the pipe from bucket to bucket".

Marie (5.7): "it was good that you thought about us and did it for us. Thank you".

The teacher is part of the feedback circle when the child guides the activity. She empowers the child in front of all the children and always thanks the child and the group. An example of this can be seen in Film 10.

The teacher says to Marie (5.7): "Marie, you had the patience to prepare the subject that interested you and to guide the group. You paid attention to each child and tried to explain what you knew to the children. Well done and thank you".

Thus too, analysis of the qualitative data from the interviews revealed that "the MDA empowers the children … it positions the child so that he is visible" noted Karen, while Bilha remarked that "the individual, the child is empowered when he works on something and then he comes and presents it to everyone". "This approach can empower the individual child, but also from the group perspective it can empower the group that works together," added Carmel. From a social aspect, "I think that the MDA offers the children a sort of social springboard" noted Noam, while Karen added: "Using this approach, the children are strengthened; they are very dominant, more socially empowered". "The child expresses himself and transmits something that he likes and the children come and listen to him and participate; its social empowerment," noted Liron. "When a child is empowered from an emotional point of view, then it is easier for him socially, in interpersonal relations with other children, and this is what this approach enables," added Karen. "I think that it is very good for the children's confidence and self-image and personal empowerment," emphasized Liron, while Karen said: "We can see the social, academic and intellectual empowerment that the MDA can provide for the children. Their minds work differently".

According to the MDA children are empowered socially, emotionally and academically and they learn to empower each other as part of the social- communication patterns developing in the kindergarten.

In the comparison between the MDA and the traditional approach, the following findings emerged from the analysis of this theme in the transcripts of the teachers' interviews:

1. Life skills – the MDA offers more opportunities for communication between the children than the traditional approach. This was explained by Edna: "I think that the MDA really prepares the children for life, more than the traditional approach. It develops life skills because it encourages and develops friendships and communication between the children".
2. Consideration, tolerance and recognition of the "other" – the MDA trains the children to address situations with consideration, tolerance and recognition for others more than the traditional approach as Dina explained: "The MDA is based on and works according to principles of tolerance, respect, containment and acceptance of others, diversity, knowing that there are several opinions, knowing that I am not the only one and that even if I do not think like someone else, I should respect what they say. In this approach they practice this. In the traditional approach they say that they do this, but they don't really practice it".
3. Ability to demonstrate initiative and leadership – the MDA trains the children to take the initiative and to lead others, more than the traditional approach, as noted by Hana: "In the MDA, the initiative actually comes from them; they can

demonstrate their strengths and show their knowledge in fields that would not perhaps emerge if another approach were used. In the traditional approach this does not happen. It is the teacher who decides what they learn and do".

4. The child as an active member of society – in the interviews of teachers working according to the traditional approach they did not relate to this category as a type of ability and practice that develops in the kindergarten and so no comparison can be drawn between the two approaches for this category.
5. Cooperation between children – the MDA encourages the children to practice cooperation in order to learn about a common field of interest more than the traditional approach, as explained by Anat: "the MDA provides a sense of belonging that is created within the work group or within groups that unite and cooperate for some sort of goal and some sort of common and meaningful learning that is derived from the children's field of interest. This affiliation and cooperation do not exist in such a strong way in the traditional approach because the learning there usually does not stem from the children's field of interest".
6. Empowerment – the MDA empowers the child and their initiatives more than the traditional approach does. "When you work according to the MDA, the children really feel that their ideas receive positive reactions, both from the staff and from the other children. In the traditional approach the children don't initiate so much and are not so active and so the empowerment is less," explained Hana. "The individual is empowered. In the MDA, the child is empowered when he works on something, and then comes to present it to everyone. This is a language that is not used in the traditional approach," added Bilha.

III.3 Quantitative Findings

The data received from the questionnaire were encoded and processed with SPSS software. The descriptive statistics are presented first, in order to portray the socio-demographic characteristics of the two groups compared in the research: kindergarten teachers working or studying according to the Multi Dialogical Approach (hereinafter: "MDA teachers") and kindergarten teachers who were working according to the traditional approach (hereinafter: "traditional teachers"). This sub-chapter describes the distribution of different characteristics in percentages and in absolute numbers for the categorical variables, such as the type of settlement where the kindergarten was situated, education level of kindergarten teachers and more. In addition, it presents measures of tendency to center, such as means and medians and also measures of tendency to dispersal, such as standard deviations and minimum and maximum values for the continuous variables (level on a rational scale), such as years of experience in teaching, number of children attending the kindergarten, etc.

The chapter then presents the distributions (in percentages) of the responses to the research questionnaire, on which the respondents were asked to grade the degree of their agreement with the various statements on a scale of 1-5, where 1 = "not at all" and 5 = "very much". Additionally, measures of means and standard deviation are presented for each of the questionnaire items.

It is noted that different items are incorporated into indices to form a composite calculated mean, in accord with the internal reliability of the research indices that were examined during the analysis of the questionnaire findings. Reliability was examined by ascertaining that the Cronbach's α that was obtained was sufficiently high (at least 0.6) to determine that the items composing those indices belonged to them and measured the same world of content. The following are the internal reliability values (Cronbach's α) obtained for the main research indices: Extent of attentiveness expressed in the MDA = 0.89; extent of difficulties and resources required to implement the MDA = 0.70; extent of giving and accepting feedback as part of the MDA = 0.84;

extent of contribution of the MDA to the development of the children's social-communication patterns = 0.95; extent of children's participation in their learning processes = 0.79; extent of dialogical styles in the kindergarten =0.95; manner of discourse in the meeting = 0.80; extent of guidance in a meeting by children = 0.68; extent of activity planning in a teacher-child meeting = 0.91; extent of feedback giving by the teacher to the child = 0.66; extent of feedback giving by child to child = 0.86; extent to which there is philosophical discussion = 0.89.

Finally, t-tests were used (statistical inference tests) to identify significant differences between the evaluations of the two compared groups (independent samples): MDA teachers and traditional teachers regarding the different research variables and indices.

III.3.1 The quantitative tools

III.3.1.1 T-tests for the two independent samples

These tests aimed to examine the existence of significant differences between the two groups (which had no connection between them) in relation to the dependent variable measure on a continuous rational scale. In the present study, comparison was conducted between MDA kindergarten teachers and traditional kindergarten teachers, both with regard to the different indices measured on a rational scale whose internal reliability is presented above and also for individual items that composed those indices. It is noted that t-tests were also used for the two independent samples in the section describing the sample in order to examine whether there were significant differences in the continuous socio-demographic characteristics of the two groups, such as years of experience in teaching number of children attending the kindergarten etc. In addition, another test was used for statistical inference in the chapter describing the sample – the Chi squared test (χ^2).

III.3.1.2 Chi squared test (χ2)

This test examines significance of difference between several groups in relation to a dependent variable that is at a level on a nominal-categorical scale. In the present study a comparison was made between the socio-demographic characteristics, such as education level and type of settlement where the kindergarten was located of the two groups: MDA teachers and traditional teachers.

III.3.1.3 Correlation matrices (Pearson correlation coefficients)

Lastly, Pearson correlation coefficients are presented for each of the compared groups in order to examine whether there were significant statistical linear correlations between the research variables measured on a continuous rational scale. In the present study, correlations were measured between all the research indices detailed above.

III.4 The findings from the questionnaire

III.4.1. Description of the sample

130 kindergarten teachers participated in the present study. 56.1% (73 teachers) were MDA teachers and 43.85% (57 teachers) were traditional teachers. Since the research involved two groups of teachers working according to two entirely different educational approaches, the research work focused on a comparison between the two groups. Thus, the overall findings for all the teachers who participated in the research will not be presented. The following is a description of the profiles of the two compared groups of kindergarten teachers.

Table III.8: Description of the teachers' characteristics – by type of work approach, for categorical variables (distribution in percentages and absolute numbers)

Index	Level	MDA teachers		Traditional teachers		χ2-value
		N	%	N	%	
Education	Bachelor's degree	N=54	73.97%	N=53	92.98%	
	Master's degree	N=18	24.66%	N=1	1.75%	
	Qualified kindergarten teacher	N=1	1.37%	N=3	5.26%	
	Total	**N=73**	**100.00%**	**N=57**	**100.00%**	
Type of settlement in which kindergarten is situated	Kibbutz	N=47	64.38%	N=17	29.82%	
	Urban settlement	N=4	5.48%	N=17	29.82%	
	Community settlement	N=22	30.14%	N=23	40.35%	
	Total	**N=73**	**100.00%**	**N=57**	**100.00%**	
Does the kindergarten operate according to the MDA?	Yes, fully	N=24	32.88%	N=2	3.51%	
	Yes, partially	N=43	58.90%	N=8	14.04%	
	No, but the possibility of joining is being considered	N=5	6.85%	N=18	31.58%	
	No	N=1	1.37%	N=29	50.88%	
	Total	**N=73**	**100.00%**	**N=57**	**100.00%**	

**p<0.01

Most of the teachers from both compared groups have a bachelor's degree. Nevertheless, significant differences were found between the two groups with regard to the level of education ($\chi2=14.47$, $p<0.01$). Thus, the proportion of those with a bachelor's degree was found to be higher among the traditional teachers than among the MDA teachers (92.98% in contrast to 73.97% respectively). Additionally, the proportion of those with a master's degree was found to be higher among the MDA teachers than among the traditional teachers (24.66% in contrast to 1.75% respectively).

The research findings indicate that there were significant differences between the two groups in relation to the type of settlement in which the kindergarten is situated ($\chi2=20.47$, $p<0.01$). Thus, most of the kindergartens in which the MDA teachers worked were in kibbutzim (64.38%), while contrastingly, most of the kindergartens in which the traditional teachers worked were situated in community settlements (40.35%). Moreover, a higher proportion of MDA teachers work in kibbutz kindergartens in comparison to the proportion of traditional teachers working in kibbutz kindergartens (64.38% in contrast to 29.82% respectively). Thus too, the proportion of MDA teachers working in kindergartens in urban settlements is lower in comparison with the proportion of traditional teachers working in kindergartens in urban settlements (5.48% in contrast to 29.8% respectively).

Analysis of the research findings indicates that significant differences were found between the two compared groups in relation to the question of whether the kindergarten operates according to the MDA ($\chi 2=75.29$, $p<0.01$). Most of the MDA teachers reported that the kindergarten in which they worked partially operated according to that approach (58.90%). In contrast, most of the traditional teachers reported that the kindergarten in which they worked did not operate according to the MDA (50.88%). Moreover, 31.58% of the traditional teachers reported that the kindergarten in which they worked did not operate according to the MDA, but the possibility of implementing this approach was being considered.

III.4.2 The Findings

Tables III.9 and III.10 present the findings that emerged from the responses of teachers working and/or studying according to the MDA. Tables III.11-III.24 present the comparison between responses of MDA teachers and responses of traditional teachers.

Figure III.1 below is a figurative representation of the comparison between the MDA and traditional approaches as seen by the teachers who responded to the research questionnaire.

Figure III.1: Summary of the research indices (means): Comparison of grading by MDA teachers and by traditional teachers

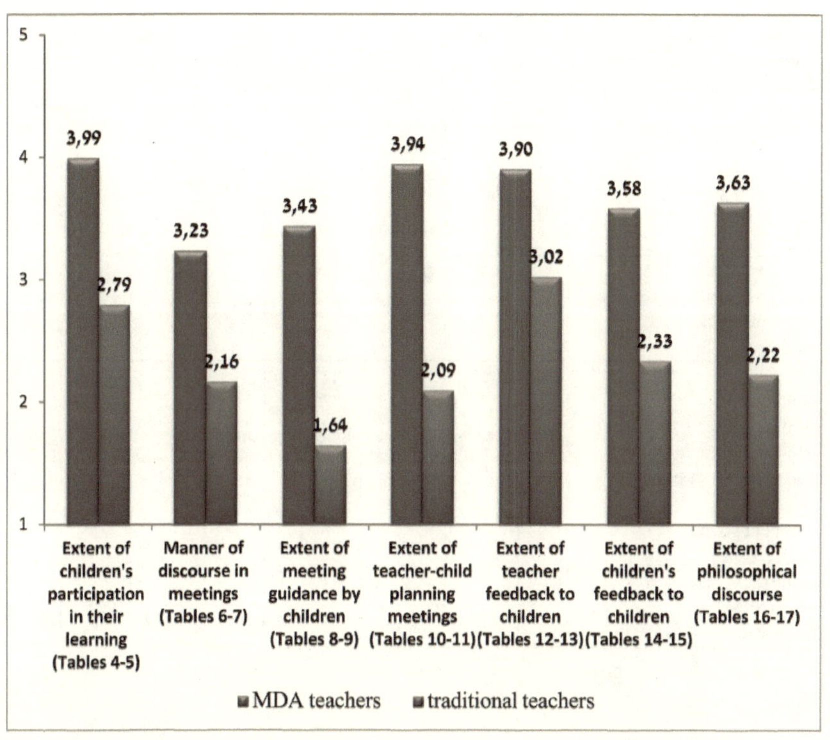

Figure III.1 summarizes the overall findings presented in this chapter by displaying the means of the research indices for the MDA teachers and also for the traditional teachers. It is important to emphasize that all the differences presented in this diagram between the two comparison groups were found to be statistically significant. It was found that all the indices were given significantly higher grades by the MDA teachers in comparison with the traditional teachers.

Table III.9: Description of the extent of giving and accepting feedback as part of the MDA by the MDA teachers (Distribution in percentages, means and standard deviations)

Extent of giving and accepting feedback as part of the MDA	**1 Not at all %**	**2 %**	**3 %**	**4 %**	**5 Very much %**	**Total %**	**Total (N)**	**Mean**	**SD**
The MDA encourages children to give and accept feedback			6.85	35.62	57.53	100	73	**4.51**	.63
The teacher is an inseparable part of the feedback circle			4.11	19.18	76.71	100	73	**4.73**	.53
From the children's feedback to each another, I learn about my work as a teacher			5.48	26.03	68.49	100	73	**4.63**	.59
Extent of giving and accepting feedback as part of the MDA – calculated index							**73**	**4.62**	**.51**

It was found that the mean extent of giving and accepting feedback as part of the MDA was high-very high (mean of 4.62 out of 5.0). The highest extent of agreement was found among the MDA teachers in relation to the statement that "the teacher is an inseparable part of the feedback circle" (4.73). On the other hand, the lowest extent of agreement was found in relation to the statement that "the MDA encourages the children to give and accept feedback" (4.51). **It seems that 'feedback' emerges from the findings as a central component in the MDA.**

Table III.10: Description of the extent of contribution of the MDA to the development of the children's social-communication patterns by MDA teachers (Distribution in percentages, means and standard deviations)

The contribution of the MDA to development of children's social-communication patterns	1 Not at all %	2 %	3 %	4 %	5 Very much %	Total %	Total (N)	Mean	SD
The MDA encourages communication			2.74	19.18	78.08	100	73	**4.75**	.49
The MDA encourages friendships between children		1.37	5.48	31.51	61.64	100	73	**4.53**	.67
The MDA contributes to the children's sense of responsibility			2.74	24.66	72.60	100	73	**4.70**	.52
The MDA encourages sensitivity to others			2.74	26.03	71.23	100	73	**4.68**	.52
The MDA encourages respect and tolerance			1.37	19.18	79.45	100	73	**4.78**	.45
The MDA encourages initiative			1.37	13.70	84.93	100	73	**4.84**	.41
The MDA encourages creativity			2.74	17.81	79.45	100	73	**4.77**	.49
The MDA		1.37	2.74	30.14	65.75	100	73	**4.60**	.62
The MDA encourages collaboration			1.37	23.29	75.34	100	73	**4.74**	.47
The MDA encourages the child's sense of efficacy				17.81	82.19	100	73	**4.82**	.39
The MDA contributes to the development child's self-confidence				20.55	79.45	100	73	**4.79**	.41
Extent of contribution of MDA to development of children's social-communication patterns – calculated index							**73**	**4.73**	**.41**

It was found that the mean extent of contribution of the MDA to the development of the children's social-communication patterns was high-very high (mean 4.73 out of 5.00). The MDA teachers expressed the strongest agreement with the statement that "the MDA encourages initiative" (4.84) and that "the MDA encourages the children's sense of efficacy" (4.82). Contrastingly, the lowest extent of agreement was in relation to the statement that "the MDA encourages friendships between children" (4.53). **It seems that 'initiative' emerges from these findings as a central component that the children acquire in the MDA.**

Table III.11: Description of the extent of the children's participation in their learning: Comparison of grading by MDA teachers and traditional teachers (Distribution in percentages, means and standard deviations)

Results for MDA teachers									
Participation of the children in their learning	**1 Not at all %**	**2 %**	**3 %**	**4 %**	**5 Very much %**	**Total %**	**Total (N)**	**Mean**	**SD**
In my kindergarten children participate in determining contents that will be discussed and planning the program		9.59	30.14	32.88	27.40	100	73	3.78	.96
The children learn fields of interest that are important and meaningful for them		2.74	16.44	39.73	41.10	100	73	4.19	.81
The extent of the children's participation in their learning processes – calculated index							**73**	**3.99**	**.83**
Results for traditional teachers									
Participation of the children in their learning	**1 Not at all %**	**2 %**	**3 %**	**4 %**	**5 Very much %**	**Total %**	**Total (N)**	**Mean**	**SD**
In my kindergarten children participate in determining contents to be discussed and in planning the program	15.79	49.12	26.32	7.02	1.75	100	57	2.30	.89
The children learn the fields of interest that are important and meaningful for them	7.02	15.79	24.56	47.37	5.26	100	57	3.28	1.03
The extent of the children's participation in their learning processes – calculated index							**57**	**2.79**	**.78**

Table III.12: The extent of the children's participation in their learning: Comparison of grading by MDA teachers and traditional teachers (means and SD)

	MDA teachers			Traditional teachers				
Item	Total (N)	Mean	SD	Total (N)	Mean	SD	t-value	Df
In my kindergarten the children participate in the determination of contents they deal with and their planning	73	3.78	.96	57	2.30	.89	9.03**	128
The children learn the fields of interest which are important and meaningful for them	73	4.19	.81	57	3.28	1.03	5.48**	104.24
Extent of children's participation in their learning processes – calculated index	**73**	**3.99**	**.83**	**57**	**2.79**	**.78**	**8.34****	**128**

**p<0.01

Significant differences were found in the reports concerning the extent of children's participation in their learning processes between the MDA teachers and the traditional teachers. Thus, the level of children's participation in their learning received higher grading from the reports of the MDA teachers than the grading given by the traditional teachers (3.99 in comparison to 2.79 respectively, t=8.34, p<0.01). More specifically, it was found that the level of children's participation in the different learning processes that were examined in the questionnaire was significantly higher according to the grading by MDA teachers in comparison to the grading by traditional teachers.

Table III.13: Description of the manner of discourse in meetings: Comparison of grading by MDA teachers and traditional teachers (Distribution in percentages, means and standard deviations)

Results for teachers working/studying according to MDA									
Manner of discourse in meetings	**1 Not at all %**	**2 %**	**3 %**	**4 %**	**5 Very much %**	**Total %**	**Total (N)**	**Mean**	**SD**
I give the right to speak to the children who raise their hands according to the order that I determine[1]	19.18	19.18	32.88	23.29	5.48	100	73	2.77 (3.23)	1.17
The children join in the conversation without raising hands, as they have learnt to do	5.48	15.07	39.73	31.51	8.22	100	73	3.22	.99
Manner of discourse in meetings – calculated index						**100**	**73**	**3.23**	**.98**
I give the right to speak to the children who raise their hands according to the order that I determine[1]	7.02	7.02	19.30	38.60	28.07	100	57	3.74 (2.26)	1.16
The children join in the conversation without raising hands, as they learnt to do	35.09	38.60	14.04	10.53	1.75	100	57	2.05	1.04
Manner of discourse in meetings – calculated index							**57**	**2.16**	**.97**

[1]The scale was reversed so that 1= “strong agreement” and 5=

"strong disagreement". This was to ensure that all the statements in the index would have the same meaning – insofar as the values were higher, so the discourse in the meetings was less organized and freer.

Note: The means provided in brackets were calculated after the reversal.

Table III.14: The manner of discourse in meetings: Comparison of grading by MDA teachers and traditional teachers (means and SDs)

	MDA teachers			Traditional teachers				
Item	Total (N)	Mean	SD	Total (N)	Mean	SD	t-value	Df
I give the right to speak to the children who raise their hands according to an order that I determine[1]	73	3.23	1.17	57	2.26	1.16	4.70**	128
The children join in the conversation without raising hands as they have learnt to do	73	3.22	.99	57	2.05	1.04	6.52**	128
Manner of discourse in meetings – calculated index	**73**	**3.23**	**.98**	**57**	**2.16**	**.97**	**6.20****	**128**

**p<0.01

[1]The mean for this statement emerged after reversal of the index so that 1 = "very much" and 5 = "not at all".

Significant differences were found in the manner of discourse employed in meetings in the kindergarten between the reports of MDA teachers and the reports of traditional teachers. The manner of discourse in the kindergarten meeting was found to be less organized and freer in the reports of MDA teachers in comparison to the reports of traditional teachers (3.23 in comparison to 2.16 respectively, t=6.20, p<0.01). More specifically, it was found that the extent of freedom in the discourse in kindergarten meetings according to different characteristics examined in the questionnaire was significantly higher in the reports of the MDA teachers than in reports of the traditional teachers.

In the following table too, the scale was reversed so that 1 = "strong agreement" and 5 = "strong disagreement". This was to ensure that all the statements in the index would have the same meaning –

insofar as the values were higher, so the discourse in the meetings was less organized and freer.

Table III.15: Description of the extent to which children guide meetings: Comparison of grading by MDA teachers and traditional teachers (distribution in percentages, means and SDs)

Results for teachers working/studying according to MDA									
Manner of discourse in meetings	**1 Not at all %**	**2 %**	**3 %**	**4 %**	**5 Very much %**	**Total %**	**Total (N)**	**Mean**	**SD**
The children learn from their friend who pre-plans and guides the whole meeting (mediated to some extent by the teacher) and actively participate according to the child's guidance	1.37%	9.59%	15.07%	39.73%	34.25%	100	73	3.96	1.01
The children don't guide the activity. They learn from the teacher and actively participate in the meeting, speaking, singing, dancing, acting etc. according to her guidance[1]	6.85%	20.55%	38.36%	24.66%	9.59%	100	73	3.10 (2.90)	1.06
Extent to which children guide meetings: calculated index								**3.43**	**.81**
The children learn by listening to the teacher and the meeting is based on quiet attentiveness to the teacher[2]	36.99	21.92	26.03	13.70	1.37	100	73	2.21	**1.13**

Results for traditional teachers									
Manner of discourse in meetings	**1 Not at all %**	**2 %**	**3 %**	**4 %**	**5 Very much %**	**Total %**	**Total (N)**	**Mean**	**SD**
The children learn from their friend who pre-plans and guides the whole meeting (mediated to some extent by the teacher) and actively participate according to the child's guidance	59.65	29.82	5.26	3.51	1.75	100	57	1.58	.89
The children don't guide the activity. They learn from the teacher and actively participate in the meeting, speaking, singing, dancing, acting etc. according to her guidance[1]		1.75	7.02	50.88	40.35	100	57	4.30 (1.70)	.68
Extent to which children guide meetings: calculated index						**100**	**57**	**1.64**	**.62**
Children learn by listening to the teacher. The meeting is based on quiet attentiveness to the teacher[2]	24.56	22.81	29.82	17.54	5.26	100	57	2.56	1.20

[1] The index was reversed so that 1 = "strong agreement" and 5 = "strong disagreement". This was performed so that the statements in the index would all have the same meaning – insofar as the values were

higher this meant that the children guided the meetings more and learnt more from their friend and less from the teacher. The means provided in brackets were calculated after the reversal.

[2] This statement was not included in calculating the index

Table III.16: Extent to which children guide meetings: Comparison of grading by MDA teachers and traditional teachers (means and SDs)

	MDA teachers			Traditional teachers				
Item	Total (N)	Mean	SD	Total (N)	Mean	SD	t-value	Df
The children learn from their friend who pre-plans and guides the whole meeting (mediated to some extent by the teacher) and actively participate according to the child's guidance	73	**3.96**	1.01	57	**1.58**	.89	14.10**	128
The children don't guide the activity. They learn from the teacher and actively participate in the meeting, speaking, singing, dancing, acting etc. according to her guidance[1]	73	**2.90**	1.06	57	**1.70**	.68	7.86**	123.88
Extent to which children guide meetings: calculated index	**73**	**3.43**	**.81**	**57**	**1.64**	**.62**	**14.31****	**127.95**
The children learn by listening to the teacher and the meeting is based on quiet attentiveness to the teacher[2]	**73**	**2.21**	1.13	**57**	**2.56**	1.20	-1.74	128

**p<0.01

[1] The mean for this statement was calculated after the index was reversed, so that 1= "strong agreement" and 5= "strong disagreement".

[2] This statement was not included in calculating the index

Significant differences were found in relation to the extent of children's guidance of the meetings in the kindergarten between the reports of the MDA teachers and the reports of the traditional teachers. Grades given for the extent of children's guidance of the meetings in the kindergarten were higher in the reports of the MDA teachers in comparison to the reports of traditional teachers (3.43 in contrast to 1.64 respectively, $t=14.31$, $p<0.01$). More specifically, it was found that the extent to which children guided the meetings in the kindergartens according to different characteristics examined in the questionnaire was significantly higher in the reports of the MDA teachers in comparison to the reports of traditional teachers.

Table III.17: Description of the extent to which there are teacher-child meetings to plan activities: Comparison of grading by MDA teachers and traditional teachers (distribution in percentages, means and SDs)

Results for teachers working/studying according to MDA									
Manner of discourse in meetings	**1 Not at all %**	**2 %**	**3 %**	**4 %**	**5 Very much %**	**Total %**	**Total (N)**	**Mean**	**SD**
The concept of "teacher-child meetings" is clear and recognized		1.37	15.07	27.40	56.16	100	73	**4.38**	.79
I conduct meetings with children to plan activities		9.59	17.81	45.21	27.40	100	73	**3.90**	.92
I conduct planning meetings with the children as a planned part of my daily and weekly agenda	4.11	10.96	36.99	23.29	24.66	100	73	3.53	1.11
Extent to which there are teacher-child meetings to plan activities – calculated index						**100**	**73**	**3.94**	**.84**
Results for traditional teachers									
Manner of discourse in meetings	**1 Not at all %**	**2 %**	**3 %**	**4 %**	**5 Very much %**	**Total %**	**Total (N)**	**Mean**	**SD**
The concept of "teacher-child meetings" is clear and recognized	17.54%	29.82%	19.30%	17.54%	15.79%	100	57	**2.84**	1.35
I conduct meetings with children to plan activities	43.86%	33.33%	12.28%	8.77%	1.75%	100	57	**1.91**	1.04
I conduct planning meetings with the children as a planned part of my daily and weekly agenda	61.40%	29.82%	5.26%	3.51%		100	57	1.51	.76
Extent to which there are teacher-child meetings to plan activities – calculated index						**100**	**57**	**2.09**	**.89**

Table III.18: Extent to which there are teacher-child meetings to plan activities: Comparison of grading by MDA teachers and traditional teachers (means and SDs)

	MDA teachers			**Traditional teachers**				
Item	Total (N)	Mean	SD	Total (N)	Mean	SD	t-value	Df
The concept of "teacher-child meetings" is clear and recognized	73	**4.38**	.79	57	**2.84**	1.35	7.67**	85.54
I conduct meetings with children to plan activities	73	**3.90**	.92	57	**1.91**	1.04	11.60**	128
I conduct planning meetings with the children as a planned part of my daily and weekly agenda	**73**	**3.53**	1.11	**57**	**1.51**	.76	12.36**	126.06
Extent to which there are teacher-child meetings to plan activities – calculated index	**73**	**3.94**	**.84**	**57**	**2.09**	**.89**	**12.15****	**128**

**p<0.01

Significant differences were found in the extent of teacher-child meetings held to plan activities in the kindergarten between the reports of the teachers working/ studying according to the MDA and the reports of traditional teachers. The extent of teacher-child meetings held to plan activities in the kindergarten was reported as higher in the reports of the MDA teachers than among the traditional teachers (grade 3.94 in contrast to 2.09 respectively, t=12.15, p<0.01). More specifically, it was found that the existence of teacher-child meeting to plan activities according to specific characteristics examined in the questionnaire was reported as significantly higher by the MDA teachers than by the traditional teachers.

Table III.19: Description of the extent of feedback given by the teacher to the children: Comparison of grading by MDA teachers and traditional teachers (distribution by percentages, means and SDs)

Results for teachers working/studying according to MDA									
Feedback given by teacher to child	**1 Not at all %**	**2 %**	**3 %**	**4 %**	**5 Very much %**	**Total %**	**Total (N)**	**Mean**	**SD**
There is feedback between me and the child	1.37%	6.85%	23.29%	41.10%	27.40%	100	73	**3.86**	.95
I give feedback (unplanned) to the child according to what the child is doing, I talk, ask questions etc.		4.11%	19.18%	47.95%	28.77%	100	73	**4.01**	.81
I provide planned feedback to the child regarding activities initiated by the child	4.11%	12.33%	13.70%	36.99%	32.88%	100	73	**3.82**	1.15
Extent of teacher's feedback to the child – calculated index						**100**	**73**	**3.90**	**.81**
Results for traditional teachers									
	1 Not at all %	**2 %**	**3 %**	**4 %**	**5 Very much %**	**Total %**	**Total (N)**	**Mean**	**SD**
There is feedback between me and the child	5.26%	19.30%	28.07%	38.60%	8.77%	100	57	**3.26**	1.04
I give feedback (unplanned) to the child according to what the child is doing, I talk, ask questions etc.	3.51%		19.30%	49.12%	28.07%	100	57	**3.98**	.90
I provide planned feedback to the child regarding activities initiated by the child	43.86%	38.60%	12.28%	3.51%	1.75%	100	57	**1.81**	.91
Extent of teacher's feedback to the child – calculated index							**57**	**3.02**	**.70**

Table III.20: Extent of feedback given by the teacher to the children: Comparison of mean grades given by MDA teachers and traditional teachers (means and SDs)

	MDA teachers			**Traditional teachers**				
Item	Total (N)	Mean	SD	Total (N)	Mean	SD	t-value	Df
There is feedback between me and the child	73	3.86	.95	57	3.26	1.04	3.43**	128
I give feedback (unplanned) to the child according to what the child is doing, I talk, questions etc.	73	4.01	.81	57	3.98	.90	.21	128
I provide planned feedback to the child regarding the child's initiated activities	73	3.82	1.15	57	1.81	.91	10.84**	128
Extent of teacher's feedback to the child – calculated index	**73**	**3.90**	**.81**	**57**	**3.02**	**.70**	**6.56****	**128**

**p<0.01

Significant differences were found in relation to the extent of feedback given by the teacher to the child between the reports of the MDA teachers and the reports of traditional teachers. The extent of feedback given by the teacher to the child was found to be highest according to the reports of the MDA teachers in comparison with the reports of the traditional teachers (3.90 in contrast to 3.02 respectively, t=6.56, p<0.01). More specifically, it was found that the extent of feedback given by the teacher to the child according to the different characteristics examined by the questionnaire was significantly higher according to the reports of the teachers working according to the MDA than in the reports of traditional teachers.

Table III.21: Description of the extent of feedback given by children to other children: Comparison of grading by MDA teachers and traditional teachers (distribution by percentages, means and SDs)

Results for MDA teachers									
Feedback by children to children	**1 Not at all %**	**2 %**	**3 %**	**4 %**	**5 Very much %**	**Total %**	**Total (N)**	**Mean**	**SD**
The children give feedback to one another	2.74%	13.70%	21.92%	41.10%	20.55%	100	73	**3.63**	1.05
There is feedback action-reaction (the child does something and another child reacts)	1.37%	12.33%	31.51%	39.73%	15.07%	100	73	**3.55**	.94
The children are asked by me to give feedback to the child that guides the activity	5.48%	13.70%	23.29%	34.25%	23.29%	100	73	**3.56**	1.15
The extent of feedback by children to children – calculated index							73	**3.58**	**.95**
Results for traditional teachers									
Feedback by children to children	**1 Not at all %**	**2 %**	**3 %**	**4 %**	**5 Very much %**	**Total %**	**Total (N)**	**Mean**	**SD**
The children give feedback to one another	12.28%	29.82%	35.09%	19.30%	3.51%	100	57	**2.72**	1.03
There is feedback action-reaction (the child does something and another child reacts)	14.04%	28.07%	26.32%	28.07%	3.51%	100	57	**2.79**	1.11
The children are asked by me to give feedback to the child that guides the activity	64.91%	28.07%	3.51%	1.75%	1.75%	100	57	**1.47**	.80
The extent of feedback by children to children – calculated index						100	57	**2.33**	**.82**

Table III.22: Extent of feedback given by children to other children: Comparison of mean grades given by MDA teachers and traditional teachers (distribution by percentages, means and SDs)

	MDA teachers			Traditional teachers				
Item	Total (N)	Mean	SD	Total (N)	Mean	SD	t-value	Df
The children give feedback to one another	73	3.63	1.05	57	2.72	1.03	4.95**	128
There is feedback action-reaction (the child does something and another child reacts)	73	3.55	.94	57	2.79	1.11	4.20**	128
The children are asked by me to give feedback to the child that guides the activity	73	3.56	1.15	57	1.47	.80	12.14**	126.49
The extent of feedback by children to children – calculated index	**73**	**3.58**	**.95**	**57**	**2.33**	**.82**	**7.92****	**128**

**p<0.01

Significant differences were found in the extent of feedback by children to children between the reports of the MDA teachers and the reports of the traditional teachers so that the extent of feedback given by children to children was found to be higher according to the reports of the MDA teachers than in the reports of the traditional teachers (3.58 in contrast to 2.33 respectively, t=7.92, p<0.01). More specifically, it was found that the extent of feedback by children to children according to different characteristics examined in the questionnaire was significantly higher in the reports of the MDA teachers than in the reports of the traditional teachers.

Table III.23: Description of the extent to which philosophical discourse is conducted in the kindergarten: Comparison of grading by MDA teachers and traditional teachers (distribution by percentages, means and SDs)

Results for MDA teachers									
Existence of Philosophical discourse	**1 Not at all %**	**2 %**	**3 %**	**4 %**	**5 Very much %**	**Total %**	**Total (N)**	**Mean**	**SD**
I am familiar with the term "philosophical discourse"	5.48	5.48	16.44	39.73	31.51	100	73	**3.85**	1.11
Random philosophical discourse occurs throughout the day	5.48	5.48	32.88	31.51	23.29	100	73	**3.60**	1.09
There is planned, structured philosophical discourse on subjects that the children ask to discuss as part of the curriculum	6.85	6.85	20.55	38.36	17.81	100	73	**3.44**	1.17
Extent of philosophical discourse – calculated index							73	**3.63**	**1.01**
Results for traditional teachers									
Existence of philosophical discourse	**1 Not at all %**	**2 %**	**3 %**	**4 %**	**5 Very much %**	**Total %**	**Total (N)**	**Mean**	**SD**
I am familiar with the term "philosophical discourse"	31.58	19.30	19.30	21.05	8.77	100	57	**2.56**	1.36
Random philosophical discourse occurs throughout the day	33.33	21.05	22.81	21.05	1.75	100	57	**2.37**	1.20
There is planned, structured philosophical discourse on subjects that children ask to discuss as part of the curriculum	54.39	28.07	10.53	3.51	3.51	100	57	**1.74**	1.03
Extent of philosophical discourse – calculated index							57	**2.22**	**1.03**

Table III.24: Extent to which philosophical discourse is conducted in the kindergarten: Comparison of mean grades given by MDA teachers and traditional teachers (means and SDs)

	MDA teachers			Traditional teachers				
Item	Total (N)	Mean	SD	Total (N)	Mean	SD	t-value	Df
I am familiar with the term "philosophical discourse"	73	**3.85**	1.11	57	**2.56**	1.36	5.78**	107.01
Random philosophical discourse occurs throughout the day	73	**3.60**	1.09	57	**2.37**	1.20	6.12**	128
There is planned, structured philosophical discourse on subjects that the children ask to discuss as part of the curriculum	73	**3.44**	1.17	57	**1.74**	1.03	8.69**	128
Extent of philosophical discourse – calculated index	**73**	**3.63**	**1.01**	**57**	**2.22**	**1.03**	**7.83****	**128**

**p<0.01

Significant differences were found in the extent of philosophical discourse reported by MDA teachers and reports of traditional teachers. Thus, the extent of philosophical discourse was found to be highest in the reports of the MDA teachers in comparison to the reports of the traditional teachers (3.63 in contrast to 2.2 respectively, t=7.83, p<0.01). More specifically, the extent of philosophical discourse in the kindergarten according to different characteristics examined in the questionnaire was found to be significantly higher in the reports of MDA teachers in comparison with the reports of the traditional teachers.

From the quantitative findings described above, it is clear that in the comparison between MDA and traditional teachers, the components of the multi-dialogical kindergarten emerge as follows:

1. Initiative expressed by the child
2. Child's ability to lead
3. Provision of feedback
4. Children's participation in learning processes.

Chapter 4

Discussion of the Findings

IV.1 Preview

This chapter discusses the findings presented in Chapter III in consideration of extant literature on the studied issues surveyed in the literature review in Chapter I: Theoretical Fundamentals. The discussion is organized in line with the research questions. Qualitative findings are used to answer Research Question 1, while quantitative findings are used to answer Research Question 2.

IV.2 Answering Research Question 1: Qualitative findings

The first research question asked: "What unique social, behavioral and interpersonal communication patterns develop among kindergarten children in a multi-dialogical kindergarten?"

The research drew on the premise that a connection exists between the use of the MDA in kindergartens and the development of kindergarten children's social-communication patterns. The findings reveal a connection between the implementation of the MDA in kindergartens and the development of the kindergarten children's social-communication patterns.

Discussion of Finding 1: It seems that the multi-dialogical kindergarten is characterized by the teacher's strong need to be attentive, including attentiveness beyond the spoken words. The teacher learns to assimilate this attentiveness as part of the social-communication patterns that characterize a kindergarten working according to this approach, and in the teacher uses this attentiveness to foster the growth of children's initiatives and work out of their strengths. Explanation: It seems that children's initiatives are created as a result of the teacher's attentiveness, since the moment that she assigns planned time during the day's schedule to pay attention and observe the children, she is able to identify what they are occupied in doing and what are their real fields of interest, which she then uses to construct her activities in the kindergarten. In fact, this attentiveness constitutes the foundation for the teacher's planning of the learning and work curricula in the kindergarten. This finding is supported by the writings of Rogers, who said that growth begins from moments characterized by attentive communication. This is because it is at these moments that equality is formed between the educator and the learner, and both of them change as a result of the interaction between them (Harari, 2008). Clark and Moss (2005) went deeper, reinforcing Rogers' statement, and arguing that it is impossible to capture the concept of attentiveness as listening that leads to the reception of knowledge, rather it should be seen as a reflective process aimed at thinking about meanings, forming connections and revealing new understandings. **Conclusion from this discussion: social- communication patterns are shaped in a multi-dialogical kindergarten by the teacher's attentiveness through which she enables the children's initiatives to be expressed, and this constitutes the foundation for the kindergarten's work and learning curricula.**

Discussion of Finding 2: The multi-dialogical kindergarten is characterized by the attentiveness of the children one towards the other, while the teachers learn to facilitate this as part of the MDA and as part of the social- communication patterns that develop in

the kindergarten. Explanation: It seems that the reason that the children learn to be attentive to each other is pinned in their strong participation in their studies. This is expressed in several dimensions: firstly – the teacher enables the children to guide each other in various activities. Secondly –the teacher coaches the children, showing them how to discuss things without needing to raise their hands in the meeting or group, and teaches them how to express their opinions while paying attention to others. These discourse components allow the children to develop social-communication patterns of attentiveness to one another. This finding correlates with theoretical literature that argues that participation of children in the planning of the kindergarten's activities and learning allows them to accumulate personal experience in social abilities such as attentiveness and involvement, expression of personal opinions, acquisition of a way in which to share their experiences with their friends, practicing decision-making in their daily life, being able to conduct negotiations and learning to wait and to contribute to and share with their friends (Clark & Moss, 2005; Leinonen & Venninan, 2012; Venninen, Leinonen & Ojala, 2010). **Conclusion from this discussion: Paying attention to a friend is a social-communication pattern acquired in the multi-dialogical kindergarten and this is given an important place through practice under the teacher's guidance.**

Discussion of Finding 3: The multi-dialogical kindergarten is characterized by the ability of the teacher and the children to assimilate the social-communication pattern of active listening, a type of listening that they exercise as part of the social-communication patterns that develop in the kindergarten. Explanation: In this sense, active listening can be seen as one of the factors that help the children's growth and learning that comes from within them and with its help, the children can develop social-communication patterns of thinking ability and autonomous action and empathy for others. The concept of "active listening" expressed in this finding was a central concept in the theory of Karl Rogers. This type of listening is a mental activity that requires strong concentration by the listener, so that the listener does not merely hear but also absorbs the message with all their senses, succeeding in paying attention not only to what is said explicitly but also to what is said between the lines and taking note of both verbal and non-verbal messages of the speaker (Zamir, 2006). **Conclusion from this discussion: Social-communication patterns such as autonomy and empathy are shaped through the practice of active listening that the teacher and children exercise in the multi-dialogical kindergarten.**

Discussion of Finding 4: In the MDA one of the teacher's ways of paying attention is to observe the children's actions and she is thus able to identify their areas of interest in any place and time. Explanation: It seems that through observation, which is one of the teacher's ways of paying attention, the teacher is able to allow the children to relate to fields that interest them, while she observes them. As a result of the children's interest their desire to learn and go more deeply into their studies increases. This deep consideration leads them to acquire social-communication patterns that are expressed in taking responsibility for their learning, practicing decision-making regarding their learning and collaborative learning. Broad support for this can be found in the professional literature that argues that when the kindergarten teacher has the opportunity to observe and pay attention, this allows her to be attentive to the children, to observe them and what they are doing in depth, coming closer to their world, to observe their viewpoints and out of this to guide them in matters that interest them. In this manner she actually allows them to become learners who are responsible for their own learning (Bengtsson, 2005; Emilson, 2007; Fiore & Rosenquest, 2010; Johansson, 2004; Sheridan, 2001).

Additionally, previous research indicates that children of kindergarten age can mediate the experiences that they have undergone to their environment, including their emotions and thoughts. This can happen on the condition that the educators try to identify this, observing and paying attention and interpreting the children's expressions. If they succeed in doing so then the children will experience true involvement in their learning (Pramling-Samuelsson & Sheridan, 2003) while reinforcing their self-confidence and acquiring social skills such as collaboration and decision-making (Emilson &

Folkesson, 2006). **Conclusion from this discussion: Social-communication patterns such as taking responsibility for learning, decision-making and collaboration are shaped and acquired through observation of the children's activities by the teacher, which is another form of paying attention to them in the multi-dialogical kindergarten.**

Discussion of Finding 5: Implementation of the MDA in a kindergarten necessitates a change in the teacher's educational perception. In other words, in order to work according to the MDA, the teacher needs to relinquish complete control of everything relating to discourse and contents in the kindergarten and to pay attention to subjects that interest the children. Explanation: When the teacher takes the approach that she should foster or block the development of social-communication patterns in the kindergarten and plans a learning curriculum that is completely closed, determining what she teaches and what the children do at any given moment in the kindergarten, this prevents the expression of the children's fields of interest and initiatives. Broad support for this finding can be found in the work of Callander (2013), who argues that the dialogical approach to education is not a program but a philosophical belief that represents a change in thinking on the role of the educator, so that all the children can participate in their learning, something that depends on the teacher's approach and the extent to which she allows this (Nyland, 2009). It seems that when the daily activities of the kindergarten are only formulated by the teacher, this constitutes an obstacle to the influence of the children on their daily life in the kindergarten (Emilson, 2007). In this situation the teacher's viewpoint has the sole control over the planning of the curriculum and activities in the kindergarten leading to an increasing gap between the children's viewpoint and that of the teacher. This gap is the cause of the children's low level of influence over the manner and content of their studies (Arner & Tellgren, 1998; Aspan, 2005; Ekholm & Lindvall, 1991; Selberg, 1999; Sheridan, 2001). Thus, if it is desirable that the children should have a greater influence over their lives in the kindergarten, the teacher should relinquish some of her absolute control over the contents dealt with in the kindergarten and the activities that take place there, so that she can in practice be more available to observe and pay attention to the children (Bengtsson, 2005; Emilson, 2007; Fiore & Rosenquest, 2010; Johansson, 2004; Sheridan, 2001). **This finding permits the conclusion that the shaping and acquisition of the children's social-communication patterns in the kindergarten depends on the teacher's approach that may or may not enable the children's fields of interest and initiatives to be expressed.**

Discussion of Finding 6: In order to implement the MDA in a kindergarten, the teacher needs to learn how to organize, plan and effectively manage time in the kindergarten. Moreover, she needs courses on the subject, guidance and modeling by a mentor and a support group of kindergarten teachers working according to this approach. Explanation: It seems that the teacher working according to MDA has a clear program concerning the learning in the kindergarten. She knows what she will apply the time to and what she will do in this framework. But within the framework there is much freedom and this is exploited to pay attention to the children and their initiatives and to develop learning curricula from this. Because of the great freedom in the educational frame, the teacher needs to have strong skills for the planning and management of time since if not, the kindergarten may have no boundaries. For this reason, she also needs close guidance and a support group to provide her with feedback and allow her to reflect on her work. **This finding expands on and brings new knowledge to literature on time organization and planning. It is concluded that the shaping and acquisition of children's social-communication patterns depend on the teacher's ability to create a clear framework for activities and learning in the kindergarten, determining boundaries within which both she and the children have much freedom. This is facilitated by the teacher's learning and educational reflection regarding MDA under professional guidance and the teacher's participation in a support group of colleagues who are working according to this approach.**

Discussion of Finding 7: In a kindergarten that works according to the MDA the teacher learns together with the children

and out of her attentiveness to their fields of interest and also constitutes a model of flexibility and creative thinking for them as part of her communication patterns with them. Explanation: It seems that the MDA teacher understands that her job is not to transmit knowledge to the children rather to construct the knowledge out of the children's fields of interest, and this means that she is more flexible in her learning with the children. Moreover, it seems that for the children, this work method constitutes a model to exercise social-communication patterns such as flexibility and thinking outside the box.

On the one hand, the professional literature supports this finding since it suggests that the teacher should be more flexible and that this should be expressed in her attentiveness to the children, using this to build her work curriculum in the kindergarten (Fumoto, 2011), Freire reinforces this approach, saying that the dialogical process mediates between the teacher's role and the role of the children, which seem to be contradictory. However, he notes that they do not really contradict each other, since both of them simultaneously learn and teach. Moreover, this educational dialog creates a process of cooperation and joint investigation and reciprocal influence is formed through the dialog between equals (Aliakbari & Faraji, 2011; Darom, 1989; Gover, 2008). On the other hand, this finding adds to and brings new knowledge to extant literature relating to children's cognitive development since it proposes that the teacher's flexibility constitutes a model for the child's flexibility and thinking outside the box. **Conclusion from this discussion: The teacher's ability to act as a model for the children helps to shape and teach social-communication patterns such as flexibility and thinking outside the box.**

Discussion of Finding 8: The learning and work curricula in the MDA kindergarten stem from the children's fields of interest combined with contents that the teacher brings, where the role of the teacher in the children's learning is expressed in attentiveness to them and identification of their fields of interest and meaningful mediation for them. Explanation: It seems that the children's interest in learning engenders significant learning involving social-communication patterns such as in-depth learning, investigation and the ability to ask questions. Support for this conceptualization can be found in Rogers' assertion that the learning program should be based on the children's fields of interest, while the teacher is involved in this and helps the children to construct and implement the program (Harari, 2008). Thus too, according to Gardner's theory, the teacher should conduct dialog with the child about his strengths and fields of interest (Willingham, 2004), since learning based on the children's fields of interest will be significant learning (Renninger, 1992). The role of the educator is expressed in the identification of the children's initiatives, support for them and development of these initiatives together with the children through mediation (Lasri, 2004). **Conclusion from this discussion: The foundation for social-communication patterns such as the desire to learn, in-depth learning and ability to ask questions begins with the construction of a learning program that will enable these patterns to be expressed.**

Discussion of Finding 9: The children's ability to go deep into their learning and develop expertise in their field of interest, to learn about their abilities, to think independently and draw conclusions, to explain themselves to a group and to transmit knowledge that they have acquired to their friends through peer learning are all central patterns that develop as consequences of learning in a multi-dialogical kindergarten. Explanation: The children are helped to learn about their abilities since the learning that the multi-dialogical kindergarten offers them is learning that poses problems and relies on the asking of questions and drawing conclusions. Thus too, because it is based on the children's fields of interest, the variety of learning contents is challenging, varied and non-conventional. Moreover, because of the children's deep consideration of the subjects that interest them and the mediation that they receive regarding this field, they become experts on these subjects and can teach their friends about them. This becomes peer learning. Extant literature supports this finding; for example: Socratic dialog involves the use of questions that are not based on prior knowledge, which constitute the key to learning (Cohen, 2008). The participants take the responsibility for the dialog and discourse: asking questions about their questions, correcting their mistakes and examining their ways of thinking (Reed & Johnson, 1999). In this way they are helped to see the contradictions in their words and to draw conclusions (Cohen, 2008). Moreover, there is an understanding that different children have different languages and ways of expression and they should be considered as equal participants in any dialog and experts with regard to the subjects that interest them (Clark & Moss, 2005).

Additionally, according to the Theory of Multiple Intelligences, coined by Gardiner, when conducting a dialog with children, it should be taken into account that dialog is based on the assumption that not everyone learns in the same manner, not everyone has the same fields of interest or the same capabilities. This means that it is necessary to relate to the particular child's strengths (Willingham, 2004) and learning should develop from that point. Previous research indicates that effective peer learning can take place in early childhood in the kindergarten (Fuchs et al., 1997; Mathes et al., 1998). It is noted that the present finding adds to and brings innovative knowledge to the extant literature in the field of learning programs for early childhood since it points up that there is a large variety of learning contents in the multi-dialogical kindergarten because it is based on the children's area of interest; it is challenging and varied and unconventional. **Conclusion from this discussion: In the multi-dialogical kindergarten, social-communication patterns such as the development of expertise, learning about one's abilities, drawing conclusions, independent thinking and peer learning are acquired and shaped out of and as a result of learning according to the MDA.**

Discussion of Finding 10 – Feedback that children give and accept emerged as a central pattern in the work of the multi-dialogical kindergarten. Feedback is seen by the teacher as a communication tool that children can acquire to use throughout their lives. Explanation: It seems that when the children learn to give and accept feedback, interaction and dialog are formed between them that enable them to examine what they have done, to relate to their friends and to express their opinions in a group. Feedback is a tool that teaches the children to express their emotions and helps them to tell their friends what they enjoy, what interests them, what they find difficult and what can help them. With the help of feedback they learn to cope with difficulties and strengths and to take time in order to think more deeply. The role of the teacher is to coach the children to give feedback to one another, while the feedback also allows the teacher to get to know about the children's world. The teacher constitutes part of the feedback circle and the emphasis that she puts on feedback relates to values, relationships and communication between the children. Support for this finding is found in previous research, which found that kindergarten children are able to understand that everyone has different feelings, desires and thoughts, and also that the ability to understand diversity develops as a result of children's interactions in a peer group (Astington & Jenkins 1995; Slomkowski & Dunn, 1996). It, therefore, seems that feedback is used to raise doubts, to ask questions and to reexamine things (Ben-Yosef, 2009), to enable participants to suggest different ways to do things (Mercer & Littleton, 2007). The adult turns to the child in a containing and personal manner as one person to another, and not from a position of all-knowing authority (Ben-Yosef, 2009). **Conclusion from this discussion: Social-communication patterns such as consideration of friends, voicing one's opinion and expressing emotions in a group, coping with difficulties and strengths, are acquired and shaped through mediated learning employed by the teacher in the multi-dialogical kindergarten, imparting the tools of giving and accepting feedback to the children.**

Discussion of Finding 11: Negotiation between the teacher and the children and shared learning of contents and involvement in the kindergarten's life emerged as patterns evident in the work of the multi-dialogical kindergarten. Explanation: Negotiations between the teacher and the children influence kindergarten life and generate the inclusion of contents that turns the children into active and significant participants in the life of the kindergarten. This leads them to become active participants in their learning, in the organization of their learning, and as a result in their development. This finding is broadly supported by the professional literature that argues that the heart of the dialogical approach to education is the existence of continuous negotiations concerning ideas and action programs between the educator and the children in order to assist the development of meaningful learning (Forman & Fyfe, 1998; Lasri, 2004) between all those who participate in the learning (Lyle, 2008). Thus, the teacher and the children, who are involved in negotiations about the learning program and learning processes, contribute one to the other (Jhong, 2008). The development process actually begins with the interaction between the children and the teacher, a process that is internalized over time and becomes an inner cognitive tool that is available to the child to cope with other assignments. Interaction between the teacher and the children, in fact, constitutes the basis for the children's development of cognitive tools (Vygotsky, 1978). Moreover, MDA education is characterized by the participation of the children in decision-making concerning activities in all areas of the kindergarten and not only in the academic area. This decision-making occurs through negotiations between the teacher and the children (Efrat & Ungureanu, 2015). **Conclusion from this discussion: Social-communication patterns such as the ability to be active in learning, in activities and the organization of the kindergarten are acquired and shaped when the children are helped to become active partners in the planning of the kindergarten life and contents.**

Discussion of Finding 12: In the MDA, brainstorming by the children together with the teacher constitutes a tool for dialogical work, which the teacher can use to construct a learning curriculum that is relevant for the children's knowledge and fields of interest. Explanation: Brainstorming is used to discover together with the children what they already know on the discussed subject and what they would like to know and to do concerning that subject. Thus, the children become active participants in their learning and the subject studied is relevant for them. This helps the children to develop the ability for interactive learning, to be able to learn from their friends, to express an opinion, to take responsibility for what they would be interested to learn and to be flexible in their learning. The professional literature supports this finding, indicating that this approach to education affords a pattern of interaction characterized by relevant questions posed by the teacher and the children participating in the dialog, by the fact that the answers are not predetermined, rather they are given as part of the dialog, and the fact that the subject being discussed can be altered (Nystrand et al., 1997). This deepens the children's basic understanding, under the assumption that children in early childhood have knowledge and experience and consequently hold opinions and ideas of their own which they can express in dialog (Lansdown, 2001). The goal of the teacher in this process is to clarify the knowledge that the children have and to get to know the subject from their viewpoint in order to plan its learning (Feld-Elhanan, 2007). **Conclusion from this discussion: Social-communication patterns such as learning in a group, expressing an opinion and taking responsibility for one's learning alongside the ability to be flexible in learning are acquired and shaped through brainstorming between the teacher and the children. This tool constitutes one of the foundations for negotiation between the children and the teacher.**

Discussion of Finding 13: A personal meeting between the teacher and the child, in one of two forms of meeting: a personal emotional meeting or a meeting to plan an activity, emerged as one of the main patterns of work in the multi-dialogical kindergarten. Explanation: These personal meetings are a facet of the teacher's dialog with the child and constitute part of their attentiveness and the work method of the teacher in the MDA. In these meetings, the teacher can understand in depth how the child thinks, how she can support the child in their thinking, to demonstrate their belief in the child's abilities and understand their viewpoints. In this manner the child is given the opportunity to plan, initiate, and think about additional directions for the presentation of their viewpoint. The initiative for the meetings comes from the children and the teacher as one and it constitutes a part of the work and learning curricula for the kindergarten working according to the MDA. Support for this finding can be found *inter alia* in the theories of Buber and Rogers. One of the fundamental elements in Buber's educational perception is the "educational encounter" that constitutes the focal point of the educational process (Avnon, 2008).

This is a human encounter underpinned by a meaningful dialog, which creates a sense of confidence, empathy, intimacy and support (Ministry of Education, 2010). Rogers also viewed dialog between an educator and children as a direct, personal and humane encounter of one person with another, a meeting founded on trust, honesty and authenticity (Anderson & Cisna, 1997).

The literature also notes that the integration of children's viewpoints in the planning, implementation and evaluation of activities and learning in the kindergarten should be done together with them and not imposed upon them (Leinonen & Venninan, 2012). The ability to see the children's viewpoint and to focus on their world and way of thinking enables dialog and involvement of the children in the planning of their learning (Emilson & Johansson, 2009; Pramling-Samuelsson & Sheridan, 2003). In order to enable the children to plan activities in the kindergarten they need to communicate in an optimal manner with the teacher, out of trust and the clear knowledge that she relies on their abilities (Thomas, 2002). If the teacher does not allow the children opportunities to participate in the planning of their own activities and learning, then the children cannot choose them for themselves (Emilson & Johansson, 2009). **Conclusion from this discussion: Social-communication patterns such as planning, initiative and thinking about additional directions are shaped through dialog expressed in the personal meetings between the child and the teacher in the multi-dialogical kindergarten.**

Discussion of Finding 14: The children's guidance of their friends emerged as a main pattern in the multi-dialogical kindergarten. Explanation: When children guide their friends in different activities, this offers them experience in leadership, guidance, and strengthens their skills for guiding the group. They do this by thinking of an idea that interests them and which they want to share with their friends, planning the idea together with the teacher in a planning meeting (according to the MDA model of activity planning) and finally by guiding the group in the activity according to the idea that they had thought of. This finding adds knowledge to literature concerning social-communication development in early childhood since it relates to the learning of leadership skills at an early age to guide others on ideas that the children themselves suggest. Moreover, it suggests a practical way to perform this guidance through a model for activity planning in a multi-dialogical kindergarten. This is supported by the literature, which claims that in order to help children to learn how to guide others, the educator must coach them on this skill and allow each child who wishes to do so to guide activities under their mentorship. This mentorship strengthens the child's confidence and their social standing and allows them to learn how to guide others without being over-controlling or aggressive (Ben-Yosef, 2009). **Conclusion from this discussion: Social-communication patterns in the multi-dialogical kindergarten, such as leadership, guidance, and leadership skills, are constructed and shaped through the children's guidance of their friends, which is a unique pattern for children in kindergartens working according to the MDA.**

Discussion of Finding 15: Discourse in general and philosophical discourse, in particular, emerged as types of dialog employed in the MDA. Explanation: Dialogical discourse is based on practicing attentiveness to others and respect for their words. This practice is performed with the help of learning mediated by the teacher. This learning teaches the children to say their words without waiting for permission to speak from the teacher but rather out of attentiveness, and it teaches them when is the appropriate time to enter the discourse. With this help the children learn to discuss out of the attention they pay to others. Additionally, when they do not agree with the words of another member of the group, they learn not to negate their friend's words but instead to note their disagreement in a respectful way. When philosophical discourse is involved, raising different viewpoints on one subject, the children are exposed to the possibility of examining a particular subject from multiple angles and the fact that there is not just one way of thinking. On this point, previous research shows that children have the ability to state their own opinion and attitudes (Harcourt, 2011), and that it is possible to teach kindergarten children to discuss things (Mercer & Dawes, 2010; Mercer & Littleton, 2007). However, to do this requires the teacher's awareness and the teacher and children need to train and exercise their participation in discourse (Wells, 1986; Wells & Ball, 2008). In practice, during the discourse the participants need to learn the rules: timing – when to enter the discourse and say your piece, speaking without interrupting others, respectful consideration of other participants even if their opinions contradict one's own opinions (Blum-Kulka 2008; Cohen, 2008) and the use of expressions such as "in my opinion" or "I think" (Callander, 2013). Such discourse aims to develop communication patterns and skills including attentiveness, listening and tolerance for the words of others out of a desire to understand their viewpoints, and also helps to develop the ability to restrain judgmental reactions even when things are said that contradicts the opinion of the listener (Ben-Yosef, 2009). With regard to philosophical discourse, it seems that children's philosophical investigation is constructed on their natural curiosity, so such investigation helps to develop the ability to ask questions (Fisher, 2007). Therefore, in guiding the children's philosophical discourse, the MDA teacher demonstrates respect for diversity and different directions of thinking are welcomed (Firstater & Efrat, 2014; Lipman, 2003). **Conclusion from this discussion: In the multi-dialogical kindergarten, social-communication patterns such as the ability to discuss in a manner that involves attentiveness and tolerance for others, without judgment, while demonstrating restraint and acceptance of the opinions of others are acquired and shaped with the help of coaching in the rules of discourse in general and philosophical discourse in particular.**

Discussion of Finding 16: Mediation and documentation were revealed as central patterns in the work of the multi-dialogical kindergarten. Explanation: It seems that helped by the teacher's mediation, the children are given the opportunity to go deeper into contents, to illustrate them, to cooperate and to make decisions in their learning. The documentation produced jointly by the teacher with the children constitutes an additional tool that allows the children to broaden their learning and to become independent learners; since it is accessible to them, it serves as the basis for the continuation of their learning. Extant literature supports this finding, indicating that dialog formed as a result of mediation develops higher mental functions in the area of social-communication (Vygotsky, 1978). Vygotsky argued that humans, including children, are social creatures and so they form relationships with those around them. With a little help and mediation they can learn as a result of these social relations, far more than they would without mediation (Lyle, 2008; Tzuriel & Shamir, 2007). Feuerstein expanded this conceptualization saying that the first performances of children are external actions that are then internalized and enrooted in the children through the mediation of educators (Feuerstein, Klein & Tennenbaum, 1991; Isman & Tzuriel, 2008).

With regard to documentation, the relevant literature indicates that documentation can be performed in various ways such as written records, photography, recording, or any other means, and both children and the teacher can participate in this. Through this documentation, the shared learning of the teacher and children becomes accessible and available to them (Rinaldi, 2005). Thus, children who experience genuine participation in their learning (Pramling-Samuelsson & Sheridan, 2003) will acquire the social skills of collaboration and decision-making (Emilson & Folkesson, 2006). Moreover, it is emphasized that if the teacher knows how to mediate learning to the children, learning will be optimal and this is one of the things that most influences the acquisition of skills and social interaction between the children (Cornu & Peters, 2005; French, 2007; Stance & Kao, 2010). **Conclusion from this discussion: Social-communication patterns such as deep learning, illustration, collaboration, independence and decision-making in learning are acquired and shaped in the multi-dialogical kindergarten through the mediation of the teacher and joint documentation by the teacher together with the children.**

Discussion of Finding 17: Life skills emerged as one of the patterns of behavior evident in the multi-dialogical kindergarten, expressed in respectful consideration, tolerance, acceptance of diversity, mutual assistance, cooperation, initiative, leadership, guidance, independence in learning and in society, ability to empower and become empowered by the peer group. Explanation: The involvement of the children in the planning of the kindergarten's life, and the social interaction that ensues, allows them to be exposed to and to practice these patterns of life skills. Extant literature supports this finding, indicating that with this support early childhood children aspire to attain a sense of self-confidence that is expressed by their independence. In order to form strong foundations for this life stage it is important to notice that the development of children's initiative and independence depends directly on their participation and involvement in decision-making processes relating to themselves and their daily agenda (Hill et al., 2004). It, therefore, seems that children are able to practice and develop social skills as a result of their participation in different activities (Berk & Winsler, 1995) since they create meaning out of their experiences (Vygotsky, 1978), learn to take responsibility, to cooperate, to initiate and to lead (Claxton & Carr, 2010). Additionally, cooperation and mutual assistance between the children increase their understanding of the social map and the development of social and communication skills (Wright et al., 2003). More specifically, scholars claim that children's experiences of social-communication interaction and the attempt to understand the desires of their friends and of adults enhance these abilities (Han & Kemple, 2006; Missall & Hojnoski, 2008). It should be added that a personal sense of empowerment, self-confidence and self-belief are constructed through interactions with the teacher, children's participation in decision-making, in negotiations and by providing opportunities for children to choose, investigate and cope with problem-solving (Erhardt-Weiss, 2008; Firstater & Efrat, 2014). **Conclusion from this discussion: Social-communication patterns expressed in the children's acquisition of life skills are shaped in the multi-dialogical kindergarten as a result of the children's involvement in the life of the kindergarten, and the social interaction that this involvement affords.**

IV.3 Answering Research Question 2: Quantitative findings

The second research question asked: "What social, communication and interpersonal differences can be found between children educated in multi-dialogical kindergartens and children educated in traditional kindergartens? This question was answered by the quantitative findings collected in this study. The hypothesis proposed that differences would be found in social and communication patterns between children educated in multi-dialogical kindergartens and children educated in traditional kindergartens and in relation to:

- *Participation:* The extent of participation by the children in their learning processes.
- *Peer education:* The extent to which the children guide their friends on a learning subject.
- *Feedback:* the extent to which planned feedback is provided by the teacher to the child regarding the child's initiated activities; the extent to which children are asked by the teacher to give feedback to the child that guides the activity.
- *The manner of discourse:* the extent to which children participate naturally in meetings.
- *Philosophical discourse:* the topics that were developed from the children's theories which were then discussed in the kindergarten.

This hypothesis was affirmed by the data collected in the research.

Discussion of Finding 18 indicates that feedback emerges as a main component of the multi-dialogical kindergarten, and a significant difference was found between the reports of MDA teachers and reports of traditional teachers in the extent of feedback given by the teacher to the child and in the extent of feedback given by the child to other children. Explanation: Feedback seems to constitute a part of the dialog that is conducted according to the MDA and it is awarded an important position in the learning curriculum in the multi-dialogical kindergarten. The teacher allots time for it in the daily schedule and participates in the feedback circles taking place in the kindergarten, while she guides the group, constitutes a part of it and serves as a model for the children regarding how to provide feedback. Her role is to coach the children as to how to provide feedback to their friends, which words to use, when to talk and how to empower their friends, as part of the planned learning curriculum constructed by her. Feedback allows the children to learn to pay attention to others, to endorse each other and consequently to go deeper into their learning from each other. Moreover, children that learn to accept positive feedback from their friends develop learning patterns out of a sense of success and a pattern of reflective thinking. Contrastingly, the traditional approach also gives feedback to children, but not as part of the learning curriculum. It is more like "action-reaction" feedback, meaning that the child does something considered positive or negative and the teacher or another child reacts accordingly. Support for the MDA conceptualization in extant literature stresses the importance of allowing children to practice giving positive feedback, the rationale being that giving such feedback allows the child to learn out of success. The child, who guides an activity, can learn effectively from this so that the feedback can be a very powerful tool for the child's empowerment (Ben-Yosef, 2009). The teacher is part of the circle of feedback and also gives feedback to the child (Firstater & Efrat, 2014). It is noted that the feedback that the teacher gives to the child is not an attempt to evaluate the child's performance (Lasri, 2004). The feedback should focus on successes but not ignore difficulties (Ben-Yosef, 2009). This finding adds a practical facet to the views in professional literature indicating that the MDA aims to transform the children into partners, who are responsible for their learning in the kindergarten. They acquire the ability to initiate, plan and guide activities for all the children, while feedback constitutes an integral part of this activity since it is, in fact, part of the discourse circle (Firstater & Efrat, 2014). **Conclusion from this discussion: In the multi-dialogical kindergarten, the acquisition of social-communication patterns is shaped by feedback that helps to form patterns such as tolerance, empowerment, peer learning and reflective thinking. The quantitative findings support the qualitative findings on this matter. These patterns are acquired and formed through:**

- **Prior planning and structured and practical coaching of the children by the teacher who shows them how to practice these patterns.**
- **When learning, feedback is a planned part of the**

learning curriculum in the kindergarten and a planned part of the daily schedule.

- **Through the model that the teacher presents for the children when she is part of the feedback circle.**

Discussion of Finding 19: Significant differences were found in the level of the children's initiative, in the extent to which there is children's guidance of meetings and in the extent to which teacher-child meetings take place to plan activities between the reports of the MDA teachers and reports of the traditional teachers. Explanation: In a multi-dialogical kindergarten, the structured learning curriculum includes guidance of children by children and meetings between the teacher and the children to plan activities. The children's guidance of group meetings by children encourages and necessitates the child's initiative to propose a subject that they want to guide. It also necessitates prior planning of the subject expressed in a planning meeting with the teacher. Additionally, while the child guides the meeting, he/she, in fact, leads and guides the other children and thus, they practice and develop leadership skills. Contrastingly, in a traditional kindergarten, children's guidance of other children and meetings held to plan activities only happen occasionally and by chance and not as part of the structured learning curriculum. This finding is in line with professional literature that indicates how important it is to understand that the development of children's initiative and independence depends directly on their participation and involvement in decision-making processes relating to themselves and their daily schedule (Hill et al., 2004). This finding adds innovative knowledge to extant literature regarding children's social development in early childhood since it relates to children guiding other children, and the practical way in which planning meetings for these activities can be conducted with the early childhood child. **Conclusion from this discussion: Social-communication patterns of initiative, guidance, planning activities and leadership are acquired and shaped when there is structured and practical coaching for children preparing them to perform these**

skills as part of the structured learning curriculum in the kindergarten.

Discussion of Finding 20: Significant differences were found in the level of children's participation in their learning processes between the reports of the MDA teachers and reports of the traditional teachers. Explanation: This participation depends on the teacher's approach, to what extent the teacher facilitates this participation, whether the contents and what is done in their regard are based principally on her choices or on the children's areas of interest and initiatives. The children in a traditional kindergarten also participate in their learning processes, but since the contents and what is done with regard to them are mostly the result of the teacher's choices, the children's participation in the learning processes is less. Extant literature supports this finding indicating that children's participation in their activities and learning in the kindergarten allows them to accumulate personal experience in social abilities such as attentiveness and involvement, expressing a personal opinion, acquiring the ability to know how to share their experience with their friends, practicing decision-making in their daily life, ability to conduct negotiations, learning to wait for their turn in a dialog and how to share things with friends (Clark & Moss, 2005; Leinonen & Venninan, 2012; Venninen, Leinonen & Ojala, 2010). In this light it is noted that all children can, in fact, participate in their learning; this depends on the teacher's approach and the extent to which she is willing to allow this (Nyland, 2009). Additionally, it depends on the learning curriculum, which may simply be a set of facts that everyone must know with very little choice or which can become a genuine learning curriculum based on interest and investigation and relying on the child's strengths (Gardner, 1996). **Conclusion from this discussion: Social-communication patterns such as involvement, the ability to express oneself and to share experience and a personal opinion, ability to conduct negotiations, to share, and to make decisions are shaped and depend on the learning curriculum constructed in the kindergarten and on the extent of children's participation in its planning and in the learning in the kindergarten.**

Discussion of Finding 21 – Significant differences were found in relation to the manner of discourse in meetings between the reports of the MDA teachers and reports of the traditional teachers. Explanation: According to the MDA the discourse is led by the teacher and not managed by her. Such discourse encourages responsibility, trains children in group discourse and sharpens their attentiveness. In practice, the children do not raise their hands and wait for the teacher's permission to speak. They speak freely out of their attentiveness and learn when to enter into the discourse in an independent manner. The teacher coaches the children using structured practical rules which show them when to enter the discourse. In contrast, in the traditional approach the children raise their hands and the teacher manages the discussion and gives permission to speak. This finding is supported by the conceptualization of the philosopher, Buber that there are two situations in which man relates to his world: a situation of dialog expressed in the concept of "I-Thou", and a situation which is the opposite of dialog, which is expressed in the concept "I-It". In the situation of "I-Thou," a genuine dialog is conducted, an encounter between a person and the one who is met, each of the sides really focuses on the other, recognizing their existence and turning to them in order to form authentic mutual relations between them. From this dialog, real responsibility grows (Cohen, 1976; Friedman, 2002). In contrast, in the state of "I-It" there is no dialog, rather this is a conversation between people who do not really pay attention one to the other (Aloni, 2008; Buber, 1980; Friedman, 2002). It is important to note that it is impossible to force someone to conduct a dialog, the person does not have to enter into a dialog, but he can if he wants to, since dialog is open to all (Bartholo, Tunes & Tacca, 2010). **Conclusion from this discussion: In the multi-dialogical kindergarten social-communication patterns such as taking responsibility for the discourse, paying attention to others, and group discussion skills are shaped as a result of the manner of conversation in the meetings which are guided by the teacher, allowing the children to learn when to integrate within the discourse, and the children's contributions are not managed by the teacher.**

Discussion of Finding 22: Significant differences were found in the extent to which philosophical discourse is conducted in the kindergarten between the reports of the MDA teachers and reports of the traditional teachers. Explanation: According to the MDA, philosophical discourse is a structured part of the learning curriculum. Underpinning this type of discourse is the belief that there is no need to teach the children an opinion rather, they should be allowed to ask questions, to think about their own theories, to test them, to try to draw conclusions from this process and in this way to investigate and develop their thoughts. In contrast, in the traditional approach philosophical discourse only occurs occasionally and randomly and not as part of the structured learning curriculum. Extant theory supports the concept that philosophical discourse with children is not intended to teach the children philosophy, rather to encourage them to create their own philosophy that will be an interrogative, dynamic, testing, open, explorative and creative philosophy (Cohen 2008). Philosophical investigation is based and constructed on the children's natural curiosity and so it develops their ability to ask questions. In addition, it develops their social skills such as consideration and concern for others and the ability to conduct a genuine discourse out of attentiveness.

Despite different opinions concerning the age at which it is possible to take part in a philosophical discourse, it was found that kindergarten children are able to ask and deal with philosophical questions (Fisher, 2007). This conceptualization is supported by the Socratic theory that argues that discourse is conducted through questions and answers, examining both the questions and the answers and drawing conclusions from what can be understood from the answers (Tauber, 2008). The questions are not based on prior knowledge, and this enables participants to reveal far more about the world from the questions than from the answers (Cohen, 2008). The practice of this type of discourse allows the acquisition of tools that a person needs to make better decision-making, clarifying every subject and issue from different angles and allowing them to find different ways to examine each subject discussed. All the aspects discussed lead in the end to enrichment of the individual's ability to make decisions (Phillips,

2004). An additional facet of Socratic dialog is the understanding that "silence" represents strong power because it causes answers to emerge, challenges thinking and thus opens it up (Cohen, 2008). **Conclusion from this discussion: In the multi-dialogical kindergarten, social-communication patterns such as ability to ask questions, to test things from different angles, to draw conclusions and to make decisions, to consider others and to be attentive are shaped through philosophical discourse that is a structured part of the kindergarten's learning curriculum.**

Chapter 5

Conclusions

V.1 Preview

This chapter presents conclusions drawn from the discussion in Chapter IV, in response to the two research hypotheses regarding the differences between the MDA and the traditional approaches in kindergartens and regarding the influence of these approaches on kindergarten children's social-communication patterns. It then presents conceptual conclusions from the research findings, summarizing the unique contribution of these findings in an original theoretical model entitled "Opening the gate for social-communication patterns". This is followed by general conclusions including practical implications of the findings, and further discussion relating to the contribution of the research findings to the corpus of knowledge on the studied issues and the limitations of the present research, indicating possible new directions for investigation.

V.2 Conclusions regarding the differences between the MDA and the traditional kindergartens

Hypothesis 1: Differences will be found in social and communication patterns between children educated in multi-dialogical kindergartens and children educated in traditional kindergartens. Hypothesis 1 was confirmed.

In the multi-dialogical kindergarten, social-communication patterns are shaped through the teacher's "attentiveness", which enables the children's initiatives to come into expression, and these initiatives form the basis for the work and learning curricula in the kindergarten. Moreover, it seems that the children's attentiveness to their friends is a social-communication pattern that is acquired in the multi-dialogical kindergarten and receives an important place through the coaching and guidance of the teacher. The "active listening" that is exercised by the teacher and the children helps the children to develop additional patterns such as autonomy and empathy, so that in practice, it can be seen that taking responsibility for learning, decision-making abilities and cooperation are all acquired through the teacher's observation of the children's actions (through attentiveness and active listening). This observation is an additional way to pay attention to them.

More specifically, it is concluded that the way in which children are equipped with social-communication patterns depends on the teacher's approach that, unlike the approach of the teacher in the traditional kindergarten, facilitates the expression of the children's initiatives and fields of interest. The way to equip the children with social-communication patterns such as flexibility and thinking outside the box depends on the teacher's own ability to do this and thus to act as a "model". Moreover, patterns such as the children's desire to learn, learning in depth and the ability to ask questions are encouraged by the construction of a learning curriculum that will enable these patterns to be expressed out of the children's fields of interest.

V.3 Conclusions regarding the social-communication patterns

Hypothesis 2: Differences will be found mainly in the extent of participation by the children in their learning processes and in peer education: the extent to which the children guide their colleagues on a learning subject, the feedback, the manner of discourse, and the extent to which philosophical discourse is conducted. Hypothesis 2 was confirmed.

In a similar spirit, patterns of expertise, developing abilities, drawing conclusions, independent thinking and peer learning are shaped as implications of learning according to the MDA. The children's consideration of their friends, expression of their opinions and feelings in a group, identifying difficulties and strengths, and respecting the time needed for deep thinking are acquired through "mediated learning". The teacher coaches the children to use the tools of "giving and accepting feedback".

The fact that the children become active partners in the planning of the kindergarten life and the determination of its contents and play an active part in the kindergarten activities and events allows the children to become equal participants in their learning. Moreover, the teacher's use of "brainstorming" together with the children allows them to develop the ability to learn in a group, to express an opinion and to take responsibility for learning alongside the ability to be flexible in learning. This tool constitutes the basis for "negotiation" between the children and the teacher.

Social-communication patterns such as planning, initiative and thinking about additional directions of thought are connected to "dialog" conducted in the "personal meeting" between the teacher and a child in the multi-dialogical kindergarten. It can also be concluded that the patterns of guidance, leadership and leadership skills are imparted to the children when the children act as "guides for their friends" which is a unique pattern of behavior for children educated in the multi-dialogical kindergarten. Additionally, patterns such as the ability to discuss with attentiveness and tolerance towards others, avoiding judgment, while demonstrating restraint and accepting the opinions of others are derived from the practicing of discourse in general and "philosophical discourse" in particular.

The patterns of deep learning, illustration, cooperation, independence and acceptance of decisions in learning are shaped and acquired in the multi-dialogical kindergarten through the "mediation" of learning by the teacher and "documentation" by the teacher together with the children. Moreover, the children acquire life skills as a result of their involvement in the planning of the life of the kindergarten and the social interaction that this involvement offers. It, therefore, seems that the children's initiative, guidance, planning activities and leadership are evident when there is "structured practical coaching" for the children, showing them how to do this.

The children offer and receive "feedback" so that they play an authentic part in the communication. It seems that the feedback is an important component helping to equip the children in the multi-dialogical kindergarten with social-communication patterns such as tolerance, recognition of others, empowerment, peer education and reflective thinking. These patterns are acquired and shaped through prior planning and structured practical coaching for the children by the teacher showing them how to do these things. Additionally, the teacher represents a "model" for the children when she participates in the feedback circle, and feedback is also a planned part of the kindergarten learning curriculum and a planned part of the daily schedule. The manner of discourse involves the children's natural participation in the education process. It can be seen that social-communication patterns such as taking responsibility for discourse, paying attention to others and the skills of group discourse are shaped in the multi-dialogical kindergarten as a result of the manner of discourse in the meetings guided by the teacher and this enables the children to learn when to enter the discourse, and they are not managed by her. In their "philosophical discourse" the children propose particular topics to discuss in the kindergarten. Additionally, the ability to ask questions, to examine things from different angles, to draw conclusions and to make decisions, to consider others and to pay attention are realized through philosophical discourse that is a structured part of the learning curriculum in the multi-dialogical kindergarten.

V.4 Conceptual conclusions: Opening the gate for social-communication patterns

Figure IV.1: A theoretical model: "Wheels of Dialog"

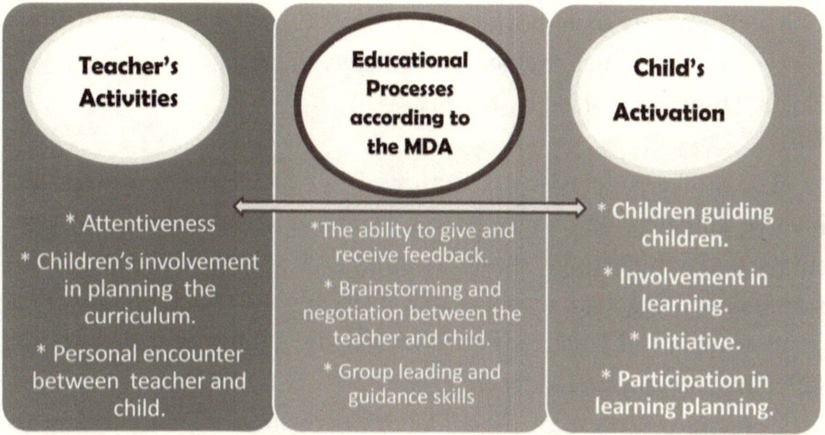

The conceptual conclusions from the research findings relate to education for early childhood. The conclusions derived from the research allowed the researcher to develop a theoretical model that explains the educational processes that advance children's social-communication processes in early childhood through the implementation of the MDA.

As can be seen from the model shown above there are three main dimensions involved in the implementation of the MDA in the kindergarten: *the teacher's activities, educational processes and the child's activation*. Sample components of these three dimensions are shown in the model.

In addition to the components shown in the diagram, *the teacher's activities* include the following components:

- The teacher's attentiveness

- Coaching and guidance
- Teacher's approachability
- Organization and time management
- Collegiality, group support and guidance
- Role modeling
- Children's involvement in planning the curriculum
- Children's participation in planning kindergarten life
- Personal encounters between teacher and child
- The ability to empower the child
- Structured and practical coaching by the teacher
- Discourse guided by teacher

The teacher's approach is expressed in *educational processes* that involve empathy, autonomy, active listening, collaboration and peer study, decision-making, ability to give and accept feedback, brainstorming and negotiations between the teacher and the child, as well as group leading and guidance skills, leadership abilities, discourse skills, reflective thinking and independence.

The entire process of the *children's activation* is connected in an optimal manner with the children's initiatives, so that they are able to take responsibility for their learning and to develop the ability to study in a group, the ability to ask questions, to draw conclusions, to think independently and to express emotions in a group. Other abilities developed by the children are the ability to take time to think, to converse, and to use in-depth learning, to conceptualize, to share experience and personal opinions and to examine things from different perspectives. It is possible to see how these processes lead the children to become involved in their learning and to develop a strong desire to learn, to be active in their learning, and to participate in learning planning. In this sense they are able to deal with difficulties and strengths, be flexible and open in their thinking, guide their friends, be attentive and tolerant to others, and practice restraint and acceptance.

To summarize: The model shows that the integration of the teacher's approach regarding the important place of the child as an active partner in the kindergarten and the reciprocity that is created between teacher and child engenders educational processes and that allow different strengths to be combined, in other words, a synergy is formed. The formation of this synergy enables the shaping and maximization of social-communication processes among children in early childhood.

V.5 General Conclusions

V.5.1 Practical implications

The practical implications of the research findings relate to four areas: implications for the kindergarten teacher's work, implications for teacher training programs, implications for the design of learning curricula for early childhood and implications for education policy for early childhood.

- Implications for the teacher's work – the teacher needs to increase her own awareness regarding the substance of attentiveness in the educational act, and to learn how to apply this at her own personal level and in the kindergarten.
- Implications for kindergarten teachers' training programs – A framework is needed for the teachers' professional development to focus on and develop expertise in education according to the MDA for early childhood.
- Implications for the design of learning curricula for early childhood – The conclusions from this study could inform those who draft curricula for early childhood and wish to incorporate the MDA into the learning curricula.
- Implications for education policies for early childhood – A change is needed in the perception of early childhood education to reduce the gap between the declared education policies of the Ministry of Education and extant practice as expressed in kindergartens.

V.6 Further discussion

V.6.1 Contribution to knowledge

The contribution of this study to the extant corpus of knowledge is expressed by filling the gap in knowledge in the domain of children's developmental psychology and by proposing a modular model, which explains the development of children's social-communication patterns in early childhood through the MDA in kindergartens. This model can be implemented in various ways. The findings draw on and add to Socratic theory, which argues that dialog is conducted through questions and answers, and to the "I-Thou" theory coined by Buber, to Dewey's theory of negotiation between the individual and society, to Roger's theory of "active listening", to the theory of equal discourse between learners and educators proposed by Freire, to Gardner's theory of multiple intelligences, to the theory of the "Zone of Proximal Development" of Vygotsky, and to Feuerstein's theory of "mediated learning" by combining the concepts of these different scholars into a single theoretical model that can be applied in educational practice. In other words, the theoretical model constructed in this research constitutes an integrative practical model for operation that can guide learning in a multi-dialogical kindergarten for early childhood. Moreover, since this model was developed by the researcher on the basis of the findings of the present study and stemmed from the field, it can be said that this is an original, innovative, evidence-based model based on data collected in the field.

The study's contribution to practical knowledge can be seen in the modular-adaptive nature of the model that allows various possible applications to be adapted to different learning approaches. It, therefore, seems that this unique model can provide guidelines for a kindergarten desiring to work according to the MDA. More specifically, it is noted that the approach that allows the kindergarten teacher to rely on attentiveness and that is accompanied by reflective educational processes is optimally connected to the children's acquisition and development of social-communication patterns that become tools for life.

An additional contribution to the gap in knowledge from the findings of the present study relates to knowledge that can inform and stimulate a change in educational policy for early childhood and in the training of educators for early childhood. This is so because the implementation of the model that was constructed from the research findings could reduce the gap between goals and aims of education in general and education for early childhood in particular as they are shaped and declared by the Ministry of Education and the practical implementation of these goals in the field by kindergarten teachers. In other words, the model can facilitate the reduction of the gap between the aforesaid declarations and practice in the field by stimulating a change in perception by field practitioners, i.e., the kindergarten teachers, supervisors and mentors for the kindergartens. In addition, the model may have an influence on perceptions of training for early childhood education through the adoption of the principles of the MDA in kindergartens, the opening of a special course in frameworks for early childhood and the development of settings for professional development of early childhood practitioners (kindergarten teachers, supervisors and mentors for the kindergartens) according to the MDA.

V.6.2 Limitations of the research

It is accepted that there is no perfect academic research. When discussing the limitations of a study, four elements are usually discussed: the research method, research tools, the researcher and the generalizability of the study. The following limitations should therefore be noted with regard to the present study:

1. Limitations associated with the research tools – this study employed filmed and transcribed participatory structured observations, semi-structured interviews and closed-ended questionnaires. In the participatory observations, the fact that the researcher was present in the field could influence the behavior of the research participants. However, the many hours of filming and observation meant that the participants became used to the presence of the researcher and the camera and consequently ignored them.

2. No limitations arose regarding the data collected by the questionnaires in the present study since the questionnaire was composed in reliance on data collected from the qualitative stage in order to ensure the validity of the questionnaires.
3. Limitations relating to generalizability. This research had no such limitations since the researcher used triangulation as a strategy, so that the findings are strong and can be generalized at a high level.

To summarize: the present mixed methods study used triangulation as a strategy to reinforce the findings and to increase the level of generalizability, and so the study can claim a high level of generalizability.

V.6.3 New directions for investigation

The study reported here indicates that the implementation of MDA educational processes can promote children's social-communication patterns in early childhood. It is suggested that future studies should investigate different ways to implement the MDA in a large number of kindergartens. Additionally, it would be useful to examine what the kindergarten teachers and education systems employing this approach need in terms of human resources and strategies in order to implement the MDA in kindergartens.

References

Alexander, R., 2006. *Towards dialogic teaching: Rethinking classroom talk,* 3rd ed. Cambridge: Dialogos.

Aliakbari, M. & Faraji, E., 2011. Basic principles of critical pedagogy. In *2nd International Conference on Humanities, Historical and Social Sciences IPEDR*, 17, pp. 78-85.

Aloni, N., 2008. Introduction. In N. Aloni, ed. *Empowering dialogues in humanist education.* Tel Aviv: Hadekel. pp. 16-47. [Hebrew]

Aloni, N., 2013. Philosophical-educational empowerment for students in the 21st century. *Gilui Dea*, 3, pp. 13-30. [Hebrew]

Alpert, B., 2011. From qualitative research to high quality writing: Interest, investigation and creativity. MOFET Institution: *Shvilei Mehkar,* 17, 114-150. [Hebrew]

Anderson, R. & Cissna, K. N., 1997. *The Martin Buber Carl Rogers dialogue. A new transcript with commentary.* Albany, State University of New York Press.

Aram, D. & Shlak, M., 2007. The safe kindergarten: Promotion of communication and social skills among kindergartners. *Early Education and Development,* 19, pp. 865-884.

Ares, N., 2006, Political aims and classroom dynamics: Generative processes in classroom communities. *Radical Pedagogy*, 8 (2), pp. 12-20.

Arner, E. & Tellgren, B., 1998. Children's views of adults – the meaning of conversation to find and understand children's perspective. *Poang I Pedagogic, Pedagogiska institutionen, Orebro Universitet*, pp. 61-80.

Ashkenazi, M., 1986. *Research methods in social sciences: Research principles and styles.* Unit 4, Ethnographic Research in Anthropology. Ramat Aviv: Open University. [Hebrew]

Aspan, M., 2005. *To do oneself justice: Children's and adults' perspective of a school project to increase pupils' influence*. Stockholm, Utvecklingspsykologiska seminariet, Stockholms universitet.

Assaf, M., 2011. Can the wolf lie down with the sheep?: About mixing methods from different approaches in educational research. *Kolot*, 1, 17-19. [Hebrew]

Astington, W. & Jenkins, J. M., 1995. Theory of mind development and social understanding. *Cognition and Emotion,* 9, pp. 151-165.

Avnon, D., 2008. The Buberian dialogue: Personal meetings, humanistic learning. In N. Aloni, (Ed.) *Empowering dialogues in humanist education*. Tel Aviv: Hadekel, pp. 143-156. [Hebrew]

Bae, B., 2009. Children's right to participate – challenges in everyday interactions. *European Early Childhood Education Research Journal,* 17, pp. 391–406.

Bakhtin, M. M., 1984. *Problems of Dostoevsky's Poetics*. Manchester: Manchester University Press.

Baniwal, V., 2014. A response to Jane Sahi's 'Dialogue as Education: Martin Buber. *Contemporary Education Dialogue,* 11, pp. 179–195

Barnett, R., 2007. *A will to learn: Being a student in an age of uncertainty*. Open University Press.

Bartholo, R., Tunes, E. & Tacca, M. C. V. R., 2010. Vygotsky's and Buber's pedagogical perspectives: Some affinities. *Educational Philosophy and Theory*, 42(8), pp. 867–880.

Becker, E., 2009. *Who did you play with in kindergarten today: The social world of pre-school children.* Tel Aviv: Research and Curriculum Development, Mofet. [Hebrew]

Bengtsson, J., 2005. *The life-world as a foundation.* Lund, Studentlittertur.

Ben-Yosef, A., 2009. *Circles of connection: Concerning the fostering of a discourse culture in a humanistic educational institute.* Rannana: MOFET Institute. [Hebrew]

Berk, L. & Winsler, A., 1995. *Scaffolding children's learning: Vygotsky and early childhood education.* Washington, DC, National Association for the Education of Young Children.

Berthelsen, D., 2009. Participatory learning: Issues for research and practice. In D.

Berthelsen, J. Brownlee & E. Johansson (Eds.), *Participatory learning in the early years: research and pedagogy*, London, Routledge, pp. 1-11.

Blum-Kulka, S., 2008. Language, communication and literacy: Outlines for the development of literate discourse. In P.S. Klein and B. Yablon, eds., *From research to action in early childhood education* (pp. 117-154). Jerusalem: Keter.

Bocos, M., 2007. *The theory and praxis of pedagogical research. [Teoria şi practica cercetării pedagogice].* (in Romanian), Cluj-Napoca, Editura Casa Cărţii de Ştiinţă.

Bodrova, E. & Leong, D., 2005. Why children need play. *Scholastic Early Childhood Today,* 20, pp. 1-6.

Bodrova, E. & Leong, D. J., 2007. *Tools of the mind. The Vygotskian approach to early childhood education.* New Jersey, Pearson.

Bowman, B. T. & Donovan, M. S., 2001. *Eager to learn.* Washington D.C., National Academy Press.

Boyd, M. & Galda, L., 2011. *Real talk in elementary classrooms: Effective oral language practice.* New York, NY, Guilford Press.

Boyd, M. & Markarian, W., 2011. Dialogic teaching: Talk in service of a dialogic stance. *Language and Education,* 25(6), pp. 515-534.

Bradburn, N., Sudman, S. & Wansink, B., 2004. *Asking questions.* San Francisco, CA: Jossey Bass.

Bruner, J., 1996. *The culture of education.* Cambridge, MA, Harvard University Press.

Bryman, A., 2001. *Social research methods.* Oxford: Oxford University Press.

Bryman, A., 2004. *Social research methods.* NY: Oxford.

Buber, M., 1980. *Secret discourse.* Jerusalem: Bialik. [Hebrew]

Buber, M., 2002. *Between man and man.* New York, Routledge.

Buchs, C., Butera, F. & Mugny, G., 2004. Resource interdependence, student interactions and performance in cooperative learning, *Educational Psychology,* 24, pp. 291-314.

Callander, D., 2013. *Dialogic approaches to teaching and learning in the primary grades.* Doctoral dissertation, University of Victoria.

Campbell, S. B., 2002. *Behaviour problems in preschool children.* New York, Guilford Press.

Carpendale, J. I. M. & Lewis, C., 2004. Constructing an understanding of mind: The development of children's social understanding within social interaction. *Behavioural and Brain Sciences,* 27, pp. 79–151.

Caspi, M., 1979. *Education tomorrow.* Tel Aviv: Am Oved. [Hebrew]

Ciot, M. G., 2009. A constructivist approach to educational action's structure. *Bulletin of University of Agricultural Sciences and Veterinary Medicine (BUASVM) Cluj-Napoca Horticulture*, 66(2), pp. 1-6.

Clark, A. & Moss, P., 2005. *Spaces to play: more listening to young children using the Mosaic approach.* London, National Children's Bureau.

Claudie, T., 2012. Emphasizing the importance of early childhood education at the beginning of the 21st century: opportunities, risks and dilemmas in long-term strategic planning or implementation of the "here and now"? *Journal of the MOFET Institute,* 47, pp. 25-31.

Claxton, G. & Carr, M., 2010. A framework for teaching learning: The dynamics of Disposition. *Early Years: An International Research Journal,* 24(1), pp. 87-97.

Cohen, A., 1976. *The educational theory of Martin Buber.* Tel Aviv: Yahadav. [Hebrew]

Cohen, A., 1983. *A revolution in education*. Tel Aviv: Reshafim. [Hebrew]

Cohen, A., 2008. *Small philosophers, philosophy for children and with children*. Haifa: Amatzia. [Hebrew]

Cohen, I., 2001. Value-oriented experiences in Jewish philosophical literature. In I. Baruch, S. Iram, I Skolnikov, Cohen, I. & Shechter, A. , eds., *Crossroads – Values and education in Israeli society*. Jerusalem: Ministry of Education and Culture, pp. 39-68. [Hebrew]

Cohen, P. A., Kulik, J. A. & Kulik, C. C., 1982. Educational outcomes of tutoring: A meta-analysis of findings. *American Educational Research Journal,* 19, pp. 237-248.

Council of Europe, 2011. *Consultation on the draft Council of Europe Strategy on the Rights of the Child.* Strasbourg, 20 July 2011.

Cohen, L., Manion, L. & Morrison, K., 2007. *Research methods in education.* 6th ed. London: Routledge Falmer.

Cornu, R. L. & Peters, J., 2005. Towards constructivist classroom: the role of the reflective teacher. *Journal of Educational Inquiry,* 6(1), pp. 50-64.

Creswell, J. W., 2013. *Research design: Qualitative, quantitative, and mixed methods approaches*. UK: Sage publications.

Creswell, J. W. & Plano Clark, V. L., 2011. Designing and conducting mixed-methods research. Thousand Oaks, CA: Sage Publications, Inc.

Creswell, J. W., Plano-Clark, V. L., Gutmann, M. L. & Hanson, W. E., 2003. 'Advanced mixed-methods research designs', In A.Tashakkori and C.Teddlie (Eds.), *Handbook of mixed-methods in social and behavioral research,* Thousand Oaks, CA: Sage, 209–240.

Danner, S. & Jonyniene, Z., 2012. Participation of children in democratic decision-making in kindergarten: Experiences in Germany and Lithuania. *Socialinis Darbas/Social Work*, 11, pp. 411-420.

Darom, D., 1989. *Climate of growth, liberty and commitment in education*. Tel Aviv: Hakibbutz Haartzi. [Hebrew]

Denzin, N. K. & Lincoln, Y. S., 2000. Introduction: The discipline and practice of qualitative research. In N.K. Denzin and Y.S. Lincoln, eds. *Handbook of qualitative research,* 2nd ed. London: Sage Publications, 1-28.

De Souza, L. M., Nakano, F., De Bragança Pereira, C. A. & Stern, J. M., 2012. Intentional sampling by goal optimization with decoupling by stochastic perturbation. *AIP Conference Proceedings*, 1490, 189-201.

Dewey, J., 1938. *Experience and education.* New York: Macmillan

Dewey, J., 1956. *The child and the curriculum and the school and society.* Chicago, Phoenix

Dewey, J., 1961. *Democracy and education* (1916). New York: Macmillan

Dewey, J., 1988. *The ethics of democracy*. University of Michigan, Philosophical Papers, Second Series, No. 1, Ann Arbor: Andrews and Com.

Dewey, J., 1997. *Experience and education*. NY: Touchstone Book.

Dey, I., 1993. *Qualitative data analysis.* London: Routledge.

Dheram, P., 2007. Empowerment through critical pedagogy. *Academic Leadership*, 5(2).

Dushenik, L. & Sabar Ben-Yehoshua, N., 2002. Ethics of qualitative research, In N. Sabar Ben-Yehoshua (Ed.), *Traditions and genres in qualitative research.* Or Yehuda: Dvir, pp. 343-368. [Hebrew]

Edwards, C., Gandini, L. & Forman, G., 1998. Introduction: Background and starting points, In C. Edwards & L. Gandini & G. Forman (Eds.), *The hundred languages of children: The Reggio Emilia approach- advanced reflections,* London, Ablex, pp.5-25.

Efrat, M. & Ungureanu, D., 2015. Is the egg spoiled? A big question from a small child. *Proceeding of the International Conference on Education Reflection and Development*. Romania: Cluj-Napoca, pp. 294-312.

Egan, K., 1992. *Imagination in teaching and learning.* New York, Routledge.

Ekholm, M. & Lindvall, K., 1991. Pupils and democracy in school, Forskningsrapport, 91, 6, Hogskolan i Karlstad.

Emilson, A., 2007. Young children's influence in preschool. *International Journal of Early Childhood,* 39, pp. 11-38.

Emilson, A. & Folkesson, A. M., 2006. Children's participation and teacher control. *Early Child Development and Care,* 176(3-4), pp. 219-38.

Emilson, A. & Johansson, E., 2009. The Desirable toddler in preschool: Values communicated in teacher and child interactions. In D. Berthelsen, J. Brownlee & E. Johansson (Eds.), *Participatory learning in the early years: research and pedagogy,* London, Routledge, pp. 61-77.

Erhardt-Weiss, D., 2008. Independence and selfhood: parents, children and the development of autonomy in early childhood. *Psychoactuality – A Spotlight on Developmental Psychology,* July 2008. 28-33. [Hebrew]

Feld-Elhanan, N., 2007. When the other is invisible, unheard and unrecognized. From education as friendship and as culture for teaching and as accessible and inclusive: Some examples from discourse with immigrant children. *Bemiclala,* 19, pp. 39-76. [Hebrew]

Fetters, M. D., Curry, L. A. & Creswell, J. W., 2013. Achieving integration in mixed-methods designs - principles and practices. *Health services research,* 48(2-6), 2134-2156.

Feuerstein, R., Klein, P. S. & Tennenbaum, A., 1991. *Mediated Learning Experience (M.L.E)*. London Freund Pub., House.

Fiore, L. & Rosenquest, B., 2010. Shifting the culture of higher education: Influences on students, teachers, and pedagogy. *Theory into Practice*, 49(1), pp. 14-20.

Fiore, L. & Suares, S.C., 2010. This issue. *Theory into Practice*, 49(1), pp. 1-4.

Firestone, W.A., 1993. Alternative arguments for generalizing from data as applied to qualitative research. *Educational Researcher.* 22(4) 16-23.

Firstater, E. & Efrat, M., (2014). Social communication patters of children in a kindergarten operating according to the dialogical education approach. *Rav Gvanim, Research and Discourse,* 14, pp. 11-48. Under the auspices of "Study and Research in Teacher Training", Jerusalem: Ministry of Education and Gordon Academic College of Education. [Hebrew]

Fisher, R., 2007. Dialogic teaching: developing thinking and metacognition through philosophical discussion. *Early Child Development and Care,* 177, pp. 615–631.

Flick, U., 2009. *An introduction to qualitative research.* London: Sage Publications.

Foley, P., 2007. A case for and of critical pedagogy: Meeting the challenge of libratory education at Gallaudet University. Paper Presented at the *American Communication Association's Annual Conference*. New Mexico, Taos.

Forman, G. & Fyfe, B., 1998. Negotiated learning through design, documentation, and discourse. In C. Edwards & L. Gandini & G. Formaneds. *The hundred languages of children: The Reggio Emilia approach- advanced reflections*, London: Ablex, pp. 239-260.

Freire, P. (2000). *Pedagogy of the oppressed.* London: Bloomsbury Publishing.

Freire, P. & Freire, A. M. A. (2004). *EPZ pedagogy of hope: Reliving pedagogy of the oppressed.* London: Bloomsbury Publishing.

French, G., 2007. *Children's early learning and development: A research paper.* Dublin: National Council for Curriculum and Assessment (NCCA).

Friedman, M. S., 2002. *Martin Buber: The life of dialogue*. London and New York: Psychology Press.

Fuchs, D., Fuchs, L. S., Mathes, P. G. & Simmons, D. C., 1997. Peer-assisted learning strategies: Making classrooms more responsive to diversity. *American Educational Research Journal,* 34, pp. 174–206.

Fumoto, H., 2011. Teacher–child relationships and early childhood practice. *Early Years,* 31, pp. 19-30.

Fumoto, H., Hargreaves, D. J. & Maxwell, S., 2004. The concept of teaching: A reappraisal. *Early Years,* 24(2), pp. 179-91.

Gardner, H., 1996. *Multiple intelligences theory in practice.* Jerusalem: Branko Weiss Institute. [Hebrew]

Gardner, H., 2011. *Frames of mind: The theory of multiple intelligences*. Basic books.

Gee, J., 1989. Literacy, discourse, and linguistics: Introduction. *Journal of Education,* 171(1), pp. 5-17.

Geertz, C., 1973. Thick description: Toward an interpretive theory of culture', In C. Geertz, *The interpretation of cultures.* New York: Basic Books.

Gibton, D., 2002. Field grounded theory: Meaning of the data analysis process and construction of theory in qualitative research. In N. Sabar Ben-Yehoshua, ed. *Traditions and genres in qualitative research.* Or Yehuda: Dvir, pp. 195-227. [Hebrew]

Gidron, A., 2011. Between qualitative and quantitative or how to define the research in which you are involved. *Kolot*, 1, 15-16. [Hebrew]

Given, H., Kuh, L., Leekeenan, D., Mardell, B., Redditt, S. & Twombly, S., 2010. Changing school culture: Using documentation to support collaborative inquiry. *Theory into Practice*, 49(1), pp. 36-46.

Goldstein, K. S., 1964. *A guide for field workers in folklore*. Hatsboro, PA: The American Folklore Society.

Gover, N., 2008. The Freirian dialogue: Empowerment, liberation, political literacy and social solidarity. In N. Aloni, ed. *Empowering dialogues in humanist education.* Tel Aviv: Hadekel. pp.195-213. [Hebrew]

Greene, M., 1995. *Releasing the imagination.* San Francisco: Jossey-Bass.

Guba, E. G. & Lincoln, Y. S., 1994. Competing paradigms in qualitative research, In N. K. Denzin and Y. S. Lincoln eds. *Handbook of qualitative research.* Thousands Oaks, CA: Sage, 105-117.

Guberman, O., 2009. Helping hand – training kindergarten assistants. Evaluation research. *Hed Hagan*, Quarterly Journal for Early Childhood Education, 14-23. [Hebrew]

Gur, H., 2007. A decade after the death of Paulo Freier, Pedagogy of hope – Dialogical teaching. *Hed Hahinuch,* 81(9), 93-95. [Hebrew]

Gutierrez, K. & Larson, J., 1995. Script, counterscript, and underlife in the classroom: James Brown versus Brown V. Board of Education. *Harvard Educational Review,* 65 (3), pp. 445-71

Han, H. S. & Kemple, K. M., 2006. Components of social competence and strategies of support: Considering what to teach and how. *Early Childhood Education Journal,* 34(3), pp. 241-246.

Harari, D., 2008. The Rogerian dialogue: To enable, to accept, to foster. In N. Aloni, ed. *Empowering dialogues in humanist education.* Tel Aviv: Hadekel. pp. 178-194. [Hebrew]

Harcourt, D., 2011. An encounter with children: Seeking meaning and understanding about childhood. In D. Harcourt & J. Eiransdottir (Eds), *Children in research: Special Issue.* European Early Childhood Research Journal, 19(3), pp. 333-345.

Harpaz, Y., 2014. Shapers of educational discourse – Pessy Sahlberg. *Hed Hakhinuch*, 6, pp. 50-55. [Hebrew]

Hecht, I. & Ram, A., 2008. The dialogue in democratic education: From personal empowerment to social activism. In N. Aloni, ed., *Empowering dialogue in humanist education* (pp. 336-257). Tel Aviv: Hadekel. [Hebrew]

Hill, M., Davis, J., Prout, A. & Tisdall, K., 2004. Moving the participation forward. *Children and Society,* 18(2), pp. 77–96.

Hobson, R. P., 2002. *The cradle of thought: Exploring the origins of thinking.* London: Macmillan.

Hockings, P., (ed.), 1995. *Principles of visual anthropology*. 2nd ed. Berlin: Mounton de Gruyter.

Holt, G., 2004. *Continual learning*. Tel Aviv: Prague. [Hebrew]

Howe, K. R., 1988. Against the quantitative-qualitative incompatibility thesis or dogmas die hard. *Educational Researcher,* 17(8), 10-16.

Howe, K. R. & Dougherty, K.C., 1993. Ethics, institutional review boards and the changing face of educational research. *Educational Researcher*, 22 (9), 16-21.

Inan, H. Z., 2009. Science education in preschool: How to assimilate the Reggio Emilia pedagogy in a Turkish preschool. *Asia-Pacific Forum on Science Learning & Teaching,* 10(2), pp. 1-11.

Isman, E. B. & Tzuriel, D., 2008. The Mediated Learning Experience (MLE) in a three generational perspective. *The British Psychological Society,* 26, pp. 545–560.

Jewitt, C., 2008. Multimodality and literacy in school classrooms. *Review of Research in Education,* 32(1), pp. 241-267.

Jhong, S. O., 2008. Children's dialogue: A hermeneutic phenomenological approach. *International Journal of Education through art,* 4(1), pp. 75-81.

Johansson, E., 2003. To come close to the child's perspective. *Pedagogisk forskning,* 8(1-2), pp. 42-57.

Johansson, E., 2004. Learning encounters in preschool: Interaction between atmosphere, view of children and of learning. *International Journal of Early Childhood,* 36 (2), pp. 9-26.

Johnson, D. W. & Johnson, R. T., 1986. *Learning together and alone,* 2nd ed. Englewood Cliffs, NJ, Prentice Hall.

Jones, D., 2007. Speaking, listening, planning and assessing: The teacher's role in developing metacognitive awareness. *Early Child Development and Care,* 177 (6-7), pp. 569-579.

Kassen, L. & Krumer-Nevo, M., 2010. *Data analysis in qualitative research.* Beer Sheva: Ben Gurion University of the Negev. [Hebrew]

Kincheloe, J. L., 2005. *Critical pedagogy primer.* New York, NY: Peter Lang Publishing.

Kirk, J. & Miller, M. L., 1986. *Reliability and validity in qualitative research.* Beverley Hills: Sage Publications.

Klein, P., 1986. *A wiser child.* Tel Aviv, Bar Ilan. [Hebrew]

Klein, P. & Yablon Y., 2007. *From research to practice in early childhood education.* Jerusalem: National Israeli Academy of the Sciences. [Hebrew]

Kohn, A., 2002. *Education that our children deserve.* Tel Aviv: Sifriat Poalim and Kibbutz Meuhad. [Hebrew]

Kozulin, A. (2004). Vygotsky's theory in the classroom: Introduetion. European Journal of Psychology of Education, XIX(1),3-7.

Kress, G., 2007. Thinking about meaning and learning in a world of instability and multiplicity. *Pedagogies: An International Journal,* 2(1), pp. 19-34.

Lam, Z., 1996. The concept of pluralism and its implementation in Israeli education. In A.G. Zeev, ed. *Education in the era of postmodernist discourse.* Jerusalem: Magnes, pp. 207-219. [Hebrew]

Lansdown, G., 2001. *Promoting children's participation in democratic decision-making.* Florence.

Lasri, D., 2004. *A place to grow.* Rosh Pinna: Haofen Tivai. [Hebrew]

Lavie-Ajayi, M., 2013. Qualitative research in educational psychology: A tool for everyday observation with new eyes. In *Observation of the work of the educational psychology services in light of principles of qualitative research.* Jerusalem: Ministry of Education, Education Unit, Education Psychology Services, 9-14. [Hebrew]

Leinonen, J. & Venninen, T., 2012. Designing learning experiences together with children. *Procedia-Social and Behavioural Sciences*, 45, pp. 466-474.

Levine, G., 1989. *Another kindergarten*. Tel Aviv: Ach. [Hebrew]

Lincoln, Y. S. & Guba, E. G., 1985. *Naturalistic inquiry.* Beverly Hills, CA: Sage Publications.

Lincoln, Y. S. & Guba, E. G., 1986. But is it rigorous? Trustworthiness and authenticity in naturalistic evaluation. In D. D. Williams, ed. *Naturalistic evaluation,* San Francisco, CA, Jossey-Bass, pp. 73-84.

Lincoln, Y. S. & Guba, E. G., 2000. Paradigmatic controversies, contradictions, and emerging confluences. In N. K. Denzin and S. L. Lincoln (Eds.), *Handbook of qualitative research.* 2nd ed. London, Sage Publications, 163-188.

Lipman, M., 2003. *Thinking in education.* Cambridge, Cambridge University Press.

Lipman, M. & Sharp, A. M., 1985. *Ethical inquiry: International Manual to accompany 'Lisa', Montclair.* N.J., Institute for the Advancement of Philosophy for Children.

Lopez, M., Tarullo, L., Forness, S. & Boyce, C., 2000. Early identification and intervention: Head start's response to mental health challenges. *Early Education and Development*, 11, pp. 265–282.

Lyle, S., 2008. Dialogic teaching: Discussing theoretical contexts and reviewing evidence from classroom practice. *Language and Education,* 22, pp. 222-240.

Mack, N., Woodsong, C., MacQueen, K. M., Guest, G. & Namey, E., 2005. *Qualitative research methods: A data collector's field guide*. Research Triangle Park, NC: Family Health International and US Agency for International Development.

Malaguzzi, L., 1998. History, ideas, and basic philosophy: An interview with Lella Gandini, In C. Edwards & L. Gandini & G. Forman (Eds.), *The hundred languages of children: The Reggio Emilia approach- advanced reflections,* London: Ablex, pp.49-99.

Mason, J., 1996. *Qualitative researching.* London: Sage Publications.

Mathes, P. G., Howard, J. K., Allen, S. H. & Fuchs, D., 1998. Peer-assisted learning strategies for first-grade readers: Responding to the needs of diverse learners. *Reading Research Quarterly,* 33, pp. 62-94.

Maykut, P. & Morehouse, R., 1994. *Beginning qualitative research: A philosophic and practical guide.* London: The Falmer Press.

McLean, V. S., 1991. *The human encounter: Teachers and children living together in preschools.* London, New York: Falmer Press.

Mercer, N. & Dawes, L., 2010. Making the most of talk: Dialogue in the classroom. *English Drama Media,* 16, pp. 19-25.

Mercer, N. & Littleton, K., 2007. *Dialogue and the development of children's thinking: A sociocultural approach.* New York, NY: Routledge.

Merriam, S. B., 1998. *Qualitative research and case study applications in education.* San Francisco: Jossey-Bass Publishers.

Merrick, E., 1999. An exploration of quality in qualitative research. In M. Kopala & L. A. Suzuki, eds. *Using qualitative methods in psychology,* London: Sage Publications, pp. 25-36.

Miller, J., 1997. *Never too young: how young children can take responsibility and make decisions.* London: National Early Years Network/Save the Children.

Ministry of Education (20.08.2001). *The role of the assistant in the kindergarten*. Circular 746ESHb. Israel: Ministry of Education, Pedagogic Administration, Department of Pre-school Education. [Hebrew]

Ministry of Education, 2010. *Guidelines for educational work in kindergartens.* Jerusalem: Department for Pre-Primary Education, Ministry of Education. [Hebrew]

Ministry of Education., 2015a. *The goal of state education.* Available at: http://edu.gov.il/owlHeb/AboutUs/MinisterEducation/EducationLaws/Pages/public-education.aspx/ [Hebrew]

Ministry of Education., 2015b. *Files for planning, management and organization.* Jerusalem: The Pedagogic Administration, Ministry of Education. [Hebrew]

Missall, K. N. & Hojnoski, R. L., 2008. The critical nature of young children's emerging peer-related social competence for transition to school. In W. H. Brown, S. L. Odom & S. R. McConnell (Eds.), *Social competence of young children: Risk, disability, and intervention,* Baltimore, MD, Brookes, pp. 117–137.

Muijs, D., 2010. *Doing quantitative research in education with SPSS*. London: Sage.

Mullender, A. & Ward, D., 1991. The practice principles of self-directed group work: Establishing a value-base for empowerment. Nottingham: The Center for Social Action.

Murphy, T., 2010. Conversations on engaged pedagogies, independent thinking skills and active citizenship. *Issues in Educational Research, 20*(1), pp. 39-46

New, R. S., 1998. Theory and praxis in Reggio Emilia: They know what they are doing, and why. In C. Edwards & L. Gandini & G. Forman (Eds.), *The hundred languages of children: The Reggio Emilia approach- advanced reflections,* London: Ablex, pp.261-284.

Nyland, B., 2009. The guiding principles of participation. Infant, toddler groups and the United Nations convention on the rights of the child. In D. Berthelsen, J. Brownlee & E. Johansson (Eds.), *Participatory learning in the early years: Research and pedagogy,* London: Routledge, pp.164 184.

Nystrand, M., Gamoran, A., Kachur, R. & Prendergast, C., 1997. *Opening dialogue: Understanding the dynamics of language and learning in the English classroom.* New York: Teachers College Press.

O'Connor, C. & Michaels, S., 2007. When is dialogue 'dialogic'? *Human Development,* 50, pp. 275-285.

Odom, S. L., McConnell, S. R. & Brown, W. H., 2008. Social competence of young children: Conceptualization, assessment, and influences. In W. H. Brown, S. L. Odom & S. R. McConnell (Eds.),

Social competence of young children: Risk, disability, and intervention, Baltimore, MD: Brookes, pp. 3–29.

Ohara, Y., Saft, S. & Crookes, G., 2000. *Teacher exploration of feminist critical pedagogy in beginning Japanese as a foreign language class*. Paper presented at the University of Hawai, Manoa.

Ojala, M., 2010. Developing multicultural early childhood education in a Finnish context. International. *Journal of Child Care and Policy*, 4, 1, pp. 13-22.

Okazaki, T., 2005. Critical consciousness and critical language teaching. *Second Language Studies*, 23(2), pp. 174-202.

Palgi, M., 2008. Introduction: Changes occurring in the kibbutz. In M. Peleg and D. Zamir, eds. *From a welfare state to a market society: Economic distress in the kibbutz.* Haifa: University of Haifa and Van Leer Institute in collaboration with the Institute for the Study of the Kibbutz and the Cooperative Concept, pp. 7-13. [Hebrew]

Palinscar, A. S., 1998. Social constructivist perspectives on teaching and learning. *Annual Review of Psychology,* 49, pp. 345-375.

Patton, M. Q., 1980. *Qualitative evaluation methods*. Beverley Hills: Sage Publications.

Phillips, C., 2004. *Six questions of Socrates*. N.Y.: Norton and Com.

Pianta, R. C., LaParo, K. M. & Hamre, B. K., 2008. *Classroom assessment scoring system*. Baltimore: Paul Brooks Publishing Co. Inc.

Peshkin, A., 1993. The goodness of qualitative research. *Educational Researcher,* 22(2), 23-29.

Pidgeon, N., 1996. Grounded theory: Theoretical background. In J. T. R. Richardson, eds. *Handbook of qualitative research methods,* Leicester: The British Psychological Society Books, 75-85.

Pidgeon, N. & Henwood, K., 1996. Grounded theory: Practical implementation. In J. E. Richardson, ed. *Handbook of qualitative research methods for psychology and the social sciences.* Leicester: British Psychological Society.

Polanyi, M., 1967. *The tacit dimension*. Chicago: The University of Chicago Press.

Pramling-Samuelsson, I. & Sheridan, S., 2003. Participation as value and pedagogic approach. *Pedagogisk forskning i Sverige,* 8(1–2.), pp. 70-84.

Rahim, S. N. F. B. A. & Rahman N. S. N.A., 2013. Children interaction patterns exhibited during learning activities: a case study at a selected public kindergarten in Malaysia. *Proceedings of the International Conference on Social Science Research*, pp. 1389-1411.

Raphaeli, V., 2011. Between quantitative and qualitative or the connection between the student's absence and success in studies. *Kolot,* 1, 11-14.

Reed, R. F. & Johnson, T. W., 1999. *Friendship and moral education - Twin pillars of philosophy for children*. N.Y.: Peter Lang.

Renninger, A., 1992. Individual interest and development: Implementation of theory and practice. In K. A. Renninger, S. Hidi & A. Krapp, eds., *The role of interest in learning and development,* Hillsdale, NJ: Earlbaum Associates, pp. 361-397.

Retting, M., 2005. Using the multiple intelligences to enhance instruction for young children and young children with disabilities. *Early Childhood Education Journal*, 32, pp. 255-259

Rhedding-Jones, J., Bae, B. & Winger, N., 2008. Young children and voice. In P. Hughes, G. Mac-Naughton & K. Smith (Eds.), *Young children as active citizens: Principles, policies and pedagogies*, London and New York, Cambridge University Press, pp. 44-59.

Rinaldi, C., 1996. Malaguzzi and the teachers. *Innovations in Early Education: The International Reggio Exchange,* 3(4), pp. 1-3.

Rinaldi, C., 1999. Overt attention. *Hed Hagan*, Kislev, 5760, 7-9. [Hebrew]

Rinaldi, C., 2005. Documentation and assessment: What is the relationship? In A. Clark, A. Kjørholt & P. Moss, eds. *Beyond listening: Children's perspectives on early childhood services*, Bristol, Policy Press, pp. 17–28.

Rinaldi, C., 2006. In *dialogue with Reggio Emilia.* London, Routledge.

Rogers, C. R. & Freiberg, H. J. 1994, *Freedom to Learn.* Columbus, OH, Charles Merrill Publishing Company.

Rogoff, B., Turkanis, C. G. & Bartlett, L., 2001. *Learning together:*

Children and adults in a school community. New York, Oxford University Press.

Rohrbeck, C. A., Ginsburg-Block, M. D., Fantuzzo, J. W. & Miller, T. R., 2003. Peer-assisted learning interventions with elementary school students: A meta-analytic review. *Journal of Educational Psychology,* 95, pp. 240–257.

Rosenstein, B., 2002. 'Video use in social science research and program evaluation'. *International Journal of Qualitative Methods*, 1(3), 22-43.

Ryle, G., 1971. *Collected essays*. London: Hutchinson.

Sabar Ben-Yehoshua, N., 2002. Ethnography in education. In N. Sabar Ben-Yehoshua, eds. *Traditions and genres in qualitative research.* Or Yehuda: Dvir, pp. 101-139. [Hebrew]

Sadan, A., 2008. Empowerment as a key concept in humanization in our times. In N. Aloni, ed. *Empowering dialogs in humanistic education.* Tel Aviv: Hadekel, pp. 48-67. [Hebrew]

Sadeghi, S., 2008. Critical pedagogy in an EFL teaching context: An ignis fatuus or an alternative approach? *Journal for Critical Education Policy Studies*, 6(1).

Salmeier, M. 2011. Data analysis in action research – A story of a quest for self-discovery. *Shvilei Mehkar,* 17, 42-52

Sargeant, J., 2008. Australian children: Locally secure, globally afraid? In R. Gerber & M. Robertson (Eds.), *Children's lifeworlds: Locating indigenous voices*, New York: Nova Science Publishers, pp. 119-133.

Schofield, J. W., 1989. Increasing the generalizability of qualitative research. In E. W. Eisner, E.W. and Peshkin, A. eds. *Qualitative inquiry in education.* New York: Teachers College Press, pp. 201-232.

Sela, L., 2002. Thoughts on dialogue in kindergarten. In: P. Klein & D. Givon, eds. *Language, learning, and literacy in pre-school children*, Tel Aviv, Ramot, pp. 233-255.

Selberg, G., 1999. *Pupils' influence in learning. A study in what happens when pupils have influence over their own learning and when pupils have different experience of such influence*. Lulea, Sweden: Universitetstryckeriet.

Seung, Y. L., Susan, L. R. & Min, S. S., 2005. Not the same kind of leaders: Four young children's unique ways of influencing others. *Journal of Research in Childhood Education,* 20(2), pp. 132-149.

Shapira, A., 2010. The kibbutz and the state. *Studies in the establishment of Israel,* 20, 193-207.

Sharpley, A. M. & Sharpley, C. F., 1981. Peer tutoring: A review of the literature. *Collected Original Resources in Education,* 5(3), pp. 7–C11.

Sheridan, S., 2001. *Pedagogical quality in preschool: An issue of perspectives*. Goteborg: Acta Universitatis Gothoburgensis.

Sheskin, D. J., 2003. *Handbook of parametric and nonparametric statistical procedures,* 3rd ed. Boca Raton: CRC Press.

Shkedi, A., 2003. *Words that attempt to touch, Qualitative research - Theory and implementation.* Tel Aviv: Ramot. [Hebrew]

Shkedi, A., 2011. *The meaning behind the words, Methodology in qualitative research – The practice.* Tel Aviv: Ramot. [Hebrew]

Shor, A. & Freira, P., 1990. *Pedagogy of liberation. Dialogs of change in education.* Tel Aviv: Sifrei Mifras. [Hebrew]

Silverman, D., 2006. *Interpreting qualitative data – Methods for analyzing talk, text and interaction,*3rd ed.. London: Sage Publications.

Sinclair, R., 2004. Participation in practice: Making it meaningful, effective and sustainable. *Children & Society,* 18, pp. 106-118.

Skidmore, D., 2000. From pedagogical dialogue to dialogical pedagogy. *Language and Education,* 14(4), pp. 283-296.

Skidmore, D., 2006. Pedagogy and dialogue. *Cambridge Journal of Education,* 36(4), pp. 503- 514.

Slavin, R. E., 1995. *Research on cooperative learning and achievement: What we know, what we need to know.* Baltimore, MD, Center for Research on the Education of Students Placed at Risk, Johns Hopkins University. Available at: http://www.successforall.com/resource/research/cooplearn.html

Slomkowski, C. & Dunn, J., 1996, Young children's understanding of other people's beliefs and feelings and their connected communications with friends. *Developmental Psychology,* 32, pp. 442-447.

Smith, A. B., 2002. Supporting participatory rights: Contributions from sociocultural theory. *International Journal of Children's Rights*, 10, pp. 73 88. *Developmental Psychology*, 9, pp. 173-188.

Sroufe, A., DeHarte, G. & Cooper, R., 2004. *The development of the child, its nature and its course*. Ramat Aviv: Open University. [Hebrew]

Stake, R. E., 1995. *The art of case study research.* London: Sage Publications.

Stake, R. E., 2005. Qualitative case studies. In N. K. Denzin and Y. S. Lincoln, eds. *The Sage handbook of qualitative research,* 3rd ed. London: Sage Publications. 443-466.

Stance, S. & Kao, P., 2010. Examining second language learning: Taking a sociocultural stance. *ARECLS*, 7, pp. 113-131.

Stanton-Chapman, T. L., Denning, C. B. & Jamison, K. R., 2012. Communication skill building in young children with and without disabilities in a preschool classroom. *The Journal of Special Education,* 46, pp. 78–93.

Stetsenko, A., 2009. Teaching–learning and development as activist projects of historical becoming: Expanding Vygotsky's approach to pedagogy. *Pedagogies: An International Journal*, 5, pp. 6-16.

Strauss, A. & Corbin, J., 1990. *Basics of qualitative research: Grounded theory procedures and techniques.* London: Sage Publications.

Tashakkori, A. & Teddlie, C., eds., 2003. *Handbook of mixed-methods in social and behavioral research.* Thousand Oaks, CA: Sage.

Tauber, Z., 2008. Socratic dialogue: Undermining and openness, pedagogic Eros and irony. In N. Aloni, ed. *Empowering dialogues in humanist education*. Tel Aviv: Hadekel. pp. 89-110. [Hebrew]

Thomas, N., 2002. *Children, family and the state. Decision-making and child participation*. Bristol: The Policy Press.

Tomasello, M., Carpenter, M., Call, J., Behne, T. & Moll, H., 2004. Understanding and sharing intentions: the origins of cultural cognition. *Behavioural and Brain Sciences,* 28(5), pp. 720–721.

Topping, K. J., 2005. Trends in Peer Learning. *Educational Psychology,* 25, pp. 631–645.

Tzuriel, D. & Shamir, A., 2007. The effects of Peer Mediation with

Young Children (PMYC) on children's cognitive modifiability. *The British Psychological Society,* 77, pp. 143-165.

Venninen, T., Leinonen, J. & Ojala, M., 2010. When the shared experience transforms to a collective joy. *Children's Participation in Day Care centers*, 3.

Vianna, E. & Stetsenko, A., 2006. Embracing history through transforming it – contrasting Piagetian versus Vygotskian (activity) theories of learning and development to expand constructivism within a dialectical view of history. *Theory & Psychology*, 16, pp. 81-108.

Vygotsky, L. S., 1978. *Mind in society: The development of higher psychological processes.* Cambridge, MA, Harvard University Press.

Vygotsky, L. S., 1999. Tool and sign in the development of the child. In R. W. Rieber, ed. *The collected works of L. S. Vygotsky: Vol. 6. Scientific legacy,* New York: Plenum, pp. 3-68.

Vygotsky, L. S., 2002. *Thought and Culture: Anthology*. Jerusalem: Van Leer Institute.

Wegerif, R., 2010. *Mind expanding: Teaching for thinking and creativity in primary education.* New York, NY: Open University Press.

Wells, G., 1986. *The meaning makers: Children learning language and using language to learn.* Portsmouth, NH: Heinemann.

Wells, G., 2000. Dialogic inquiry in education: Building on the legacy of Vygotsky. In C. Lee & P. Smagorinsky (Eds.), *Vygotskian perspectives on literacy research,* New York, NY: Cambridge University Press, pp. 51-85.

Wells, G., 2006, Dialogue in the classroom. *The Journal of the Learning Sciences,* 15(3), pp. 379-428.

Wells, G. & Ball, T., 2008. Exploratory talk and dialogic inquiry. In N. Mercer & S. Hodgkinson (Eds.), *Exploring talk in school,* London, UK: SAGE Publications, Ltd., pp. 167-184.

Wertsch, J. V. & Rogoff, B., 1984. Editor's notes. In B. Rogoff & J. V. Wertsch (Eds.), *Children's learning in the 'zone of proximal development'.* San Francisco, CA, Jossey-Bass, pp. 1–6.

Westerman, M. A. & Yanchar, S. C., 2011. Changing the terms of the debate: Quantitative methods in explicitly interpretive research. *Theory and Psychology,* 21(2), pp.139–154.

White, J., 2007. League tables damaging to society's future. *Irish Independent,* 19.

Whitehead, J. 2009. Using a living theory methodology in improving practice and generating educational knowledge in living theories, *Educational Journal of Living Theories,* 1(1), 103-126. Retrieved from: http://ejolts.net/node/80

Willingham, D. T., 2004. Reframing the mind. *Education Next*, 4, pp. 18-24.

Wolensky, A., 2014. Shapers of educational discourse – Passi Salberg. *Hed Hahinuch*, 6, pp. 40-41. [Hebrew]

Wolf, D., 1998. Qualitative interaction in the classroom. *The Kindergarten Echo,* 62, pp. 396-409.

Wong, A., 2009. Dialogue engagements: Professional development using pedagogical documentation. *Canadian Children*, 34(2), pp. 25-30.

Woods, P., 1996. *Researching the art of teaching: Ethnography for educational use.* London: Routledge.

Wright, K. C., Stetson, R. W., Rourke, M. & Zubernis, L. S., 2003. The relationship between psychological understanding and positive social behaviours. *Social Development, 12*, pp. 198-221

Zamir, S., 2006. Attentiveness – A cornerstone of the learning process. *Al Hagova*, 5, 13-16. [Hebrew]

Appendix

Appendix 1: Video-films that were transcribed

Transcript of Film 8	Researcher's notes
Yahel (5.0): "Ohad, thank you. I loved doing this, transferring the water with the hosepipe from bucket to bucket". Mari (5.7): "It was good that you thought about us and did this for us. Thank you ". Naveh (4.9): "I also swallowed a little water in the activity, but I didn't choke, and you (turning to the child guiding the activity) helped me". Mari (5.8): "It was difficult and I tried it a lot. But in the end you (turning to the child guiding the activity) explained it to me again and again until I understood". Ronen (4.5): "Ohad, it was good that you did this; it was interesting". Teacher: "Ohad, you had so much patience for each child. Even someone who didn't succeed, at the end of the activity you took him and tried to explain to him by himself so that he succeeded. I also saw that you knew how to give compliments to the children and to encourage them. Well done and thanks to everyone".	The children sat in a circle and gave feedback to the child guiding the activity Ohad. The teacher also sat in the circle. Each time another child spoke. The teacher spoke at the end.

Appendix 2: Structured participatory observations

Protocol from Observation 6 – observed activity	Researcher's notes
Naveh (4.8): Pointing to the painting that he received from Yarden: "that's the atmosphere and he was in the atmosphere and he fell". Yarden (5.6): "I have a question, what is the atmosphere?" Naveh (4.8): "The atmosphere is …", Yarden (5.6): "Space?" Naveh (4.8): No, atmosphere is a sort of circle in a spaceship. If you pass through it then that means you enter space". Yarden (5.6): "I understand".	The children sat in a circle and talked about a painting painted by Naveh (see below). The teacher also sat in the circle. The children observed the painting and pointed to it, asking Naveh questions about it.

The painting by Naveh discussed in the participatory observation

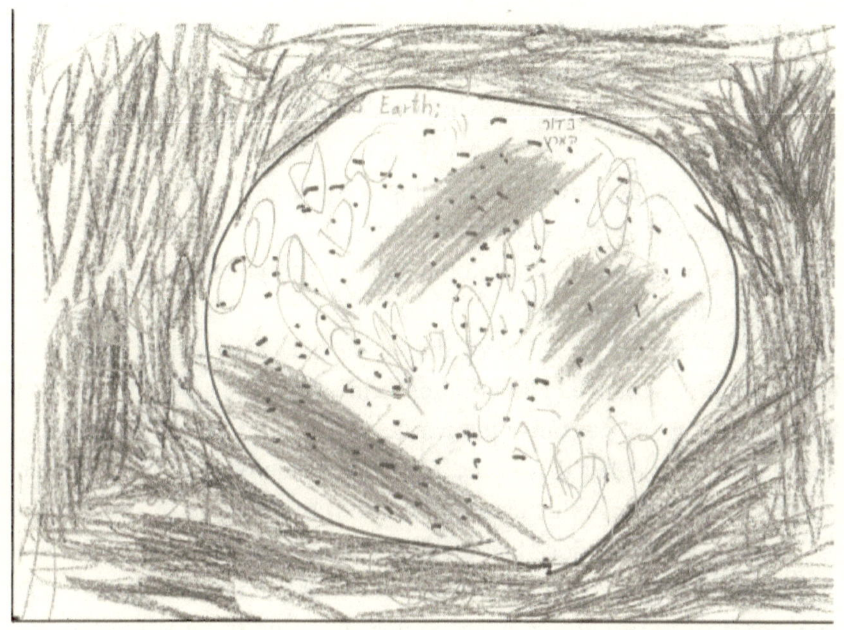

How was the earth born?
Naveh: God made the earth and then everything started – for instance, trees and water and bears and stones, planes and sky and clouds and stars and the moon and sun and aliens and planets and houses and toys and slides. After God (כדור פורח) created the earth, he died because he fell out of a plane. He wanted to parachute with balloons (hot air balloons) but he didn't have any so he fell and died (Naveh, 4.8 years old)

נווה - איך נולד כדור הארץ? 20-10-2014
״אלוהים ברא את כדור הארץ ואז התחילו
להיות כל הדברים – למשל עץ, ומים, ודובים,
ואבנים, מטוס, שמיים, ועננים, וכוכבים, וירח, ושמש,
וחייזרים, וכדורי לכת, ובתים, וצעצועים ומגלשות.
אחרי שאלוהים ברא את כדור הארץ
הוא מת, כי הוא נפל ממטוס.
הוא רצה לצנוח עם כדורים שנופלים (כדור פורח)
ולא היה לו אז הוא נפל ומת.
(נווה בן 4,8)

Appendix 3- Semi-structured interviews

Example of part of an interview conducted with one of the kindergarten teachers

Interviewer:Do you know what the Multi-Dialogical Approach for kindergartens is?

Teacher:Yes, but in the most general way.

Interviewer:Can you explain the approach to me according to what you know? And if you do not know about it can you explain what you understand the approach to be?

Teacher: It's the creation of dialog on the basis of the children's educational experience. The children bring from their own world and through dialog and discourse the whole operation of the kindergarten is produced. I think that this is the way, out of dialog, out of giving an equal weight to things that emerge from the children.

Interviewer:What does that mean, an equal weight?

Teacher:That the program suggested by the children, subjects that they want to deal with, is at least equal in value to what the teacher brings, to contents that the teacher brings and out of this dialog the whole activity and work of the kindergarten is actually derived.

Interviewer:What in your opinion are the disadvantages of the Multi-Dialogical Approach from a social viewpoint?

Teacher:I can think that perhaps the child who does not feel sufficiently confident and sure about his abilities to suggest his ideas, children lacking confidence may feel slightly outside of things, that his opinion may be less expressed. I think that this could be one of the social problems.

Interviewer:And can you think about another social problem that might arise, another social disadvantage in this approach?

Teacher: It's possible that if the children determine the workgroups, they might only invite particular children to their activities and not invite other children with whom they are less connected.

Appendix 4: The closed-ended questionnaire

Questionnaire specially composed for an academic research as part of the requirements for a doctorate on the subject: "The multi-dialogical approach in a kindergarten" by Molly Efrat

General questions

Please answer as appropriate in the underlined space:

1. Years of teaching experience __________
2. Education: (1) First degree ____ (2) Second degree __ (3) Third degree ____.
3. (1) I have experience in teaching according to multi-dialogical approach ____.

(2) I have no experience in teaching according to the multi-dialogical approach ____.

1. Type of settlement in which your kindergarten operates (1) kibbutz ____ (2) town/city ___ (3) village ____ (4) other ___.
2. Number of children attending the kindergarten this year _________.
3. The age group of the children attending the kindergarten this year (more than one option may be selected: (1) one year olds ____ (2) two year olds ____ (3) three year olds ____ (4) four year olds ____ (5) five year olds ____ (6) six year olds ____ (7) other (please detail) ____.
4. Number of staff members working in the kindergarten including the teacher ______.
5. Does the kindergarten operate according to the Multi-Dialogical Approach (a) Yes fully (b) Yes partially (c) no, but the possibility of using it is being considered (d) no (e) another answer ________________.

Part A

1. Please mark the two most outstanding advantages in your opinion of the multi-dialogical approach in comparison with other approaches:

1. The kindergarten programs are varied and not always conventional.

2. Planning of the curriculum for the kindergarten is created as a framework rather than a pre-determined program in which the kindergarten teacher knows what she will do at any given moment.

3. In activities, a single child from the kindergarten is at the center and the teacher focuses on that child's initiative.

4. In the discourse and the circle time the children speak without raising hands to ask for permission to speak.

5. The children ask questions and express their opinions.

6. There are no advantages

7. Other (please detail)

____.

1. Please mark the three most outstanding disadvantages in your opinion of the multi-dialogical approach in comparison with other approaches:

1. The kindergarten programs are varied and not always conventional.

2. Planning of the learning programs for the kindergarten is created as a framework for the program and not as a pre-determined program in which the kindergarten teacher knows what she will do at any given moment.

3. In activities, a single child from the kindergarten is at the centre and the teacher focuses on that child's initiative.

4. In the discourse and the circle time the children speak without raising hands to ask for permission to speak.

5. The children ask questions and express their opinions.

6. There are no advantages

7. Other (please detail)

Part B (Intended for kindergarten teachers who work according to the multi-dialogical approach)

Please grade the extent of your agreement with each of the following statements on a scale of 1-5 where 1= I do not agree at all and 5 = I agree to a large extent:

No.	Statement	1 Do not agree at all	2		4	5 Agree to a large extent
1	When I listen to the children, they produce new ideas	1	2	3	4	5
2	The approach allows me to pay more attention than is conventional to the children's varied and different expressions, and not necessarily verbal expressions	1	2	3	4	5
3	The multi-dialogical approach encourages the children to listen to one another	1	2	3	4	5
4	The multi-dialogical approach encourages the teacher's active listening	1	2	3	4	5
5	The multi-dialogical approach allows the teacher to make new discoveries through her attentiveness	1	2	3	4	5
6	The multi-dialogical approach encourages dialogue between equals (dialogue among the peer group)	1	2	3	4	5

Part C: (intended for all the teachers, apart from sections which are marked otherwise)

Please note, to the extent that they exist, several examples of the products of **attentiveness** according to the multi-dialogical approach in your kindergarten:

____

Part D:

Please grade the extent of your agreement with each of the following statements relating to your work in the kindergarten on a scale of 1-5 where 1= I do not agree at all and 5 = I agree to a large extent:

No.	Statement	1 Do not agree at all	2		4	5 Agree to a large extent
1	I found that the transition to the multi-dialogical approach was difficult for me	1	2	3	4	5
2	I think that the multi-dialogical approach allows me to listen more to the children	1	2	3	4	5
3	As a teacher, working according to the multi-dialogical approach means I need to do more planning	1	2	3	4	5
4	As a teacher using the multi-dialogical approach I need to be more flexible and invest more care in time management	1	2	3	4	5
5	In order to work according to the multi-dialogical approach, courses on this subject are needed	1	2	3	4	5
6	Working according to the multi-dialogical approach means that the teacher needs to be very flexible	1	2	3	4	5
7	Working according to the multi-dialogical approach means that the teacher must be very receptive to new ideas that come from the children	1	2	3	4	5
8	The multi-dialogical approach creates interest for the children	1	2	3	4	5
9	The multi-dialogical approach contributes to the development of children's independent thinking in the kindergarten	1	2	3	4	5

10	I feel that the multi-dialogical approach contributes much to the children's development in various and new areas	1	2	3	4	5
11	The multi-dialogical approach enables the children to develop their creativity and imagination	1	2	3	4	5
12	The multi-dialogical approach contributes to development of relationships and cooperation between the children	1	2	3	4	5
13	The multi-dialogical approach contributes to the development of a culture of discourse among the children	1	2	3	4	5

Part E:

Please grade the extent of your agreement with each of the following statements relating to your work in the kindergarten on a scale of 1-5 where 1= I do not agree at all and 5 = I agree to a large extent:

No.	Statement	1 Do not agree at all	2		4	5 Agree to a large extent
1	The multi-dialogical approach encourages the children to give and accept feedback	1	2	3	4	5
2	The teacher is an inseparable part of the feedback	1	2	3	4	5
3	As the teacher, I can learn about my work through the feedback that the children provide for one another	1	2	3	4	5

Part F:

Please grade the extent of your agreement with each of the following statements relating to your work in the kindergarten on a scale of 1-5 where 1= I do not agree at all and 5 = I agree to a large extent:

No.	Statement	1 Do not agree at all	2		4	5 Agree to a large extent
1	The multi-dialogical approach encourages communication	1	2	3	4	5
2	The multi-dialogical approach encourages creation of friendships between the children	1	2	3	4	5
3	The multi-dialogical approach contributes to the children's sense of responsibility	1	2	3	4	5
4	The multi-dialogical approach encourages sensitivity towards others	1	2	3	4	5
5	The multi-dialogical approach encourages respect and tolerance	1	2	3	4	5
6	The multi-dialogical approach encourages initiative	1	2	3	4	5
7	The multi-dialogical approach encourages creativity	1	2	3	4	5
8	The multi-dialogical approach encourages the children to be active.	1	2	3	4	5
9	The multi-dialogical approach encourages cooperation and collaboration	1	2	3	4	5
10	The multi-dialogical approach encourages the children's sense of self-efficacy	1	2	3	4	5
11	The multi-dialogical approach contributes to the development of self-confidence	1	2	3	4	5

Part G:

The next two questions are intended for kindergarten teachers who do not work according to the multi-dialogical approach (1=not at all, 5=to a very large extent). Please mark appropriate box with an X.

1. To what extent are you familiar with the multi-dialogical approach?

1 = not at all	2	3	4	5 = to a very large extent

2. To what extent are you interested in working according to the multi-dialogical approach?

1 = not at all	2	3	4	5 = to a very large extent

Part H:

Please grade the extent of your agreement with each of the following statements relating to the multi-dialogical approach on a scale of 1-5 where 1= I do not agree at all and 5 = I agree to a large extent:

No.	Statement	1 Do not agree at all	2		4	5 Agree to a large extent
1	In my kindergarten the children constantly participate in the planning of contents and their application in the kindergarten	1	2	3	4	5
2	The children learn areas of interest that are important and meaningful for them	1	2	3	4	5

Part I:

Please grade the extent of your agreement with each of the following statements relating to the multi-dialogical approach on a scale of 1-5 where 1= I do not agree at all and 5 = I agree to a large extent:

No.	Statement	1 Do not agree at all	2		4	5 Agree to a large extent
1	There is good communication between the children in the kindergarten	1	2	3	4	5
2	I feel that I use a participatory approach in my communication with the children	1	2	3	4	5
3	The communication created between the children has unique features	1	2	3	4	5
4	I use brain-storming with the participation of the children and the teacher for different subjects in the kindergarten	1	2	3	4	5
5	I often initiate personal meetings with the children	1	2	3	4	5
6	The children often initiate meetings with me	1	2	3	4	5
7	I tend to hold personal meetings with the children to plan activities	1	2	3	4	5
8	The children in the kindergarten develop the ability to guide and manage discussions, meetings and group activity	1	2	3	4	5
9	The activity in the kindergarten encourages the children to talk about philosophical questions and issues	1	2	3	4	5
10	I examine various subjects with the child and think about how we will present and lead them for the kindergarten children	1	2	3	4	5
11	I document the contents that are raised in the discussion with the children	1	2	3	4	5
12	The children draw and write down the plan for the activity on which they will focus together with the teacher	1	2	3	4	5
13	In my kindergarten the children learn to give and accept feedback.	1	2	3	4	5

Part J: Manner of discourse. Intended for all teachers

Please grade the extent of your agreement with each of the following statements concerning your work in the kindergarten on a scale of 1-5 where 1= I do not agree at all and 5 = I agree to a large extent:

No.	Statement	1 Do not agree at all	2		4	5 Agree to a large extent
1	I give the turn to speak to the child that raises their hand according to an order that I determine	1	2	3	4	5
2	The children enter into the discussion in the meeting without raising hands as they have learnt to do.	1	2	3	4	5

Another response ______________________________

Part K: The learning program – intended for all the teachers

Please grade the extent of your agreement with each of the following statements concerning your work in the kindergarten on a scale of 1-5 where 1= I do not agree at all and 5 = I agree to a large extent:

No.	Statement	1 Do not agree at all	2		4	5 Agree to a large extent
1	I plan the program ahead of time according to subjects that I choose and according to the Hebrew calendar and that is how we work.	1	2	3	4	5
2	I prepare the program ahead of time according to subjects that I choose and according to the Hebrew calendar and it includes subjects that the children suggest randomly according to their interests and that is how we work.	1	2	3	4	5
3	I plan the learning program ahead of time in such a way that some of the subjects will be determined by the children's desires and interests, in a manner that is not random.	1	2	3	4	5

Another response ______________________________

Part L: Children's activities in the circle time, intended for all teachers

Please grade the extent of your agreement with each of the following statements concerning your work in the kindergarten on a scale of 1-5 where 1= I do not agree at all and 5 = I agree to a large extent:

No.	Statement	1 Do not agree at all	2		4	5 Agree to a large extent
1	The children learn from their friend who guides the entire circle time (with a certain amount of mediation by the teacher). The circle time is pre-planned by him and the children take an active part according to his guidance.	1	2	3	4	5
2	The children do not guide the circle time, they learn from the teacher and take an active part in the circle time – talking, singing, dancing, play-acting etc. according to her guidance.	1	2	3	4	5
3	The children learn as they pay attention to the teacher in the circle time. The meeting is founded on their quiet attentiveness to the teacher.	1	2	3	4	5

Another response

____

Part M: The teacher's attentiveness to the children's ideas and fields of interest as part of the daily schedule. Intended for all the teachers

Please grade the extent of your agreement with each of the following statements concerning your work in the kindergarten on a scale of 1-5 where 1= I do not agree at all and 5 = I agree to a large extent:

No.	Statement	1 Do not agree at all	2		4	5 Agree to a large extent
1	I pay attention to the children as part of the regular activities	1	2	3	4	5
2	I put aside time as part of the daily schedule to pay attention to the children while conducting planned structured observation every day, in order to identify the children's areas of interest and ideas	1	2	3	4	5

Another response____________________________________

Part N: Teacher-child meetings to plan activities

Please grade the extent of your agreement with each of the following statements concerning your work in the kindergarten on a scale of 1-5 where 1= I do not agree at all and 5 = I agree to a large extent:

No.	Statement	1 Do not agree at all	2		4	5 Agree to a large extent
1	The term "activity planning meetings" is known and clear for me.	1	2	3	4	5
2	I conduct activity planning meetings with the children	1	2	3	4	5
3	I conduct activity planning meetings with the children as a planned part of the daily and weekly schedule	1	2	3	4	5

Another response ________________________________

Part O: The teacher's feedback to the child. Intended for all teachers

Please grade the extent of your agreement with each of the following statements concerning your work in the kindergarten on a scale of 1-5 where 1= I do not agree at all and 5 = I agree to a large extent:

No.	Statement	1 Do not agree at all	2		4	5 Agree to a large extent
1	Feedback takes place between me and the child	1	2	3	4	5
2	I give (unplanned) feedback to the child according to the things he does, says, asks etc.	1	2	3	4	5
3	I give planned feedback to the child in respect of innovative activities that the child performs.	1	2	3	4	5

Another response

____

Part P: Child-child feedback. Intended for all teachers

Please grade the extent of your agreement with each of the following statements concerning your work in the kindergarten on a scale of 1-5 where 1= I do not agree at all and 5 = I agree to a large extent:

No.	Statement	1 Do not agree at all	2		4	5 Agree to a large extent
1	The children give feedback to each other	1	2	3	4	5
2	There is action-reaction feedback (the child does something and another child reacts)	1	2	3	4	5
3	The children are asked by me to give feedback to the child who guides the activity	1	2	3	4	5

Another response ______________________________________

Part Q: Philosophical discourse. Intended for all teachers

Please grade the extent of your agreement with each of the following statements concerning your work in the kindergarten on a scale of 1-5 where 1= I do not agree at all and 5 = I agree to a large extent:

No.	Statement	1 Do not agree at all	2		4	5 Agree to a large extent
1	Philosophical discourse takes place throughout the day	1	2	3	4	5
2	Planned and structured philosophical discourse takes place on subjects that the children ask to discuss as part of the learning program	1	2	3	4	5
3	I know about the concept "philosophical discourse"					

Would you like to add, to clarify/ to note something concerning this questionnaire in particular or regarding the multi-dialogical approach in general?

Appendix 5: Consent form and permission for the videotaping of children

The research in which your children will participate aims to investigate the "development of social-communicative skills of children in a kindergarten that operates according to the multi-dialogical approach."

I promise to use the pictures and films that are taken only for research purposes, not for publication and I will not transmit them to any other entity or distribute them on any sort of network.

I will use the videotaped material at academic conferences in Israel and abroad out of the desire to contribute to educational learning and practice.

Best wishes
Molly Efrat
Signature Molly Efrat I.D. No. 0505914004

****

I know that my child will participate in the research by Molly Efrat on the subject "Development of social-communicative skills of children in a kindergarten that operates according to the multi-dialogical approach".

I know that the researcher has given her promise to me, as the guardian of my child, to use the videotaped material at academic conferences in Israel and abroad out of the desire to contribute to educational learning and practice.

As the child's guardian, I hereby declare that I consent to this willingly

I know that I can request that my child leave the research at any stage.

I know that the researcher promised me, as the child's guardian that she will use the filmed video-films only for research purposes, not for publication and she will not transmit them to any other entity or distribute them on any sort of network.

Date ____________________

Name of parent(s) ____________________

Name of child____________

Parent(s) signature ________________________

Appendix 6: Statement of confidentiality

Dear participant,

The research in which you will participate aims to examine the "development of social-communicative skills of children in a kindergarten that operates according to the multi-dialogical approach".

I promise to use the materials from this research only for research purposes and to maintain anonymity and discretion with regard to all the stages of the research.

No identifying details of the participants will appear in any publication of the research.

Best wishes,
Molly Efrat
Signature Molly Efrat I.D. No. 0505914004

****

I know that I will participate in the research by Molly Efrat on the subject "Development of social-communicative skills of children in a kindergarten that operates according to the multi-dialogical approach".

I hereby declare that I am willing to participate in this research.

I know that I can leave the research at any stage.

I know that the researcher promises to maintain anonymity and confidentiality at all stages of the research.

Date ____________________
Name ____________
Signature ________________________

Appendix 7: Children's documentation

<u>Children's documentation- The teacher writes in words and the child draws so that he can understand what is written</u>

Work plan for the preparation of a game made by the child and the teacher

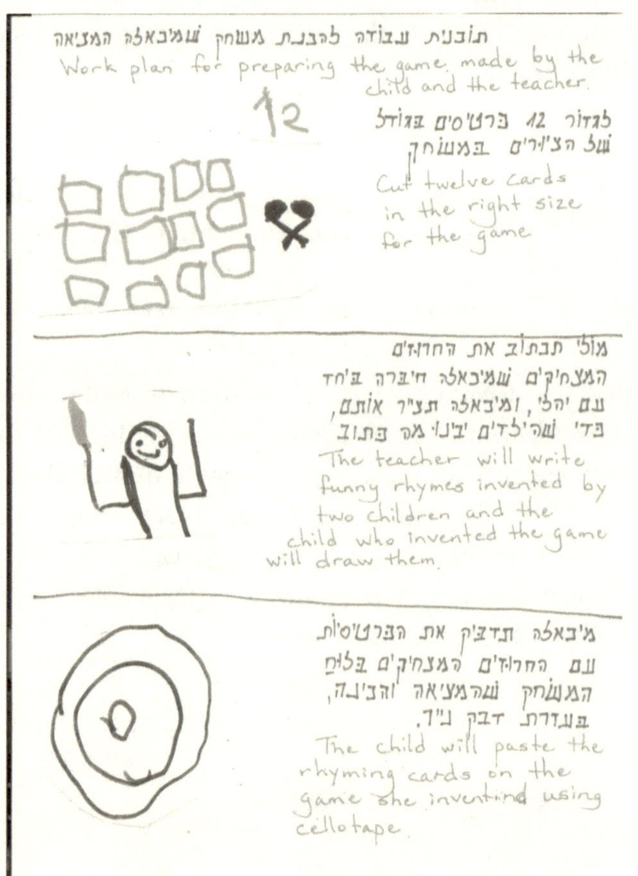

www.ingramcontent.com/pod-product-compliance
Lightning Source LLC
LaVergne TN
LVHW091255150826
845673LV00006B/1423